Put Your Potatoes on the Desktop

Christian Version

A Practical Approach to Emotion Intelligence

Put Your Potatoes on the Desktop

Christian Version

A Practical Approach to Emotion Intelligence

by Ralph D. Sinn, M.D.

iUniverse, Inc.
New York Bloomington

Put Your Potatoes On The Desktop - Christian Version
A Practical Approach to Emotion Intelligence

iUniverse books may be ordered through booksellers or by contacting:

iUniverse
1663 Liberty Drive
Bloomington, IN 47403
www.iuniverse.com
1-800-Authors (1-800-288-4677)

ISBN: 978-1-4401-4063-1 (pbk)
ISBN: 978-1-4401-4064-8 (ebk)

Library of Congress Control Number: 2009926931

Printed in the United States of America

iUniverse rev. date: 5/7/2009

Acknowledgements

Special thanks to my mother Edith and to my wife Barbara for your support, encouragement, and help with writing what I have to say. Thanks to Barbara Every for your editing expertise. Thanks to countless patients who have encouraged me to write and have persevered to get me to do so.

Introduction

A discussion about emotions is never an easy venture to tackle, because emotions are not scientific. In other words, you cannot weigh or measure emotions. Yet, emotions are a real dimension of our existence as humans. There is a kind of truth to emotions, but it cannot be understood within the scientific realm. It is a rather nebulous truth.

Any presentation about emotions is therefore limited. My limitation in discussing emotions lies within the framework of my point of view, or angle, or bias of what emotions are about. I cannot, however, present to you the entire picture. The idea is similar to posing for your portrait in a studio. What is the angle or point of view that best describes your appearance? Any angle portrays *you*, but you may have a sense that the portrait does not represent the entire you.

The same is true with any discussion about emotions. Books, lectures, or sermons regarding anger, stress, communication, relationships, and forgiveness are each that particular author's point of view, angle, or bias in describing the role of emotions. Some presentations that you have heard or read may describe an angle that is similar to the point of view I am about to present, whereas others may seem contradictory to mine. Yet, each presentation attempts to paint a picture of the reality of emotions.

The following is my attempt to portray a point of view about emotions, particularly those that are referred to as "negative." In the context of feeling your negative emotions, I will discuss the difference between the tragedy of the destructive mindset and the victory of the constructive mindset. Please read this book by starting at the first chapter. Progress through the concepts of the book by reading each chapter in sequential order. If you skip ahead to read the constructive method of emotion management without first understanding the foundation of the preceding chapters, your preparedness to understand the concepts will be limited. This book presents a practical approach to emotion management. Every step in the process is important and necessary to get as broad an understanding as possible.

The text is meant to be applicable to both genders. Any reference to a "he" or "she" or to a "him" or "her" in the examples given to illustrate points is meant to be gender interchangeable and not necessarily gender specific. Some issues may be more common to one gender than to the other, but they apply to both genders nevertheless.

Biblical Perspective

The biblical basis for learning about emotions is found in 2 Peter 1:5-8: "For this very reason, make every effort to add to your faith goodness; and to goodness, knowledge; and to knowledge, self-control; and to self-control, perseverance; and to perseverance, godliness; and to godliness, brotherly kindness; and to brotherly kindness, love. For if you possess these qualities in increasing measure, they will keep you from being ineffective and unproductive in your knowledge of our Lord Jesus Christ."

Peter begins with faith. I believe everyone has faith. Faith is an inherent quality of being human, similar to having arms and legs. What you put your faith in, however, may be different to what someone else puts his or her faith in. If your faith is in the living and loving God, then you will add goodness to your faith, because God is a good God, and you will learn to make good choices in your life.

Peter goes on to add knowledge as the next progression. Knowledge has to do with science. It is interesting that Peter states that your "science," that is, how you interpret what you observe in this world, is based on the foundation of your faith. For example, if your faith is that there is a God, then the way you interpret your science is consistent with your faith. Another way of saying this is that your faith is your bias. If, on the other hand, your faith is that there is no God, then the way you interpret your science is consistent with your bias that there is no God.

The next step after knowledge is self-control. This is a principle of education. When you learn about something, your sense of self-control within that discipline is enhanced. For example, when you first learn to drive a car, you likely do not feel that you have control. You have to think of eye-hand-foot coordination. You have to be aware of the laws of driving, the signs on the road, and so on. Eventually, your confidence increases. You drive from point A to point B. You don't have to think about your eye-hand-foot coordination. Your awareness of signs on the road becomes second nature. In other words, you are free to feel in control; you have added self-control to your knowledge of driving.

Peter adds perseverance to self-control. Just because you are more confident and self-controlled when you drive does not mean that there will not be challenges ahead. One application of perseverance is in learning to drive defensively. Things happen on the road that will test your skill. As you sort out how to handle the various challenges, you add perseverance to the knowledge and self-control that you have already obtained.

This book has to do with learning about your emotions. When you learn the difference between the destructive and constructive mindset of understanding your negative emotions, including anger, then you are free to add a sense of self-control to the knowledge you gain regarding the emotions you feel. You become free to add perseverance to the self-control you attain as your knowledge increases. Just because you learn to be increasingly constructive in the way you manage your emotions does not mean that you are without destructive challenges along the way. You therefore learn to persevere through the challenges on the foundation of the knowledge and self-control you attain.

You become free to add the next steps in Peter's progression, that is, godliness, brotherly kindness, and love. I find it interesting that Paul, in 1 Corinthians 13:13, compresses Peter's progression. Paul writes: "And now these three remain: faith, hope and love. But the greatest of these is love." Paul also begins with faith and ends with love, but he summarizes what is between with hope. Therefore, as you increase your knowledge, self-control, and perseverance, in terms of understanding your emotions, you gain hope in your life. Hope gives you the ability to believe in yourself and to keep you going forward.

Chapter 1
What Is Anger?

If you were to define the word *anger*, what would you say? Would you propose that it means that somebody is frustrated or mad, or that someone is yelling, running away, or hitting someone or something?

There seem to be two major categories of definitions for the word *anger*. One category of definitions corresponds to what I would say is an *energized state* in the body. It is as if your body has a baseline energy level, and when you are "ticked," your body is energized toward a higher energy level. People attempt to describe this phenomenon by using emotional descriptions when defining the word *anger*. They use terms such as "frustrated," "mad," or "upset," or they say "I get in a rage," or "my blood pressure goes up."

A second category of definitions people use to describe anger corresponds to some kind of action. Words such as "screaming," "hitting," "suppressing," "crying," or "I get away from there" are used for this category.

For the purposes of this presentation on anger and the negative emotions, I will limit the use of the term *anger* to the energized state category of definitions of anger. I will present anger as a secondary emotion, which describes a state of energy that the body is raised to at certain times. Sometimes a person may define anger as a certain degree of heightened energy. For example, it may be said that frustration is a little bit of increased energy, being mad is a bit more, being angry is even more, **and being in a rage is yet more energy!** For the purposes of this presentation, I will use the word *anger* as an umbrella term to include any increase in the body's energy level compared with its baseline energy level.

For the action category of definitions of anger, as opposed to labelling this category as anger, I will label it as *anger management*. Therefore, if someone is yelling, or hitting, or suppressing, these actions are to be understood as forms of anger management.

A common way of describing the energized state of anger as a secondary emotion is by calling it the *fight-or-flight response*. This is a well used and recognized term. We get this phrase by observing animals, that is, what they do in situations of threat, and then we try to understand human responses in similar terms. For instance, imagine a mouse in a field at night, rummaging here and there for food. All of a sudden, that mouse notices an owl swooping down at him. The mouse has a quick decision to make: either he gets on his hind legs and fights that owl off (as in a cartoon sequence) or he scoots for cover. Whatever that mouse chooses to do, a transformation takes place in his body. At one moment, the mouse is looking for food, and then suddenly he outruns Donovan Bailey and sets a world record! But if that mouse doesn't outrun the owl, he becomes a tasty morsel.

Humans can do unheard-of things under panic situations. For instance, an elderly person can lift a car off of someone to save a life. But under normal circumstances, that person may not have that kind of strength. Being energized to anger is not, however, an on-and-off switch. You do not always have superhuman strength every time you are ticked off. The amount of energy that you are raised to depends in part on what is on your plate at the time.

The following is a discussion about some of the physiology involved in being energized to anger. I will try to simplify as best I can, but I am sure I will not be able to tell the whole story. The way your body gets heightened to the energized state is by means of stress factors that bring up the body's energy level. There are many different stress factors—some we know a lot about, but some we probably have not discovered yet, for scientists continue to study and learn more and more about how our bodies function. One stress factor we know something about is called *adrenalin*.

A major gland in our bodies is the adrenal gland. This gland is composed of many different kinds of cells that manufacture various substances that the body uses to function properly. One of those substances is adrenalin. The cells that manufacture adrenalin continuously produce and release the adrenalin into the bloodstream. If you were to have a blood test to ascertain your blood adrenalin level, the result would be a level (one hopes) that falls within the normal range. The cells that produce adrenalin, however, tend to make more than what your body needs normally, for if your body requires more adrenalin than usual, extra is available to meet the increased demand.

When your brain senses that your body needs to have more adrenalin available to do its work, your brain sends a signal to the cells in your adrenal gland that gives them the order to release more adrenalin into your bloodstream. In turn, the cells in the adrenal gland obey the order and thus release more adrenalin into your bloodstream. The adrenalin in turn becomes a messenger to other cells in the body to deliver a message. One of the cells the adrenalin gives a message to is a muscle cell. Imagine that your forearm is a muscle cell. Your opposite hand floats around and represents the adrenalin flowing along with the blood. When the adrenalin gets close to the muscle cell, the adrenalin attaches to it and gives the muscle cell a message (your "adrenalin" hand grabs onto your "muscle" forearm). The message is "We need power!" The muscle cell in turn answers: "That is exactly what I am here for. I can deliver!" This interaction between the adrenalin and the muscle cell is similar to what happens in a typical scene in the original *Star Trek* series, when Captain Kirk delivers a message to Scotty in engineering. The message is: "Scotty! We need power! We've got to move!" Scotty replies in his typical Scottish accent, "Aye Captain, I'll give you all the powerrr I can musterrr!"

How does the muscle cell deliver the power? It relies on a fuel source. In the "Starship Enterprise," that fuel source is what Scotty refers to when he says, "I'll fire up the matter/antimatter machines! (But I don't know how much she can take.)" In the muscle cell, the fuel source is not matter/antimatter (at least if it is, we haven't discovered that yet), but rather is a form of sugar stored in the muscle cell. The muscle cell burns the sugar to derive energy from it and translates this energy to moving the muscle. Most fuel sources that we are aware of on planet Earth involve burning the fuel in the presence of oxygen to get the most efficient burn. You do not need oxygen to burn the sugar in your muscle cell, but if you do not supply oxygen, the fuel efficiency of the sugar is not as great. For example, if you start a campfire because you want to roast marshmallows, your flame is not as great and useful as it could be if you packed some logs down and lit them. If, however, you pay attention to airflow through the logs, and thus space them out, then you achieve an efficient burn with a better flame to roast your marshmallows.

The body does a similar thing with the muscle cell. Not only does the adrenalin tell your muscle cell to burn the sugar, but the adrenalin also gets your body to deliver oxygen to the muscle cell so that you can have as efficient a burn of the sugar as possible. Therefore, a chain of events transfers the oxygen from the air you breathe to your muscle cell.

Another dynamic to keep in mind is that any fuel source that you burn leaves you with waste products to deal with at the end of the burn cycle. A complete and efficient burn of the sugar in your muscle cell leaves you with waste products that your body has an effective way of disposing. Those waste products are carbon dioxide and water. Your body disposes of the carbon dioxide when you breathe out (the exhaust system). Your kidneys take care of the excess water. If, however, you do not have a complete and efficient burn of the sugar in your muscle cell, you are left with more complex waste products, which your body has a bit more difficulty dealing with. Some of the more complex waste products may put you at risk for their toxic effects. One example is a buildup of lactic acid, which can affect different people in different ways (people are not all the same). For example, developing writer's cramp may be an example of a buildup of lactic acid in the muscles that move your hand when you are writing, especially if you are under duress, as in an essay exam in which you are pressured for time. You are doing the best you can, writing frantically, and then all of a sudden you are in a situation in which your brain is trying to tell your hand what to write, but your hand muscles just … will … not … move … as you clutch your pen tighter and **tighter**. If you put your pen down and shake your hand, you get some feeling back in your hand after a while, and then you are ready to pick up your pen and get on with it. What is likely happening is that a buildup of lactic acid in the muscles of your lower arm is compromising your muscles' ability to function as they are designed to. By shaking your hand, you increase the blood flow to those muscles to deliver more oxygen and counteract the oxygen deficit. You are then able to carry on with your essay exam, likely writing at a slower pace, to better match the oxygen supply with the demand of your muscles. You then get through your exam as best as you can.

The adrenalin not only gives your muscle cell the message to produce power, but it also prepares your body to deliver more oxygen to your muscle cell. The burn of the sugar (fuel) in your muscle is designed to be as efficient as possible. To achieve the ideal fuel efficiency, a chain of events occurs in your body so that oxygen can be delivered to your muscle cells. The first link in the chain is an increased need to breathe. You may feel short of breath or that you can't catch your breath. There is a rate of breathing that provides a healthy balance of matching the supply and demand of oxygen in your body, and if you breathe within this healthy balance, you are doing just fine. If, however, your breathing rate is outside the bounds of the healthy balance, then side effects can start kicking in to work against you. Going beyond the healthy balance of breathing on the high end results in hyperventilation, which means you are breathing rapidly, or taking a lot of deep breaths that follow one after the other more closely. This situation is indeed successful in getting more oxygen into your body. Side effects happen, however, because with every breath you breathe out, you are breathing out carbon dioxide. Even though carbon dioxide is a waste product, your body needs a healthy amount of it to function properly. If you breathe out too much of the carbon dioxide, then you diminish your body's level of carbon dioxide to less than the healthy level. You then start getting symptoms of hyperventilation such as light-headedness.

Your breathing gets your body to take oxygen into your lungs. Your lungs are designed to transfer oxygen from the air that goes into your lung to the blood that flows through your lung at the time. The next link in the chain is to get oxygen in the blood flowing through your lungs to your muscle cells. Now your heart and blood vessels factor in. Your heart receives the message to beat more forcefully and rapidly. You feel your heart beating in your chest. As far as your blood vessels are concerned, your blood pressure goes up, in part because your heart is like a pump that is beating with increased force and resulting in increased pressure to make your blood flow faster. Your arteries also factor in to modulate your blood pressure and are well designed to do so. An additional fact about arteries is that they are like a tree with branches to supply blood to all parts of your body. When you are energized to anger, your arteries get a message to close off the supply of blood to your stomach area (digestive system). These digestive system arteries do not close off entirely. They close off only a little, so that more of your blood is available to be delivered to your muscles and your brain. Such an occurrence is well and fine for your muscles and brain, but the cells in your stomach area do not like this situation one bit! Your blood is good and nourishing stuff, and the cells in your stomach area believe they are not getting their fair share of it, so they protest. Signs that your stomach cells are protesting are that you feel butterflies in your stomach, or knots, or cramps, or nausea. Does any of this ever happen to you? As you can see, your blood delivers oxygen to your muscle cells. The discussion so far is what is considered normal physiology of how oxygen gets delivered to your muscle cells.

Another body adjustment when you are energized to anger is that the tone in your muscles increases. I believe this has to do with a readiness for action. Your muscles are designed to be packed with tiny fibres that relate to each other in an overlapping fashion. The energy that comes from the burn of sugar in your muscle cell is translated to your muscle fibres so that they shorten with respect to each other and thus result in linear motion. Afterward, the fibres relax and lengthen until the next time they are made to shorten. This is how you get muscle movement. In a similar way, an internal combustion engine is designed so that a piston moves in a linear fashion into an enclosed chamber to compress the air trapped inside. Gasoline is then injected into the enclosed chamber and a spark ignites the fuel to explode. The explosion forces the piston back down the cylinder in a linear fashion. The linear motion is then translated into rotary motion along the axle. Muscles are not designed to directly translate linear motion to rotary motion, but rather to produce various movements of your limbs and body as your groups of muscles interact with each other.

One way to think about how the tone in your muscles increases is to imagine sitting in your vehicle at a red light anticipating the light to turn green. As you are in the ready position, you depress the accelerator pedal somewhat, thus revving up your engine. What you are doing is increasing the engine tone as a readiness for action. Vrrroooom, vrrroooom, vrrrooom! Or, imagine you are driving along a winter road. All of a sudden, your vehicle swerves after driving over an icy spot. To keep your vehicle steady, you tighten your grip on the steering wheel. The previous moment you were holding your steering wheel in a relaxed fashion with some flabbiness of your arm muscles, but the next moment you grab onto your steering wheel with a firm grip. Your arm muscles that were flabby are now firm; that is, their tone is increased as a readiness for action.

The increased muscle tone you experience may go to specific and variable muscle groups. People react in different ways. One example is clenching your teeth together and grinding them. Over time, you might grind your teeth down, and your dentist alerts you about the effect of grinding on your teeth. Another example may be if you develop temporomandibular (TM) joint problems, as the wear and tear on the jaw mounts up over time. Yet another example is if you experience tension headaches, or tension in your neck, shoulder, or back muscles. Your other muscle groups could also be affected. Can you relate with any of these effects?

When it comes to a healthy rate of breathing, I discussed previously what happens when you go beyond the healthy balance when you breathe too rapidly. On the other hand, going beyond the balance on the low end relates to the fact that you use muscles to breathe. An example is holding your breath. When you are driving and hit that icy spot, and when you swerve and grab your steering wheel more tightly, you may also hold your breath….uhh! If you do so, then your body has already released adrenalin into your bloodstream, and the adrenalin has told your muscles to burn more sugar to produce power, but … now you are not delivering oxygen to your muscles to achieve an efficient burn! That is why you have to remember to breathe when you are stressed or energized to anger, but your breathing needs to be controlled. That is what breathing exercises for stress relaxation techniques hope to accomplish—to teach you to breathe through the stress and deliver oxygen that your body needs when it becomes energized. Even the old saying "When you are angry, take a deep breath and count to 10" (or vice versa) is consistent with breathing exercises.

The simplest example of being energized to anger starts when your body is at a baseline energy level. If you become energized to anger, your body energy level goes along a smooth upward curve, reaches a peak, and then follows a smooth curve back down to your baseline energy level. The reason that you cool down is because of the way adrenalin gives its message to your muscle cells. The adrenalin is not a drill sergeant. Adrenalin does not attach itself permanently to your muscle cells to deliver the order … "Burn! Burn! Come on! What's the matter with you? Burn!" Rather, adrenalin attaches briefly to your muscle cells and delivers its message. Your muscle cells in turn comply with the message. An adrenalin molecule then detaches from the muscle cell, having done its job, and gets broken down and sent to the wastebasket. Therefore, your energy level at any given moment likely has to do with how often a message from adrenalin is delivered to your muscle cell, as varying amounts of adrenalin are released into the bloodstream by your adrenal gland.

All of these physiological descriptions about the energized state of the body are what I refer to and call "anger." From that point of view, having anger is like having arms and legs. Anger is not a matter of good versus bad or right versus wrong. Having anger is not something sinful or inappropriate. Your body is designed to have anger, just as you are designed to have arms and legs.

If anger is a secondary emotion, then the primary emotions are hurt, frustration, and fear. In the same way that your body is designed to have anger, you are also designed to have emotions. Your brain is organized in such a way so that certain components of your brain help you to move your arms and legs in a controlled and purposeful manner. Other parts of your brain help you make sense of what you see and hear. Still other components of your brain are what are known as your emotion centres. Therefore, to have emotions is like having arms and legs; it is not something bad, wrong, sinful, or inappropriate. You are designed to have emotions.

Classification Systems

One of the problems people encounter in understanding their emotions may have to do with the classification system used to categorize emotions. The label for the group of emotions that include hurt, frustration, fear, and anger is the *negative emotions*. Referring to these emotions as negative in no way implies that they are wrong, bad, sinful, or inappropriate. The term *negative* is merely based on the classification system used. There is no intention to judge the moral value of emotions.

Classification systems do have value in helping people understand who they are, but the usefulness of these systems is limited. The reason people come up with classification systems is that we tend to ask questions as we go through our lives, such as "Who am I? What am I? Where am I? Why am I?" One of the places people seek answers to these questions is in nature. When we observe the natural realm, we get a sense that there is a certain order to nature. We then attempt to describe this order with a classification system. (If there were no order in nature, we couldn't make sense of anything.) We find that these classification systems are helpful in assisting us to get answers to our questions. But it is at this point that we start showing the limits we have as humans, that is, how we tend to put things we try to understand together. We have the tendency to conclude that the truth of nature is represented in the classification system that we have come up with. We then defend our classification system as truth and assume that nature must fit within our classification system, rather than allowing nature to be what is true.

An example of what I am describing has to do with the animal kingdom. We know how to recognize the difference between a dog and a cat because each animal has a certain set of characteristics that identifies each as a dog or a cat. So far so good. We find such a system of classification helpful. What happens, however, if we should come across an animal that has what we identify as both dog-like and cat-like features? Where do we place this animal in our classification system? This is where controversy may come in. One group of people may defend the animal as a cat, another group may defend it as a dog, and yet another group may suggest that it must be a common ancestor to both dogs and cats. Whatever that animal is, however, is not what we say it is. That animal is just ... whatever it is. We as scientists are those trying to fit this animal into our own scientific classification system. An example of an animal like this could be a cheetah. There is not much controversy that a cheetah is a member of the cat family, but the word *cheetah* has been described as meaning "dog-cat," for the cheetah has some dog-like characteristics. Other animals that can possibly be used as examples could be the hyena or the platypus.

When it comes to classifying emotions, people have come up with a classification system that divides emotions into some that are called positive and others that are called negative. There is no problem with such a classification system per se, but there is a risk in considering something called negative as being something wrong, bad, sinful, inappropriate, unwanted, or undesirable. But calling emotions negative is in no way meant to give them a negative connotation, nor is it meant to convey a statement of moral deficit. In the same way that there is a classification system of electrical charge that identifies electrons as having negative charge and there is no consideration that the use of the flow of electricity is something negative, bad, or wrong, we ought not to consider our negative emotions as something bad or wrong. We simply have emotions as part of who we are as humans. Emotions are a fact of life.

I believe the concept of positive and negative emotions is derived partly because emotions sensitize and alert people to issues of *right versus wrong* that they face in their day-to-day lives. Right versus wrong represents ideas of law, justice, truth, and so on, that a person has for various reasons. (This is what is meant by "right-wrong" in the anger model in Figure 1.1.) Therefore, if you find yourself in the presence of something you believe is right, true, or in accord with your idea of justice, you respond with what is called a positive emotion, such as being happy. Even the word *happy* is rooted from the word *to happen*, which implies that your emotions are linked to some kind of happening, as well as your idea of justice that is connected with it. On the other hand, if you find yourself in the presence of something you believe is wrong or an injustice, which is against some idea of law or truth, you respond to your idea of injustice with what is called a negative emotion, such as hurt, frustration, fear, or a combination of these emotions. These negative emotions in turn energize you to anger.

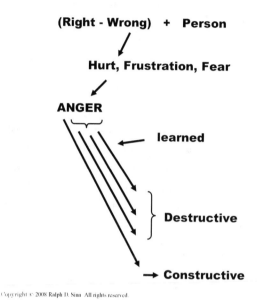

Figure 1.1 The Basic Model of Anger/Emotion Intelligence

I should mention that the energized state is not limited to the negative side of the coin of emotions. There is an energized state on the positive side as well, which may be referred to as joy or ecstasy. Perhaps the best word to describe the positive energized state is *elation*. As far as the main theme of this book is concerned, however, the discussion is limited primarily to the negative emotions.

How then can you make sense of what your emotions are about? I believe the term used to describe the energized state of anger actually does a disservice in terms of understanding what anger is about. Do you remember the phrase that is used to describe the energized state? If you remember the phrase "the fight-or-flight response," then you have remembered well. So, why would such a well-respected and well-accepted phrase to describe the energized state of anger do a disservice for understanding what anger is about? Please recall that at the start of this chapter, different definitions of anger were identified and divided into two basic categories of definitions. One way to understand anger is within a category that attempts to describe an energized state in the body (this category was labelled "anger"). The second category of definitions relates anger to an action (this category was labelled "anger management"). Dividing the definitions of anger into two categories makes sense to people. But, my claim now is that calling the energized state of anger the fight-or-flight response is a misnomer. Why would I make such a claim?

Think about anger as an energizing emotional response and anger management as an action. In these terms, why then is it a misnomer to call the emotional response the fight-or-flight response? Some people suggest that referring to the energized state of anger as such is too limiting in providing options to deal with your challenges. I agree with this suggestion, but I do not believe this to be the main point. My main objection to calling anger the fight-or-flight response is that action terms (*fight* or *flight*) are being used to describe the energized state. If anger is an energized response and anger management is the action, then using action terms such as *fight* or *flight* to refer to the energy component can fuse the energized response of anger and the action of anger management together to make it seem as if they are one and the same thing. That possible confusion is the reason that I object to calling anger the fight-or-flight response. I believe it is fundamentally important to keep the two main definitions of anger, that is, energy and action, separate.

Therefore, instead of referring to anger as the fight-or-flight response, my preference is to call it a *motivational response*. The way I paint the picture is as follows (Figure 1.1): When you find yourself in the presence of something you believe is wrong or an injustice, or is against some idea of law or truth, you respond to your idea of wrongness with what is called a negative emotion, such as hurt, frustration, fear, or a combination of these emotions. Your primary negative emotions in turn energize you to anger. Your anger is a motivational response. But what are you motivated to do? Well, you find yourself in the presence of something you believe is wrong; therefore, you believe something is unacceptable and something has to *change*. And this is what I believe anger is about ... change. I also believe that this is where concepts of anger and stress intersect. Both have to do with change. Stress has to do with being in the presence of change (for example, you have to move your place of residence), whereas anger is the sense that something is unacceptable and therefore something has to change. The energy of anger is a motivational energy in you to bring about change.

When you come up with a way to bring about change when you are in the presence of something you believe is unacceptable, you are now working within the action category of anger management. There are two ways to bring change about, and they are ... fight or flight! The words *fight* and *flight* are action terms. Therefore, the way I prefer to divide anger and anger management is to refer to anger as a motivational response that in turn leads to anger management, which is a *fight-or-flight* **action** to bring change about.

Fight or flight is also a value-neutral term. Fight does not have to mean violence, and flight does not have to mean weakness. The term *fight or flight* merely represents two ways of bringing about change. When it comes down to it, fight means you bring about change by attempting to change the wrong into a right. Flight means you bring change by removing yourself from being in the presence of what you believe is wrong. Perhaps you believe it is not possible or you are unable to change what you believe is wrong into a right, and so you remove yourself from the presence of what you perceive is wrong to bring about the change.

Sometimes a perseverance question comes into play on whether you choose a fight method or a flight method to bring change about. Relationship issues can provide an example. For instance, two people are in a relationship with each other that they both value highly. Something happens within the context of their relationship that has a sense of wrongness to one of them. Because the offended person values the relationship more than the problem, a fight method to bring about change is attempted (find a way to make the wrong turn into a right). A challenge in any relationship, however, is that all relationships are a two-way street. This means that both people have a role to play in making their relationship with each other work. Just because the offended person has a sense of wrongness within the context of their relationship does not mean the other person agrees that something wrong has happened. Even if both agree that there is a wrong, nothing may be done to bring about change. Therefore, the offended person has a perseverance question: Because they value the relationship more than the problem, they persevere with a selection of fight methods to bring about change.

As time passes, however, if there is no change to the satisfaction of the offended person, that person encounters a perseverance question, that is, "How long do I keep fighting for change?" Eventually, if no change happens, the value of the problem may start to override the value of the relationship. The offended person may think: "I've tried for a long time to bring about change, and no change has happened. When it comes down to it, this problem is more important to me than the relationship. It looks like I have to revert to a flight way to bring about change." And so the offended person brings about change by removing him- or herself from being in the presence of what is believed to be wrong, and ends the relationship. The preceding relationship dynamics are relevant to people who seek to find answers to their questions when attempting to make sense of their relationship difficulties.

Person

As you refer to the anger model in Figure 1.1, let us move our discussion to the part of the model called "+ person." This part of the anger model is not a mathematical equation. When it comes to human conflicts, there is usually a person affiliated with the concept of right versus wrong. From this point of view, your concept of injustice is usually along the lines of something said or done, or not said or not done, that you believe is unacceptable. The person in the equation is the someone who said the wrong thing, or did the wrong thing, or did not say the right thing, or did not do the right thing. Sometimes the person is you. You may think "Why did I do that?" or "Why didn't I say something?" Sometimes the person is another individual, or a group of people, or a company, or an organization of some sort. Sometimes it is a government (but there will be no political discussions here!). The person can also be an inanimate object that is personified, such as your car.

A significant factor to consider is that nobody is perfect (except Christ from a biblical point of view). This fact is complicated by two factors: quantity and quality. Quantity is about the time you spend with someone; the more time you are with a person, the more you are exposed to the fact that he or she is not perfect. If you apply this concept to yourself, you are exposed to yourself 24/7, which means you are continually exposed to the fact that you are not perfect. You may therefore think "Why did I say that?" or "Why didn't I do something?" If you apply this concept to others, you find that people you spend the most time with, such as your friends, co-workers, or loved ones, are those you are exposed to more often and to the fact that they are not perfect. There is a saying along this line that states "Familiarity breeds contempt." This is the quantity factor.

The other complicating factor is quality. No matter who you are, you have expectations. Your expectations are for yourself as well as for others, no matter whether the other people are total strangers or your loved ones. Your expectation level is an idea of perfection you have for whatever reason. Even though your expectation may be reasonable and it is your will to attain it, you discover you will fall short of attaining your mark in various ways. When applied to others, whether to a total stranger or to your loved one, your expectation level may be reasonable and it may be their will to live according to your expectation level. But, the other person will also fall short of attaining the mark, despite their wish to attain it. When it comes to a total stranger, you may have an expectation level of something you call "courteous driving." However, as you are driving, someone cuts you off and swerves in front of you in your lane. You cannot see who it is, but you will likely have some kind of response to that action.

When applied to your loved one, you also have expectations that may be reasonable. For instance, a spousal vow is basically a promise that two people make to each other in the presence of witnesses:

Person #1: "I will love and care for you."

Person #2: "I will love and care for you."

Even though two people proclaim such vows to each other and try with all their heart to fulfill their vows, they find they fall short of fulfilling the vows in various ways:

Person #1: "Why did you do that? I thought you loved me!"

Person #2: "I do love you! I wasn't trying to hurt you; I just messed up this time!"

Therefore, the bottom line is that no matter who you are, you are not perfect. Neither are other people. This means that you will deal with issues of right and wrong every day. They will especially apply to you and to those you spend the most time with, and are complicated by the factors of quantity and quality. You will therefore get a lot of energy from your emotions every day. So the next question is, what will you do with all your motivational energy to bring change? What you do with your emotions falls within the realm of anger management.

Anger Management

On the anger management side of the anger model, illustrated in Figure 1.1, there are four basic methods that we as humans come up with to bring about change. The four methods in the figure are represented by the four arrows that originate from the word "Anger" and point downward to "Destructive" and "Constructive." Each of the methods represents a way that fight or flight is realized. Some of the methods are more fight in their nature, some are more flight, and some are a combination of the two. The reason that people use the various methods is that they represent successful ways to bring change about. Therefore, they are learned. If they didn't work out successfully, they would be discarded. The word *learned* in the anger model applies to the anger management side of the equation of anger and anger management. Being energized to anger is not learned. You simply have emotions, just as you have arms and legs. How you bring the change about (how you manage your anger) is what is learned.

How do you learn the various anger management methods? Well, you learn them from your parents or your caregivers as you grow up. You are exposed to how they manage their anger. Some of their methods you pick up on and start to use yourself, and some of their methods you react against and then come up with the other ways to manage your anger. You learn which anger management methods are effective from your personal experiences, whether you are aware of it or not. You learn methods from your friends, peers, and co-workers; you observe how they manage their anger and may come up with similar ways. Or you learn methods from the telling of stories. The story you hear may be someone talking about his fishing trip, it may be a novel you are reading, or it may be a movie you are watching. A story involves some kind of conflict. The conflict gets more difficult until the story is resolved. The resolution of the story is the author's suggestion of how to resolve the conflict (and is an anger management process).

I believe everyone learns the four basic anger management strategies, but not all people are the same. Each person has a dominant method, and this is where individual differences come in. For one person, his dominant method is the first management arm of the anger model (e.g., the shortest arrow leading down from the word *anger* to the word *destructive* in Figure 1.1); for someone else, hers is the management method represented by the second arm (the next longer arrow); and for a third person, he uses a combination of the first two methods depending on the situation.

Another complicating factor to consider in understanding anger and anger management is that what you learn over the course of time eventually becomes automatic. For example, when you first learn to drive, you have to think about all kinds of rules of the road and of how to coordinate your eyes, hands, and feet to drive from point A to point B. Eventually, you drive from point A to point B automatically, not thinking about all the things you need to do to get there, but you are doing them nonetheless. The same is true with anger management methods. Over time, they become automatic. You find yourself in the presence of a situation that you believe is wrong or unacceptable and ... Zing! You manage your anger in the way you have learned. You are not necessarily thinking: "So, how am I going to manage my anger today? Will it be method number 1 or 3?" No, you tend to automatically use the management method you have learned is successful to bring about change. This is another reason that some people define anger in terms of an action. They link their energized emotional state directly to an action and therefore define anger in those terms.

It is important, however, to distinguish the increased motivational energy of anger from the action of anger management. The reason to distinguish the difference is that although there are four anger management methods representing successful ways to bring about change, three of the methods end up being *destructive*. This means that the method used to successfully bring about change also leads to a tearing down. You either tear down yourself, someone else, or a relationship. On the other hand, one of the management methods is *constructive*, which means that the method used to successfully bring about change also leads to a building up. You either build up yourself, someone else, or a relationship.

Therefore, the bulk of the work is on the management side of the anger model. As far as being energized to anger, you need to understand and accept that anger is not the problem. If you were to expect that the work you have before you is to become less angry (if you thought you had a problem with anger), or you would like to be less anxious, and so on, then I would say to you … good luck! Try not having arms and legs! This is an impossible work. The real work before you is with anger management, and the hope of this type of work is connected with the fact that the way you manage your anger is *learned*. You may or may not know how or why you learned a particular destructive anger management method, but the main point is that you learned it. And if you have learned it, then you can also learn to unlearn it. You can learn to channel the energy of your anger to the constructive method. The ability for you to do so is a real hope you can hang onto in the work you have ahead.

Actually, if you seek to be less angry, the way to achieve this goal is as a benefit of learning the constructive method of anger management. You discover over time that you experience less overall intensity of emotion when you apply whatever emotion you feel to the constructive method of anger management. You learn to accept your emotions and not to be afraid of them. You may also become less emotional. In contrast, you tend to experience more emotions and to experience them more intensely if you use the destructive methods of anger management.

Please note that I prefer to use the terms *constructive* and *destructive* when describing anger management methods, as opposed to the terms *positive* and *negative* or *the right way* versus *the wrong way*.

Personhood

Although there are three destructive methods versus one constructive method of anger management, you can lump the three destructive methods together as one, when you contrast the methods in a general way. This is because they share some common themes. What the destructive methods have in common is that the emotions you experience have control over you. Please take a moment to think about the previous statement. Have you ever thought or believed "My emotions are controlling me" or "Your emotions are controlling you!"? The belief in the dynamics of emotions having control makes logical sense to people. Sometimes I think my emotions have control over me. Even though this dynamic is a concept that most people have no problem understanding or accepting as valid, it is a concept that is problematic. The problem lies in the fact that by stating that my emotions have control over "me," I am identifying a "me" that is controlled by my emotions rather than a *me* that includes them. But I have just gone through a whole dissertation in which I hoped to convince you that having your emotions is like having your arms and legs. In other words, having your emotions is part of how you understand yourself as an individual, or as a *me*, and is also a concept that makes logical sense.

How can these two concepts be understood both ways? Are my emotions part of something I call *me*, or are they separate and can control something I identify as "me"? What am I talking about? My head is spinning! I suggest that an approach to search out these questions is within a philosophical discussion. The question that addresses this dilemma is "What makes a person a person?"

There are various proposals to answer such a philosophical question. One proposal suggests that a person comprises a body, a soul, and a spirit. Most people I have discussed the question with agree with this proposal, even though there are differences in how they understand and divide the components of a person into various explanations. The easiest component to understand is the body (the component within the realm of the senses or science). It is the soul and spirit components of a person that most people have difficulty trying to understand and explain. Many attempts to define soul and spirit use similar terms for both, even though people tend to believe the two are distinct. Whichever way that the components of soul and spirit are understood, I think most people do get a sense that they are more than mere bodies.

An example of the awareness that people are more than bodies occurs in a book written by the late Christopher Reeve.[1] He wrote an autobiographical account of the movies he was involved in before his terrible accident, including his role as Superman. He relates the story of his life and writes about the accident he endured when he fell off of his horse while riding. He describes his experience of waking up in a hospital bed, discovering he has lost his ability to move his arms and legs. He writes about his recovery and about his hope to stimulate research to learn how to reattach his severed spinal cord so that he can walk again. Unfortunately, Christopher Reeve does not survive to the point of having some kind of intervention to help him walk again. What I find interesting about his book, however, is the title he chose for it. His title for his book is *Still Me*. What does he mean by this title? Could he be referring to his still body, the body that he is unable to move? Even though such an explanation is plausible, I think there is more to it. What his title says to me is: "I continue to be somebody. I may not be able to walk or use my arms, but I am still 'me'. I sure would like to be able to walk again and hug my wife again, but even though I can't do those things right now, I continue to be a person. I'm still me."

The person that Christopher Reeve describes does not seem to me to be about his body, because he does not have the ability to use most of it. He seems to make reference to something else that he describes as "me." What is it? Is it his soul? Is it his spirit? I find that I cannot assume that I know what exactly it is he refers to, but whatever it is, it must be different from his body.

When it comes to emotions, I understand my emotions to be in the soul part of who I am. I am not suggesting this is the way emotions ought to be understood; it is only the way that makes the most sense to me. If I think about a computer, the hardware represents the body, and the software or cyberspace represents the soul—something that is real, but not something I can grab, feel, and measure. Emotions are like that, too. If my emotions are in the soul component of who I am, there is yet another "me" that I identify when I have thoughts such as "My emotions sometimes control 'me.'" This third me is what I place in the spirit component of what makes me a person. More on that later.

Destructive Mindset

Let us explore what happens when your emotions have control over you. Something you identify in yourself as "me," that is, the essence of what makes you a person, falls under the control of your emotions. Please refer to the anger model in Figure 1.1 and follow along with this scenario: You find yourself in the presence of something you believe is wrong or an injustice, which is against some idea you have of law or truth. Your negative emotions of hurt, frustration, fear, or a combination of these emotions, sensitize and alert you to your concept of injustice. Your primary emotions in turn energize you to anger, which is a motivational energy in you to bring about change. Because your emotions have control over something you identify in yourself as "me," your emotions *prevent you from focusing your thoughts on what the problem at hand is.* But you are energized! You are motivated to bring about change! So what then do you focus your motivational energy on to bring about change? You focus on the **person!** You blame. You blame yourself, or you blame somebody else, depending on who the person is that is connected with, or is responsible for, doing what you believe is wrong. This very blaming dynamic is what leads you into the destructive mindset and the resulting destructive way of managing your anger.

The reason that blaming a person (whether you blame yourself or somebody else) drives you into the destructive mindset is that when you focus your motivational energy for change onto a person, you find yourself in a dilemma. Your dilemma is that you find yourself trying to change something that is *unchangeable.* There is something about a person that is unchangeable. It is true you can change the way you do things (the body part of what makes you human); it is true you can change the way you think or understand a situation (along with your emotions, this is within the soul component of a person). But there is something that makes you human that you cannot change—you cannot change who you are or who someone else is. There seems to be something about being a human that is unchangeable.

Change and time are related terms, are they not? You need time for change to occur. But if there is an ingredient to personhood that is unchangeable, the implication is that there is something about your personhood that falls outside the realm of space-time. If this is true, there must be a component of a person that has difficulty with understanding the concept of time. I believe people indeed experience snippets of such a phenomenon, but it is hard to get a handle on understanding it. I will give you examples of situations in which I think the phenomenon applies, and you can see what you think.

Have you ever thought something like "Boy, that year sure went by fast!"? My argument is that if a person's total humanness is within the realm of space-time, your experience is most likely to notice that you are going through a year one day at a time, and that after 365 days have elapsed, you would have total awareness that you have just passed through another year of existence in this world. "I've just gone through a year, yesssir, 365 days." But this is not your experience, is it? I don't know about you, but my experience tends to be: "Wow! Was that a year that just went by? It's going by faster and faster!"

Another example: It is not uncommon for an elderly person to comment: "I can't do the things I used to do when I was 25. I am getting older and weaker. But inside I don't feel any different!" When I look at myself in the mirror, sometimes I am surprised. I see a few more grey hairs sprouting up, and I think: "Where did that come from! Is that me in the mirror?" It is me, but this me seems to be different from some other me that I am referring to in my self-talk. I believe that what I am describing is a common experience people share as they journey through their lives. You see evidence of your body passing through time, but there is something about you that is not passing through time. Aging seems to be an insult! Aging seems to have a sense of wrongness connected with it.

Biblical Relevance

I believe the sense of wrongness connected with aging may be evidence that people were not intended to age. Think about the time after the creation but before the fall of Adam and Eve. Before Adam and Eve ate of the fruit that brought death, was aging inherent to life experience?

If it is true that there is something about your humanity that is outside the realm of space-time, then there must be some way of understanding and labelling it. Whatever exists and is not within the realm of time is understood as being eternal, and this component of your humanness is therefore the *eternal-nature* part of what makes you human. I understand this eternal-nature to be within the spirit component of what you are as a person.

When you are energized to anger and focus your thoughts on blaming the person, there seems to be an awareness in you that there is something about people that is unchangeable. Yet change is required! You are thus motivated! Therefore, the method you come up with to bring change falls within the realm of **power!** *It is me versus you, buddy!* You seek to bring change by enhancing your power advantage over your adversary and/or diminishing his power advantage over you, or you conversely belittle yourself as being small and insignificant compared with your adversary who has more power than you. You therefore submit to change, but do so begrudgingly.

You then discover what are called defence mechanisms to protect yourself from others having power over you. There are various defined defence mechanisms. One example is a counterattack. For instance, somebody says something that concerns you. She says it to you in an aggressive manner. You reply: "Oh! You're pointing the finger at me, are you? Well, what about you?" This counterattack line of defence is within the *me-versus-you* mindset, which makes it difficult for you to sort through an issue that concerns you and your adversary.

The Marriage Relationship

The me-versus-you mindset is contrary to what a marriage relationship is designed to be. One way that a marriage is referred to in the Bible is according to the concept that "two become one." I try to make sense of this unifying concept by viewing the spousal relationship as a team. When a person of marrying age is single, he is on his own team in the game of life. He deals with the problems and stresses that come his way on his own, for he is on his own team.

On the other hand, a marriage vow occurs when two people vow to each other: "You and I are going to be on the same team in this game of life. The problems and stresses that come our way we will deal with together as a team." When, however, problems and stresses come and the two people deal with their challenges in a me-versus-you fashion, their sense of team will fall apart. They will build up walls of defence to shield one from the other. They seek to protect themselves from each other and perhaps to maintain a sense of dignity. Eventually, each of them may have thoughts, or ask each other questions such as "I thought you were *for* me, but you are actually *against* me!?" And so the team concept of their marriage breaks down and is in danger of a destructive end result.

Brotherly Love

Another example of the destructive mindset is the outcome of two brothers who have a project they wish to work on together. They cannot, however, agree on how they are to go forward on their project. Finally, one brother says to the other: "We have to do it my way! Why? Because that is the way Mom and Dad would do it. And the way you want to do it? Nobody in the whole world would want to do it that way—so, come on!" In this example, the brother who aligns himself with Mom and Dad hopes to enhance his power advantage over his brother. Mom and Dad represent higher authority, and the power of their authority is aligned to the brother who hopes to use it for his advantage. He also hopes to diminish his brother's advantage by isolating him. He tells his brother that no one he knows of would do it the way his brother would do it. He therefore hopes that his brother succumbs to his way of doing the project. He may succeed in his efforts. His brother pouts: "Okay! We'll do it your way!" But are they a team? Not really. The one brother has merely captured his brother to do it his way (where he may assume the control). If something goes wrong as the project proceeds, the brother who at first gives in perks up, "I told you so!" So all along the two are not actually a team.

Biblical Relevance

One of the definitions of the word *Satan* is "accuser." Therefore, if you accuse yourself or someone else (focusing on the person) when you are upset or angry, you are in a mindset consistent with the destructive mindset warned about in the Bible. The result is destruction, which is consistent with the devil's schemes. However, the scripture also informs readers that you can become aware of the devil and his schemes (2 Corinthians 2:11), you can transform your mindset (renewing of your mind; Romans 12:2), and you can capture your thoughts to make them obedient to Christ (2 Corinthians 10:5). Therefore, you are not without hope!

Constructive Mindset

Let us explore the constructive method of anger management. The major difference between the constructive mindset and the destructive mindset is that the basic "who you are" as a human (soul or spirit as discussed earlier) has the control of your life. You learn to allow yourself to experience your emotions. The *me* (or *you*, the essence of who you are) has the control of your life, rather than the dynamic of allowing your emotions to have control over you. You learn not to be afraid of your negative emotions. You may continue to dislike your negative emotions (which may never change), and since they are unpleasant, you may prefer it if you did not have to feel them (another reason that they are classified as negative), but you are not afraid of them. You learn to use your negative emotions as a tool, where the basic "who you are" has the control rather than your emotions.

The initializing event that leads into your experience within the constructive mindset is the same as the initializing event into the destructive mindset. Please refer again to the anger model in Figure 1.1 and follow along with this scenario: Something happens that you believe is wrong—an injustice or something that is against some idea of law or truth that you have for whatever reason. Your negative emotions kick in to alert you to your sense of injustice. Your emotions in turn energize you to anger. So far the process is the same as the example for the destructive mindset. This time, however, you deal with the issue within the constructive mindset. The basic "who you are" takes control of your life. You grab hold of the emotions you feel, and you are in control. You use your emotions as a tool to help you to discern as best you can what the problem is that you are facing. Sometimes the problem is easy to figure out; sometimes it is not as simple. The answer of what the problem is, however, lies in that it is usually about something said or done, or not said or not done, that you believe is wrong. Once you identify as best you can what the problem is, your thoughts focus on the *problem*. You are able to grab hold of your problem to give yourself the opportunity to work with it, where you are in control (as opposed to your emotions). For example, the problem is that the dishes need to be washed. The problem is not the person who is not washing the dishes.

The process to bring about change (the anger management approach) within the constructive mindset now becomes a *truth encounter*, rather than the *power encounter* approach of the destructive mindset. Your challenge is to communicate or testify to what you believe the problem to be. The problem is an event that is not according to your version of truth. It is to be hoped that you will find a way to communicate so as to be understood by the person you are interacting with, but there are challenges when it comes to communication issues. Having a constructive mindset does not necessarily make your life a bed of roses—there are challenges to getting your point across that you will need to work through. Your quest is to communicate that a wrong has been done, and that the wrong affects you, them, and/or both of you. The focus of your thoughts is on the problem (a truth has not been upheld), as opposed to your focus being on blaming the person responsible for the problem. This dynamic is relevant, for example, if you take offence that something of yours has been stolen; the act of stealing is offensive to you no matter who is responsible for having done it. Therefore, the problem is always the problem; the problem is never the person.

It is said that when you focus on truth, "the truth sets you free" (biblical expression). But what does truth set you free to be? It sets you free to be a team! The concept of *team* is a unity term, and unity is a spiritual dynamic. If you have an increased sense of unity with someone (fellowship, camaraderie, family, belonging, brotherhood, sisterhood, and so on), the increased unity that you sense is what I call *spiritual food*. In other words, it feels good; you have an increased sense of belonging when you feel heard or validated when you have something to say.

Another component of growth as a result of the constructive mindset occurs on occasions when you fight with someone about something. When your attention is on what you are fighting about as opposed to you defending yourself against the other person, you often discover you are fighting with that person about something you actually agree on. And this is a sad reality that people are sometimes too blind to realize; you discover you are more interested in defending yourself against someone. Or, when you look at what it is you defend, your truth may actually be a lie. You are too interested in defending yourself and you risk being blind rather than admitting that you are defending a lie. When, however, you look at your truth and discover it actually is a lie, you grow in your overall knowledge of truth.

Biblical Relevance

Jesus said, "I am the way and the truth and the life" (John 14:6). Perhaps the verse means that when you focus your thoughts and feelings on truth (the constructive mindset), your focus is on the Lord. And when your primary focus is on truth, you fulfill the first and great commandment, that is, to "Love the Lord your God with all your heart and with all your soul and with all your mind and with all your strength" (Mark 12:30, where Jesus quotes Deut 6:4, 5). In the context of fulfilling this first commandment, you are then free to fulfill the second commandment, which is to "Love your neighbour as yourself" (Mark 12:31). You are free to fulfill the second commandment only in the context of the first.

If you believe you love God by loving your neighbour first, you are in violation of loving God first. Your neighbour becomes your "god" for you to love God. You become in danger of failing to worship God "in spirit and in truth" (John 4:24). But if you worship and love God first with your "everything," then you are free to love your neighbour as well as yourself, for you do not compare yourself with others within the me-versus-you way of thinking. Rather, you recognize that the person is not the problem. By relating with yourself and with others (your neighbours) in the mindset that the person is not the problem, you are loving yourself and loving them. Since God loves you and loves your neighbour, you are free to love yourself and love your neighbour, because you love God first, and therefore love what He loves.

Now for the HOMEWORK ASSIGNMENT

To start off with, I am asking you to learn from yourself. What I mean is, work on attaining an awareness of when you are in the energized state of anger, or if you prefer, of when you are in the energized state of anxiety. When you catch yourself feeling energized by your emotions or you notice your body is in an energized state when you are in a stressful situation, try to get an understanding of where your mindset is focused at the time. For example, when are the times that you find you are within the destructive mindset, and when are the times that you find you are within the constructive mindset? There is no right or wrong answer for this homework assignment. The assignment is merely a way to assist you to become aware of and to gain insight into how you understand your emotions when you feel them by examining where your thoughts are focused when you take offence at something.

When you are energized to anger, and you catch yourself within the destructive mindset, try to switch your thoughts into the constructive mindset. Eventually you can become what is called *mindful in the moment*, which to me means that you are training your thoughts to focus in the constructive way when you are taking offence at something.

For example, when it comes to your work or profession, especially if you have confidence in your ability to do whatever job you are doing, you tend to have a constructive mindset. For instance, you are at work. A problem presents itself, and you may think: "This is a tough problem! But if I check this angle out, or check that out, I will work it through as best I can." You notice that there is inherent stress in this situation.

But you are keeping it simple by making the situation to be about the problem only.

On the other hand, if you are not confident about your ability to do a certain type of job, you tend to be within the destructive mindset when you are challenged by certain problems. For instance, the same problem as described earlier presents itself, and you may think: "This is a tough problem! I don't think I am going to be able to figure it out! I don't know what I am doing!" Do you see in this second example how you are making yourself to be the problem? Therefore, your hands are tied in finding a way to come up with a solution to the problem. You are making yourself to be the problem, when you actually are not the problem. The problem is the problem! You are not the problem nor are your emotions the problem! When you learn to understand the difference between making the person to be the problem and making the problem to be the problem, you will find life to be a lot simpler and satisfying when your anger is focused in the constructive way. You will be free to believe in yourself and to be able to tackle various challenges, finding creative ways to do so.

From now on, before every subsequent chapter, please keep track of how you are doing with the homework assignment. Assess how you are coming along with gaining insight into how you understand your thoughts when you experience your negative emotions. When are the times that you are in a destructive mindset, and when are you in a constructive mindset? If you are in a destructive mindset and catch yourself within it, what are the benefits (if any) from switching your thoughts to the constructive mindset? From now on, your life is like a game you are playing. The homework assignment is a tool to help you understand how you are making sense of your emotions and the subsequent focus of your thoughts as you play the game called *your life*.

The following chapters examine the various anger management methods in more detail. First, I will describe the various destructive methods. You will get an understanding of various dynamics to be aware of as you practise the homework assignment and increase your emotion intelligence as you learn to be more constructive in the way you understand your anger and perform your anger management.

Summary of the Homework Assignment: What Is the Problem?

When you take offence at something, think about the homework assignment. There are three ingredients in the mix:

1. The problem (the thing said or done, or not said or not done, that you believe is wrong).

2. Your negative emotions and anger (and if you believe it is wrong to feel negative emotions, then you believe that you are the problem because you feel them).

3. The person responsible for the problem (you or someone else who said it, did it, did not say it, or did not do it).

Of these three ingredients, only one of them is the problem. Which is it?

The problem is not your negative emotions, your anger, or you. The problem is not the person responsible for the wrong. The problem is the problem! Nothing else. Once you have this truth sorted out in your understanding, you become free to discern and communicate the problem within the constructive mindset and hold accountable the person who is responsible for the problem. Good luck to you as you venture forth!

Chapter 2
Express

Now let us proceed by discussing the various anger management methods in more detail. First, I will discuss what I call the *destructive* methods. This will help you to understand various dynamics to be aware of as you are learning the homework assignment. You will notice that I prefer to use the designations *destructive* and *constructive* anger management techniques, as opposed to negative versus positive or the wrong way versus the right way.

The first destructive method to discuss occurs when anger comes out within the me-versus-you mindset. This method is called *express* and is illustrated in Figure 2.1:

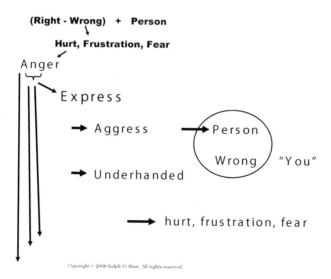

Figure 2.1 The Express Method of Emotion Management

When your anger comes out within the me-versus-you mindset, it can do so either aggressively or underhandedly. Whichever way it comes out, the result is the same. The primary focus of your thoughts is on the person (and so the arrow points to the person in Figure 2.1). The person and the problem (the "wrong") are considered to be as one and the same and so are illustrated as being circled together. It is as if the person represents the problem. The result of the destructive mindset is that you are limited to using "you" statements, and therefore you find yourself within me-versus-you thinking.

The first example of aggressiveness is physical aggressiveness. For instance, someone is upset about something connected with you (something you said, or did, or didn't say, or didn't do that he believes is wrong). But the focus of his thoughts in his anger is on you, who to him is the person doing what he believes is wrong. Since the focus of his thoughts is on the person who represents the wrong, he focuses on you and hits you with his fist (or attempts to). Society recognizes such actions as representing a destructive method of anger management, and so there are laws that address this method in order to protect citizens.

Another example of aggressiveness is verbal aggressiveness. This method can come in different forms. One form of verbal aggressiveness is the use of volume. A person is upset about something connected with you. The focus of her thoughts in her anger is on blaming you, the person. To her, the person represents the wrong, and so she yells or screams at you to bring about change (her anger management strategy). In this case, her power is represented in the volume of her speech. It is as if she is thinking, "If I yell loud enough, you will know that I mean it, and my yelling will get you to do what I want you to do so that change happens."

However, not all volume is destructive. You can have a constructive way of understanding your emotions, be communicating according to the problem, and have increased the volume of your speech. Emotions affect people in various ways. Emotions can colour your speech. Having a constructive way of communicating does not imply that you seek to converse in a monotone fashion like a robot. Having a constructive way of communicating may include increased volume. It could be said that you are animated, or *passionate*, about what you believe (when you communicate constructively with increased speech volume).

And yet, all you can do is manage your own emotions. You cannot manage other people's emotions. You may become constructive in the way you understand your emotions and communicate what you believe, but there is no guarantee that the person you are communicating with will receive your communication within a constructive mindset on her part. Communicating constructively increases the probability that the other person will respond within a constructive mindset, but it does not guarantee it.

Therefore, you will face challenges from time to time. You may find yourself communicating with someone within the constructive mindset. Despite your efforts, his response is within a destructive me-versus-you mindset. It is easy at this point to get captured into a me-versus-you way of relating with him, not because of you, but because of him. Your challenge is to learn not to take the bait of a me-versus-you response, reacting to it in like manner. Your challenge is to maintain the constructive mindset regardless of the other person's mindset. (This is sometimes illustrated in sports. For example, a star hockey player comes up against a known agitator on the opposing team. The job of the agitator is to provoke the star player so that he gets off his game and is more concerned about the agitator. If the star player strikes back at the agitator, is caught in the act, and penalized by the referee, the agitator has done his job to get the star player off his game and lose his effectiveness. Therefore, the challenge of the star player is not to "bite." He must keep focused on his own game to cater to his own strengths.)

A second example of verbal aggressiveness is the use of certain words or phrases that are thought to represent emotion or have some sense of power connected to them. Many of these words may be labelled as "swear words." (As well, the use of words that have an idea of power connected to them, such as are used as "spells" to result in some action, may also be included as forms of verbal aggressiveness. For example, in stories involving the use of magic, a magician casts a spell by saying the magic words to save the hero from certain destruction and so saves the day. Or the magician casts a spell, and the hero is covered in mud to make his or her quest all the more difficult.)

Yet another example of verbal aggressiveness could be a situation in which somebody is talking to you about a concern in a seemingly controlled and dignified manner. But as she is talking to you, she "goes up one side of you and down the other side," telling you how you let her down and asking, "How could you do such a thing?" So, she may appear cool, calm, and collected in her demeanour while talking to you, but she is verbally aggressive nonetheless. She is making you (the person) be the problem, rather than focusing on the problem itself.

Passive aggressiveness is another form of aggressiveness. This form of communication is linked to your power to withhold doing something you also have the power to do. An example is to "give" someone the silent treatment. In this case, "to give" implies something outward, but what is really happening is the withholding of contact to "give" a message. This is what makes it passive and yet aggressive. Another example is when a wife does things to help her husband, such as making breakfast for the both of them every day. One day, she is upset with her husband. She makes breakfast only for herself and carries on as if nothing happened. When he arrives at the breakfast table and notices he does not have his breakfast before him, he knows something is up. Her "message" is given to him in a passive yet aggressive way.

Underhandedness can come in different forms. This communication is not in the open but is subtle. One example is to control or manipulate things to make a point or get at somebody. It could involve gossip, which is a way within the destructive mindset to diminish the power of the targeted person and enhance the power of the person controlling the content of the gossip. Consider the following scenario in the workplace. Your colleague is upset with you at work. She manipulates things at work so that you find yourself in trouble with the boss. You approach your manipulative colleague unaware and regarding her as your friend. You seek her support in your time of distress. If you realize it is your colleague "friend" who has set you up to be in trouble, you may consider it to be just as if you had been given a slap in the face (the same as aggressiveness).

It is worthwhile discussing the use of humour when you communicate. When the humour is sarcastic, it can be considered to be aggressive. Humour can also be used defensively, as a way to soften the blow when you are attempting to communicate. For instance, your friend may wish to confront you about a concern of his. In his presentation, he tells you how terrible you are and asks how you could do such a thing, but he says it in a joking way so that you will not take it too hard.

Sometimes humour is used with the idea, "If it's a joke, it's okay." I believe the thinking here is that humour is generally thought to be connected with positive emotions. Therefore, if something is said in a humorous way, the expectation is you ought to receive the communication with positive emotions. If you receive the joke and experience negative emotions, there is thought to be something wrong with you. For example, you are at a party, and there is someone who is the life of the party. As he speaks to a group of people, he makes a comment about you that is risqué, such as a comment about your appearance or your behaviour. Everyone in earshot laughs (perhaps out of politeness), but you are not amused. Sometime later you approach this person privately and tell him you did not appreciate what he said. His defence to you is to say: "What's the matter with you? Can't you take a joke?" So you find yourself in a situation where not only does he make sport of you in a way you believe is unacceptable, but he also does not allow you to have your negative emotions even though you have them nonetheless. It becomes a difficult situation to sort out.

Not all humour is destructive. There is also constructive humour in the setting of something negative. After all, the saying goes "Laughter is the best medicine." I believe the difference between destructive and constructive humour is that constructive humour occurs in the setting of acceptance, while destructive humour is in the setting of judgment. For example, you have a friend who wishes to talk with you about something negative connected with you, yet your friend is willing to be weak as well. She may say to you: "I know you are struggling with such-and-such. I myself struggle with this and that. But hey, we've got to live! We can't let those things get us down!" Such is the setting of acceptance. On the other hand, the use of humour in the setting of judgment occurs when a person uses the power of humour to make a point or get at someone else.

Sometimes you cannot tell whether a person is being accepting or judging when he uses humour connected with something negative. It is because you have not established an understanding with him in your relationship. In such cases, I believe it is worthwhile to follow up with that person. If you do not do so, you may be at risk of writing off a relationship with someone that you may otherwise value over time. If you are not sure of how to take it, follow up with the person in question. You may say to him something like: "I don't really know you. I don't know how to take what you just said." If his intention is to be a friend to you, he will work it out with you so that you are both satisfied. Over time, he may become a friend you value. (Sometimes people use negative humour, believing it to be benign, not realizing someone whom they do not wish to hurt takes offence. The offending person really appreciates your feedback; without it, he would not know any better.) On the other hand, if you follow up with him and you discern his intention is to judge you (and you do not have a say in the matter), you have confirmation on how to understand your contact with him.

Whichever "express" method is used, whether aggressive or under-handed, the result is the same. You focus your thoughts on the person. The person and the problem are considered to be one and the same. You communicate using "you" statements.

The destructiveness of the express methods is realized when the person on the receiving side of the method (the target) responds to the method with emotions of hurt, frustration, fear, or a combination of them. In other words, the target person in turn experiences negative emotions. She is thus energized to anger and now has an anger management issue of her own to deal with. It is as if the anger model gets shifted so that the person on the receiving end of somebody being aggressive toward her becomes the person energized to anger. She takes offence at the *communication style* of the first person. (That's right! Please notice that all of the express methods described so far are merely communication styles. They are attempts to communicate, yet are destructive nonetheless.) The targeted person in turn has an anger management issue of her own to deal with.

To put it another way, if you are the one who is taking offence at something and are energized to anger, and if you manage your anger by using an aggressive method to bring change, then the very anger management method you are using is *provocative*. The very communication style you are using is understood as an issue of injustice by the person you are communicating with. He in turn is thus energized to anger. You have started the scene with one person upset and energized to anger. Your anger management method results in a second person becoming upset and energized to anger. The scene now leads toward a battle between the two over whose issue takes priority.

Escalating Cycle

There is one way in which the battle proceeds that can result in an *escalating cycle*. Imagine that someone is upset with you about something you did that he believes is wrong. But instead of focusing on the problem when he talks with you, he focuses on you and blames you. To him, you represent the problem, and he yells at you. You in turn do not like being yelled at (which I suspect is never going to change). Even though you can become very constructive in how you understand your thoughts, it does not mean you will like being yelled at. Therefore, if someone yells at you, you will likely take offence and be energized to anger.

Let us imagine that the way you in turn manage your anger is to focus right back on the first person, and you yell back at him. To yourself, you think, "I'm going to let you know how it feels, buddy!" Well, you know what? You have succeeded! In the same way that you do not appreciate being yelled at, he does not appreciate being yelled at either. He in turn may think, "Why are you yelling at me, when I'm the one yelling at you?" Instead of maintaining focus on the problem and persevering on what it is he is yelling at you about, he takes offence at you for yelling back at him. He is thus energized a little more in his anger. Therefore, not only is he energized from whatever the problem is, which he yelled about in the first place, but his energy is increased because he does not appreciate you yelling back at him. His comeback to you may be to yell again, and with more oomph, force, or gusto to drive home the point! You in turn don't appreciate his increased yelling, and therefore you are energized yet more. You retaliate at him with more force of your own. On and on the cycle continues with escalating force back and forth. The scene becomes a game between the two of you. It may become vicious. It may turn physical, and someone may get hurt. At the end of the game, there is the appearance of a winner and a loser. The person who "wins" may justify his victory. He may think, "I sure showed so-and-so how strong, or smart, or witty I am!" But is there really a winner?

Of over 12 years of asking my patients whether they believe there is a winner in the preceding situation, over 99.9% emphatically claim there is no winner. To search out an answer to the question whether there is a winner or not in such situations brings our discussion into a philosophical dimension. How you answer the following question determines whether you consider there to be a winner in such situations. The philosophical question that addresses the point is as follows: What is the basis of life? This is a deep and fundamental question. I find that two major proposals answer the question. Each proposal is summarized by one word.

The word that summarizes the first proposal to find an answer for the basis of life is *survival*. If the basis of life is survival, the concept of *survival of the fittest* follows. The belief according to this proposal is that the strongest, smartest, or fastest survive, and the weak do not. If survival is the basis of life, I suggest you could easily answer: "Of course there's a winner! That's the way life is! The strongest win and the weakest lose. It is just that simple!" But my experience is that over 99% of people I pose the question to claim there is no winner. So what is going on here? Are people answering the question according to an alternate proposal for the basis of life?

There is a saying for what it is like to "be at the top" that provides a clue to what the other proposal for the basis of life is. The saying is "It's lonely at the top." Why is it lonely? It is lonely because you have not been a friend to others on your journey to the top and you brought them down so that you could advance. And once you are at the top, you cannot consider anybody to be a friend to you, because you imagine that they are only trying to find a way to bring you down so that they can replace you at the top. Therefore, you are lonely because you have no true friends. And thus, there is the clue to what the other proposal for the basis of life is.

The word that summarizes the second proposal for the basis of life is *love*. Love implies a relationship. The concept of a relationship implies that a "story" is being told. There are two ways to end a story (Shakespeare does a good job of telling and ending stories in these two ways). One way that a story ends is called a *tragedy*. In terms of a relationship, a tragedy implies a going apart. The result is a *lose-lose* scenario. The other way a story ends is called a *comedy*, which in terms of a relationship implies a coming together. The result is a *win-win* scenario.

Therefore, if life is based on love, the outcomes are either win-win or lose-lose. If you have a scenario with the appearance of a win-lose outcome, then in reality, if one person loses, both lose. The person who believes he wins in a win-lose outcome only deludes himself into thinking he is the winner. In truth, he also loses. Over 99% of respondents to the posed question in the preceding discussion answer accordingly. Therefore, the express anger management methods are destructive, for they are communication styles at high risk for resulting in lose-lose outcomes.

Tangent

When two people battle over whose issue takes priority, an alternative avenue such a scenario can take is a *tangent*. In such situations, as with the escalating cycle, let us imagine someone is upset with you about something. In her anger, she focuses on you to blame you, for to her, you represent the problem. She yells at you. In response, you are energized to anger, for you do not appreciate being yelled at. This time, however, instead of yelling back at her, the way you manage your anger in return is to emphatically say to her: "Don't yell at me! Stop yelling!"

The person who yelled at you in turn thinks to herself: "What do you mean don't yell at you? I'm trying to tell you something!" But instead of focusing on what she is trying to tell you, she gets caught up with your concern about being yelled at, and addresses your concern in a defensive way. She replies, "When I'm upset, I can yell if I want!" You in turn reply: "No you can't! I don't like it one bit! I'm afraid for myself, or others, when you are like that." The scene may continue:

"Yes I can!"

"No you can't!"

"Yes I can!"

"No you can't!"

"Yes!"

"No!"

"Yes!"

"No!"

And on and on the discussion goes, proceeding along the detour of a tangent, where the two people are basically discussing the rules of anger management or communication. But there is not likely to be a conclusion or a resolution of the matter, for the two are not speaking the same language to each other. They are on two different wavelengths. At the end of the discussion, both walk away hurt. You walk away hurt and thinking: "What is it with her? I'm trying to tell her I don't like being yelled at (or threatened), and she just doesn't get it! How much of this can I take? I'm afraid for myself. I'm afraid for others involved (perhaps children)." And so you walk away hurt.

But the person who yelled in the first place also walks away hurt. She may struggle with thoughts like: "What gives here? Every time I'm trying to say something, instead of listening to me, it becomes about how I'm saying it! In the meantime, the thing I was trying to say is left untouched. It didn't get addressed. I don't have a voice! I'm a nobody!

I'm not allowed to say anything!" And so she also walks away hurt, and the result is another lose-lose outcome.

When examining the two different wavelengths of communication between these two people, I suggest that your point of view when you say "I don't like being yelled at!" is a fairly clear one at face value. Who likes being yelled at? I believe you would generally agree with concern about being yelled at. However, part of the issue at stake is the timing of the message. When a person is upset and energized to anger and if she manages her anger by yelling, then to her the yelling and the emotion she feels are one and the same. It is as if her yelling represents her emotion. If she hears you reply "Don't yell at me!" she will tend to understand your message in this way: "Don't feel!"

Since having feelings is like having arms and legs, she defends her right to exist when she defends her right to yell. To her, however, the yelling she is doing represents her emotions. Therefore, when she replies "I can yell if I want!" she is actually saying "I think! I feel! Can't you see?" However, it is not her feelings she is defending; it is her yelling that she is defending, which puts her on a different wavelength of understanding than you who have been yelled at. And this is the difficulty in sorting out such a situation. If the person who yells recognizes there is a difference between her yelling and her emotions, there is a way to come to an understanding between the two people in the situation of the tangent. I will address this type of scenario once more later in this chapter.

How Express Methods Are Learned

The next question to consider is, how does a person learn the express methods? Your experience likely shows you that express methods are successful ways to bring about change. For instance, it is not uncommon to hear a parent, particularly if he or she has young children, proclaim, "I can't get anything done around here with these kids unless I use an aggressive tactic!" As well, children learn how far they can get with their parent until they hit a certain point where the line is drawn. The children then stop and walk away "clean" because their parent responds to them in an aggressive manner.

After such an encounter between a parent and child, people get a sense that aggressive methods to manage anger are like using a double-edged sword. One of the edges of the sword represents the aggressive anger management method as a successful way to bring about change. You notice that as you use aggressiveness to bring about change, particularly with people that are weaker than you (such as a child), the aggressiveness is successful as an anger management method. You learn that to be aggressive helps you to accomplish your desire to bring about change. The other edge of the sword, however, represents the aggressive method that you are using to bring about change as having elements of wrongness associated with it. You get a sense that the aggressive method you are using is hurtful. You notice that there are responses to the method in the people you apply the methods to, as well as responses in observers. For example, the very parent who exclaims "I can't get anything done around here with these kids unless I use an aggressive tactic!" also struggles with her parenting skills by lamenting "But what kind of parent am I, to use such a method on my child that I love?"

People are inclined to think that aggressive anger management methods, although successful in their ability to bring about change, also have a sense of wrongness connected to them. Sometimes there are debates discussing whether there is a second edge to the sword or not. On one side of the debate, the claims are: "If so-and-so does something wrong, he deserves aggressive treatment! The responsibility is his! There is therefore no second edge to the sword." On the other side of the debate the claims are: "So-and-so may do something you believe is wrong, but that does not mean he deserves aggressive treatment! Two wrongs do not make a right!"

One way to learn express methods (such as aggressiveness) is illustrated in the following example. Imagine parents who are bringing up their children and interacting with them about issues of etiquette. Ideas of etiquette are rules of right versus wrong that society applies to certain situations. The rule of etiquette in the following example states: "It is wrong to eat with elbows on the table." The idea of rightness or correctness states it is proper to eat in a manner in which your elbows are not placed on the table. If, however, your elbows are on the table while you eat, the rule of etiquette is not adhered to and thus your action is improper.

Imagine a young child eating with his elbows on the table. His parent says to him quietly: "Get your elbows off the table. It is not proper etiquette and does not look good ... blah, blah, blah." So the child replies "Okay" and takes his elbows off the table. A rule of education, however, is repetition. The child in our example is informed of the rule of etiquette for the first time, but he does not necessarily remember the rule from then on. Similarly, the first time a child hears the concept "Two plus two equals four" does not necessarily mean he remembers the concept from then on. That is why children in school participate in repetitive exercises of mathematical concepts to help them learn the concepts.

Therefore, the next time the child eats with his elbow on the table, his parent gives him a reminder that doing so is unacceptable. His parent gives his arm a gentle nudge and says: "Remember? The elbow?" "Okay, Okay," the child replies as he removes his elbow from the table.

One day, the parent has a particularly stressful day at work and wants to come home to have a nice relaxing meal with his family. Home is a place of refuge. This parent comes home, sits at the table, and notices his child eating with elbows on the table. The parent thinks: "I've had enough stress for today. How many times have I told my child it is wrong to eat with elbows on the table, and he is still doing it!" So out comes an explosion. The parent pounds his fist on the table and screams, "Get your elbows off the table!" Whoosh! The child's elbows are off the table before you can bat an eyelid.

This aggressive method is successful at bringing about change, and therefore the method is learned. It is just that simple. It is not rocket science. People learn the aggressive methods whether they are aware of it or not.

Let us follow up this example. Sometime later, bedtime approaches. The parent wishes to give his child a kiss and a hug goodnight, but notices that since mealtime, his child has made himself scarce. The parent looks for his child and finds him in his room, slouching on his bed with a downtrodden look. The parent goes into the child's room, is lovingly concerned about his child, and says: "What's this all about? Are you okay?" The child thinks for a moment, and replies that he is upset for having been yelled at by his parent at the table. The parent responds quizzically, "Well, do you know why I yelled?" The child may not be able to give him an answer. The child looks down, shrugs his shoulders, and says, "I don't know."

"What do you mean you don't know!?" interjects the parent quickly and threateningly. "You never listen to me! Blah, blah, blah!"

So what is happening? Yes, the child is "getting it" again.

I believe one of the reasons that the child is not able to give an answer to his parent in this situation relates to the parent-child relationship dynamic, especially with a younger child. To a young child, the parent is bigger, stronger, wiser, and for the most part loving, and is teaching the child the difference between right and wrong. Therefore, to a young child, the parent is like God.

If you should ask this parent a couple of hours later "Why did you yell at your child?" the parent at this later time is more likely to answer within a constructive, problem-focused mindset. The parent may state, "The reason I yelled at my child is that I am trying to teach him that eating with elbows on the table is wrong, and that is exactly what he was doing!" Therefore, the parent's mindset at this later time is focused on the problem. At the earlier time, however, when the parent's message is delivered to the child at the table, the focus of the parent's mindset is on the child.

If you should ask the child a similar question a couple of hours later, "Why did your parent yell at you?" the child is more likely to respond within a person-oriented mindset. The child may answer "It's because I'm an idiot" or "It's because I'm no good" or "Because I'm bad" or "Because my parent hates me." These are all examples of the child's person-oriented mindset. Over time the child may continue to be related to by his parents primarily within a person-oriented mindset. If so, he is at risk of viewing himself solely within the destructive person-oriented mindset and may therefore struggle with low self-esteem. He doesn't like himself. He doesn't know why. He's never understood the difference between blaming himself and understanding that there are problems about things said, done, not said, or not done. He's seen himself as the problem and cannot split who he is as a person from problems that occur.

A second possible response to the child by the parent could be if the parent says to the child: "You're upset because I yelled at you? But that was a couple of hours ago! It's all in the past! You shouldn't feel that way. Just snap out of it!" People easily convince themselves with such thoughts. You think "I shouldn't feel this way," or you tell someone "You shouldn't feel that way." But if having emotions is like having arms and legs, try saying to someone "You shouldn't have legs!" In the context of legs, the statement sounds ridiculous, don't you think? But that is exactly what you are trying to convince yourself or others of when you think you or other people should not feel. A difference between your emotions and your arms and legs, however, is that you can learn not to feel if you believe you should not feel. The consequences of learning not to have your feelings can be health related. I will discuss this dynamic in a later chapter as the third destructive method of anger management, that is, when you learn not to feel and how doing so can affect your health.

A third possible response the parent can have toward his or her child in this situation occurs when he allows his child to have emotions. The parent does not make the fact of emotions be the problem, but instead validates his child's emotions and deals with the child's problem first. The parent then brings the whole scenario toward a constructive outcome. For example, when the parent learns his child is upset for having been yelled at, he responds to his child: "Let's see. You're upset because I yelled at you. Hmmmm. When I think about it, I would be upset if someone yelled at me the way I yelled at you. I believe I understand the way you feel. It was wrong of me to yell at you like that. Will you forgive me?" At this point the parent deals with his child's issue as best as he can. The parent then goes on to state: "The reason I yelled at you is that I am trying to teach you that eating with elbows on the table is wrong, and that is what you were doing. When I noticed your elbows on the table, I felt similar emotions to what you must have felt after I yelled. So, the real message is that it is wrong to eat with elbows on the table. But you're okay, I love you!"

Therefore, there is hope. If you have a tendency to manage your anger within the express method, especially if it tends to be in an aggressive manner, your challenge is to learn the homework assignment so that you can learn to capture the energy that anger gives you before it comes out within the destructive mindset. You can then learn to channel the energy of anger that you experience to the constructive mindset as best as you can.

But even if you are getting better at managing your anger constructively, you may continue to have challenges along your life path and to discover that you are not perfect. Sometimes your anger will come out within the destructive mindset and you will start to express. If your anger management does so, however, you will also learn to recognize the destructive dynamic you are in sooner than before, that is, before you get too far up the escalating cycle of a me-versus-you game or you go off on a tangent. You will learn to capture your anger energy sooner and then to rechannel your thoughts back toward the constructive mindset.

The way to rechannel the energy of your anger back to the constructive mindset, if your anger management initially comes out aggressively, is to humble yourself. Humbling yourself is an act of freedom. It is not an act of weakness. If you believe that humbling yourself is an act of weakness, you are more likely to justify yourself than to truly humble yourself. For instance, consider if your friend says to you in a self-justifying way "Okay! I'm sorry I yelled, all right?" Are you likely to believe he is truly sorry? No. You are aware that this form of justification is actually a sign of showing strength, and you are not fooled. An alternative response within a power mindset is to seek pity, which is about weakness. Your friend sorrowfully says to you: "I'm so sorry, I feel so bad. Please don't hold it against me!" You can get drawn in to feel sorry for your friend in order to make him feel better. The result is that it becomes about your friend's feelings rather than about the situation, and you are not sure you have a fulfilling result to the discussion. On the other hand, if your friend separates his destructive anger management method from his emotions, he is free to humble himself. He is free to say: "I'm sorry that I yelled. I do, however, feel, and this is what I was trying to say …" Such a person becomes free to talk about the problem in a constructive way.

Two Sides to the Equation

There are two sides to the equation of managing your anger in an express way. The first is the "dishing out" side of the equation, and the second is the "receiving" side of the equation. The dishing out side of the equation was discussed earlier, where your work has to do with learning to capture the energy of your anger before it comes out in a destructive way. You then channel your anger into the constructive mindset. The dynamic of bringing it back, if your anger management comes out in a destructive way, was also discussed earlier. Your challenge is to humble yourself and then rechannel the energy of your anger into the constructive mindset.

Biblical Relevance

Verses in the Bible present clues as people seek ways to understand concepts of emotion management. One relevant verse to our discussion is in 1Corinthians chapter 13, which is known as "the Love chapter." The love referred to in this chapter is the "agape," or unconditional kind of love. The relevant verse is the first part of verse 5, where it is written "Love is not rude." When you manage your anger in an express, especially aggressive way, it is easy to admit that you are being rude. You are not practising agape love when you attempt to communicate by yelling at a person. But when you read 2Corinthians 2:11, the scripture, in referring to Satan, indicates that you can be aware of his schemes. Further on in the letter, in 2Corinthians 10:5, it is written "we take captive every thought to make it obedient to Christ." Therefore, the work you have ahead is this: to capture your thoughts in conjunction with your emotions and to train your thoughts to be focused within the constructive mindset.

The second side of the equation has to do with being on the receiving end of someone else managing his anger in a destructive way. He focuses his blame on you and you are thus his target. How can the homework assignment help you to maintain a constructive mindset in this scenario? One difference, in comparison with being on the dishing out side of the equation, is that you are not the primary person who is upset. The other person is the first to be upset and energized to anger, but the way he manages his anger results in you also being energized to anger as you take offence at his anger management method (for example, if he yells at you). It means you also have an anger management question of your own to deal with.

To apply the homework assignment in this situation, first of all, if you are energized to anger by your emotions when you take offence at another person (for example, if someone yells at you), then your work is to allow yourself to experience your emotions and not to believe that your emotions are the problem. By doing so, you are free to use your emotions as a tool to discern what the problem is, and you are free in your thoughts to separate the problem from the person (constructive mindset).

The outward application of your work then becomes that if you allow yourself to have your emotions and convince yourself that emotions are not the problem, you learn to allow others to have their emotions as well. If you live the game of life in such a way that life is about emotions, your life will be a difficult road to travel. If your life is primarily about whether you or others experience positive or negative emotions, yours is a difficult, if not impossible, way to live. Sooner or later, you become aware of the reality of emotions, for to have emotions is similar to having arms and legs.

If you allow your opponent to have and experience his emotions when he manages his anger within a destructive mindset, you will learn to accept the fact **that** he is experiencing his emotions. You will learn to become confident to persevere and work through otherwise difficult circumstances. To repeat, you must learn to allow the other person to have his emotions.

The second factor I find helpful when you are on the receiving end of someone's destructive anger management is the biblical expression of "turning the other cheek." How I paint the picture of turning the other cheek is as follows: Wherever your cheek is turned is where your attention is. Therefore, if someone is upset and yelling at you, your initial response and attention is likely to be on what your issue is at the time. You will focus on the fact that you do not like being yelled at. Your initial focus on your issue is important. Depending on how aggressive the other person is, if you believe you are in danger, you will need to pay attention to your concern of trying to protect yourself as best as you can. On the other hand, if you believe you are safe (even though you do not appreciate being yelled at), then you are free to turn the other cheek. It means you are free to turn your attention away from what your issue is (that you don't like being yelled at) to what the other person's issue is (whatever his issue may be).

It is not your job to guess what the other person's issue is, since it is his issue and not yours. It is for the other person to communicate what his problem is to you. But if you focus your attention on what his problem is (not making his emotion, him, or you to be the problem), you are doing your part in listening to what he really has to say. Therefore, instead of yelling back at him (which can happen if your response is according to your issue that you don't like being yelled at and may then result in your interaction with him proceeding to an escalating cycle between the two of you) or instead of saying to him "Don't yell at me!" (which you may state, but your statement is according to your issue and may lead to a tangent between you to discuss your issue and deflect from his issue), you are instead free to reply "I can see you are upset and that is important to me. You are trying to tell me something. Is it …?"

And that is what I mean by the timing of your message to the person who is angry with you in the destructive mindset. If he is upset and yelling at you, his yelling at that time represents his emotion. If you in response turn the other cheek and focus your attention first on his issue rather than on your issue (assuming you are safe), you are free to acknowledge that his yelling only means that he is upset, and you are free to be comfortable with the fact that he is angry. You are free to validate his anger. When his emotion is validated, the connection he has between his emotion and his anger management method is severed.

Sometime later, you may not have to say anything to him about his yelling. He instead may approach you about it. For instance, he may say to you, "I'm glad we had that discussion, but I want to tell you that I am sorry I yelled at you." You are now free to possibly reply, "Yeah, I didn't like it one bit!" Please notice that the first person recognizes the double-edged nature of the sword of his aggressive anger management method and is willing to take responsibility for his part in his relationship with you.

A different scenario can occur if sometime later you decide to discuss with him the matter of his yelling. You could say to him: "I'm glad we were able to work things out the other day, but I just wanted to tell you that I did not appreciate being yelled at the way you yelled at me." He is more likely now to give ear to your concern because his yelling does not represent his emotion anymore. His emotion is validated and he is free to hear you out about your concern. This is what is meant by the timing of your message when the dynamic of the tangent occurs and you are hoping to let him know of your concern about being yelled at.

Biblical Relevance

The second half of the verse in 1Corinthians 13:5 has relevance for the receiving side of the equation. It is written, "Love is not easily angered." Keep this verse in mind in conjunction with your understanding about turning the other cheek. The verse is added fuel to help keep you in the constructive mindset when you face the various challenges that come your way.

Homework

How are you doing with your homework assignment? Are you gaining insight into the ways you understand your anger when you are taking offence at something? If you recognize the times when you understand your anger within the destructive mindset, how are you coming along with refocusing your anger onto the problem within the constructive mindset? Are you noticing a difference in how you approach a problem when you refocus on the problem rather than on blaming yourself or someone else?

Chapter 3
Suppress

The next destructive method to discuss is *suppress*. Please refer to the model of suppress in Figure 3.1. This is a peace-making method. When you find yourself in the presence of something you believe is wrong, you respond to your sense of wrongness with your negative emotions (hurt, frustration, fear, or a combination of them). You are in turn energized to anger by your emotions. In the energized state, you may think: "If I say or do anything about this, it's just going to get worse. So I better put a lid on it and keep it inside." By keeping quiet, you keep the peace.

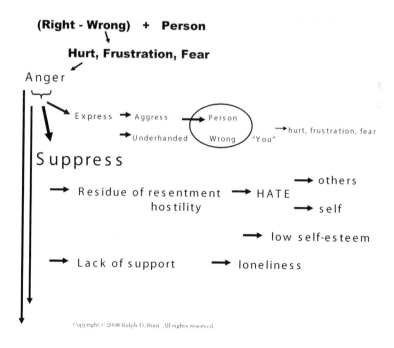

Figure 3.1 The Suppress Method of Emotion Management

The suppress method is well respected. The concept of peace is honoured in our society. Nobel Prizes are awarded for peace. The concept of peace is also valued in a spiritual context in many religions. For example, Jesus said, "Blessed are the peacemakers." If a person wishes to live according to the words of Christ, she may be convinced that the suppress method of anger management is the way to handle emotions.

But wait a minute! I am presenting the suppress method as a destructive anger management method. So what gives? Although the hope of the suppress method is focused on peace, the method is actually based on fear. Your fear (your emotions) control what you do in the situation to make the situation be about emotions. It is as if you are thinking: "If I say or doing anything about this problem, it's just going to make it worse. He will not like it if I say anything or do anything about it, and if I do say something, there is a good chance he will be energized to anger. And if he is energized to anger, and if he in turn manages his anger in an expressive—especially aggressive manner—someone could get hurt, and it could be me! So I better keep my thoughts and feelings inside, put a lid on it, and keep the peace."

You have found a successful way to manage your anger to keep the peace. When you keep your thoughts and feelings inside to keep the peace, you eventually cool down after having been in the energized state of anger. If someone else is involved in the situation and also is energized to anger, he eventually cools down as well, as long as nothing further happens. So you find a way to keep the peace, accomplishing your "noble" goal of peacekeeping.

However, there is a saying in the Bible that reads "Peace, peace … when there is no peace" (Jeremiah 8: 11). I believe the method of suppressing your anger within a destructive mindset is an example of this biblical saying. When you keep your thoughts and feelings inside within the me-versus-you mindset, you are successful in making it outwardly appear as if there is peace (as you and the other person settle down from your energized state of anger). But inwardly, in your thoughts and feelings, there is no peace.

When you keep your thoughts and feelings inside within the me-versus-you mindset, the event that has happened, which you take offence to, is recorded and saved in your memory. Imagine that your memory functions in a way that is similar to recording things on videotape. The event is saved as a portion of memory on your videotape that I call a "residue of resentment" or "residue of hostility." This event is then stored in your memory banks.

Because you accumulate a bank of memories, you will at some later time replay the videotape that is inside your mind to yourself. Each time you remember something, you recall the same issue of right and wrong that is connected with the same person. The scene is displayed to you in your mind. As you experience your memory, your emotions may kick in again, and you are in turn energized to anger. When you are in the energized state, you may think, "Every time I think about this, it's like there's a ravenous wolf inside me, and I feel ... **ugh**!" So what do you do? That's right; you suppress and keep the event to yourself. You keep the peace because you want to be that peacekeeper.

Your memories can come at different times. Sometimes you may find yourself chewing on your thoughts over and over again throughout the day about something that happened earlier that day. Sometimes you remember the next day or maybe a week later, or a month, or perhaps years later. When you have your memory and you experience new negative emotions connected with your memory, and when you keep your emotions inside to keep the peace within the me-versus-you mindset, the result is that the portion of memory on your videotape lengthens somewhat. In other words, your resentment and hostility grows.

Over time, the residue of resentment or hostility that you are accumulating is so much that you start to HATE. "Hate" is a strong word, is it not? I believe the concept of hate is that of a spectrum. Hate can occur in differing degrees for different people, with a variety of contributing factors (more than I have the ability to understand). But I believe the main point of the spectrum of hate is that the basic mindset of the person who hates is that she is focused on blaming the person, whether she hates others or hates herself. As the process of hate evolves, she is at risk of struggling with low self-worth and low self-esteem.

Linking low self-esteem with hating yourself is easy to understand, but how does hating others lead to low self-esteem? A link to self exists when you hate others because you are in the me-versus-you mindset. Notice the word "me" is present in the destructive mindset. You may hate someone else because of the way they treat you, and so your sense of self-worth or self-esteem is included in the picture of hating someone else.

Biblical Relevance

It may be easy for a Christian to believe that the way to handle emotions is by suppressing. After all, Jesus says, "Blessed are the peacemakers." For the reasons discussed earlier, however, I do not believe that the peace that Jesus talks about is within the suppress method of anger management. Suppressing your anger within a me-versus-you mindset only leads to a false peace. I believe the true peace that Jesus talks about is within the constructive mindset, and can lead to peacemaking rather than peacekeeping. I will discuss this further in chapter 5.

Low Self-Esteem

To understand the dynamic of low self-esteem, let us change the picture a little bit. Instead of the videotape example, imagine that when you are energized to anger, it means you find yourself dealing with a **hot potato** in your hands (Figure 3.2). You are tossing your potato back and forth from hand to hand because it is too hot to handle.

Figure 3.2 Hot Potatoes

The *potato* represents a concept of right versus wrong, or injustice, that you find yourself in the presence of. The heat of the potato represents your emotions, which draw your attention to the fact that you are dealing with a potato. It follows that anger management consists of what you will do with the potato in your grasp.

When you have a potato in your hands and your attention is focused on blaming the person responsible, whether you blame yourself or someone else, and when you manage your potato by using the express method, it is almost as if, with clenched teeth, you say to the person, "You gave me this potato, and so I am going to let you have it!" You throw your potato at the person you are blaming. For example, you yell at him. But if you use the express method, as discussed in the previous chapter, I hope to show that when you throw your potato at another person, you are not actually letting go of your potato. It continues to be in your grasp. However, your action of throwing a potato at another person becomes a potato to him (something he believes is wrong). If he in turn manages his potato by throwing his at you, he actually does not let go of his potato. But his action of throwing his potato at you becomes a second potato to you and now you have two potatoes to deal with. What follows can lead to an escalating cycle or to the detour of a tangent, as described in chapter 2.

If you manage your potato by using the suppress method, with your thoughts focused on blaming the person within the me-versus-you mindset, it is as if you think: "If I let you know that I have this potato, you might get upset, and then I'll have to deal with your anger, so ... what am I going to do? I know! I'll keep my potato out of sight and out of mind to keep the peace!" So what do you do with your potato? You put it in a thermally lined sack that you carry on your back (out of sight, out of mind, and you can't feel the heat). But what you are left with is a potato in the sack you are carrying around with you wherever you go (the sack represents your memory banks).

Because no one is perfect, you will deal with issues of right versus wrong every day with no matter who you meet. I have discussed this dynamic in a previous chapter and will briefly review it here. A fact of life is that no one is perfect (except Christ in the Christian faith). Two factors complicate this truth: quantity and quality. *Quantity* means the more time you spend with someone, the more you are exposed to the fact that she is not perfect. This applies especially to you (you are exposed to yourself 24/7) and to those you spend a lot of time with, such as your friends, loved ones, or co-workers (hence the saying "Familiarity breeds contempt."). *Quality* is about expectation levels that you put on yourself and on others, whether they are strangers or loved ones. Your expectation level is an idea of perfection that you have and that may be reasonable. It may be your will and the will of others to meet and fulfill your expectations, but since no one is perfect, all people fall short of your expectations, even though they try not to.

The bottom line is that you manage a crop of potatoes every day. Many of your potatoes are linked with what you have done, and many are linked with what others have done. If you place your potatoes in the sack on your back, over time your sack gets heavier and heavier and heavier (Figure 3.3). You notice the effects of your heavy sack as the load gets harder to drag around. Your knees bend from the weight, and your gait becomes more laboured. The sack weighs you down. The result is that you are stooped over as you carry around your heavy sack. I refer to this dynamic as *low self-esteem*.

Figure 3.3 Heavy Load of Potatoes

Your view of the world, and of yourself, is from the lower vantage point of low self-esteem. The weight of the sack puts a strain on you. Your sack full of potatoes becomes a lens of negative thinking. You begin to see the world from a lower vantage point, and therefore you put a negative spin on things that happen. You do not think as negatively if your walk in the world is where it is meant to be: with an upright gait, without your sack weighing you down. But seeing the world from a negative vantage point, and putting a negative spin on the events that happen, means you deal with more potatoes than you would if you were up to where you were meant to be. Your perception is that there are more wrongs, which leads to more negative feelings, which in turn leads to more anger. And when the extra potatoes that are linked with your negativity arrive, what do you do with them? That's right; you put them in your sack, because that is how you have trained yourself to handle them.

When you remember something, imagine that your memory plays out as if the potato linked to your memory comes out of your sack and goes back into your hands to grasp and mull over in real time. You then experience new emotions connected to your memory. With the heat of your fresh emotions, the result is as if your potato gets bigger or buds into two or more potatoes. And what do you do with those potatoes? Right again—you put them into your sack.

Therefore, you are at risk of falling into a downward spiral. By using the suppress method of anger management, you place your potatoes in the sack on your back. Your memories of those potatoes result in your dealing with extra potatoes associated with the same problem. After your memory, you put the original plus the extra potatoes into your sack, and the sack gets even heavier.

So you are stuck! You have a heavy sack of potatoes that you carry around with you wherever you go. Then you start asking questions: "What am I doing down here?" (Imagine that you are hunched over, carrying a heavy sack.) "Is this where I am meant to be in my life? Aren't I supposed to be up here?" (Imagine you are standing straight.) "Why am I down here?" (You are hunched over again.) Your questions are reasonable, for you are truly meant to be "up here" as opposed to "down here."

But this is where you can be at risk. A person considers the condition of being weighed down by a sack of potatoes to be like an illness. You therefore look for ways to get relief from your "condition." Seeking relief is reasonable. When you search for treatments to get the relief you seek, however, you discover that some treatments are very good, while others are risky.

Risk Assessment

One way to get an understanding of the effectiveness of any treatment is called the *risk-to-benefit ratio*. An ideal and perfect treatment results in 100% benefit to 100% of the people 100% of the time, with no risk to 100% of the people 100% of the time. Unfortunately, there is no such perfect treatment. Therefore, a favourable treatment is one that gives people the greatest benefit with the least risk.

For example, if you are diagnosed with some sort of bacterial infection and your doctor prescribes an antibiotic for you to take, the benefit side of your prescribed treatment is that the antibiotic kills those "bugs" dead so that you are cured of your infection. Limits to the benefit of the antibiotic arise if there is resistance in the bacteria to the antibiotic that you are prescribed. The effectiveness of your prescribed antibiotic is therefore limited. The question of antibiotic resistance is addressed by the Provincial Laboratories, where antibiotic resistance patterns in disease-producing bacteria that are present in your community are monitored. Physicians are notified about which favourable antibiotics to prescribe in a given locality. You therefore receive the greatest benefit possible.

On the other hand, when assessing risk, the antibiotic you take may cure your infection, but it may also introduce an illness you did not have before. You may, for instance, respond to the antibiotic with an allergic reaction. You then require additional treatment for this new health risk, with a treatment approach carrying its own risk-to-benefit ratio. And so doctors attempt to minimize the risk to a person taking an antibiotic by recording your drug allergy history. You are therefore prevented, as best as possible, from having an allergic reaction.

Treatment Options

There are two major modes of therapy, each of which comes with a supporting list of treatments to achieve the relief you seek from your heavy sack of potatoes (Figure 3.4). One of the modes of therapy is *symptomatic*. It means that the treatment used to bring relief is successful, but unfortunately nothing is done about the potatoes in the sack on your back. Symptomatic treatments get you up to where you are meant to be, but your heavy sack remains on your shoulders. You are free only from feeling the weight of your sack. The symptomatic treatments have a poor risk-to-benefit ratio.

The other mode of therapy for getting relief from the weight of your sack of potatoes is *therapeutic*. The therapeutic treatments get you up to where you are meant to be because your sack not only feels lighter, but it is lighter. There are fewer potatoes in your sack. The therapeutic treatments have a more favourable risk-to-benefit ratio. They are not without risks, but are nonetheless more favourable as treatments. Understanding the favourable treatments is based on knowledge of the constructive method of anger management. Therefore, my plan of attack in going through the anger model is to hold off on the discussion of the favourable therapeutic treatments until I discuss the constructive method in more detail.

Figure 3.4 Symptomatic versus Therapeutic Treatments for Relief from your Burden of Potatoes

I will now discuss the list of poor treatments, those that are symptomatic. Even though they have effectiveness in bringing you relief from the weight of your sack of potatoes, the risks of their use are great.

Symptomatic Treatments

Alcohol

The first treatment on the symptomatic list is alcohol. Imagine a person hunched over by the heavy weight of a sack of potatoes he is carrying on his back. He tries a drink or two. He notices that the sack feels lighter as the effects of the alcohol kick in. When he is able to stand upright, he thinks: "That's better! This is the way life is meant to be!" The alcohol does nothing about the sack of potatoes. It is still there. Only his awareness of his sack of potatoes is diminished.

There are side effects. For instance, he experiences decreased reaction time when driving (scientifically shown to occur) or he experiences impaired judgment in his thinking. A problem, however, is that the focus of our friend's response to the alcohol tends to be on the *benefits* of the treatment, rather than on the *risks*. Therefore, it is possible for him to claim, "I know I'm still a good driver, even after I've had a drink or two!" What he doesn't realize is that he puts himself and others at risk if he drives under the influence of alcohol. His reaction time, especially noticeable when driving, in reality is decreased. (Contrast the benefit-versus-risk focus of a person when treated with a medically prescribed pharmaceutical: When she takes a certain prescribed medication, her attention may primarily be on the side effects or risks, rather than on the benefits of the medication. She may become resistant to continuing the treatment. It becomes a challenge for the physician to communicate to her the balance of the benefits versus the risks of an otherwise beneficial medication for the treatment of a serious disease when providing expert medical care.)

When our friend feels a sense of relief from the weight of his sack of potatoes after a drink or two, he may also think: "This alcohol is helping me to feel better. It is helping me to be the way I am meant to be!" Such a conclusion represents the beginnings of emotional dependence on the substance.

After the effects of the alcohol wear off, he is hunched over once again by the weight of his sack of potatoes. In the meantime, new potatoes arrive. He manages them by putting them in his sack, for that is his way of dealing with potatoes. The next time he feels overwhelmed by the weight of his sack, he remembers: "The last time I felt this way I had a drink or two, and it really helped me to feel better. So why don't I try it again?" New dynamics are creeping in. He places hope in alcohol: "When I feel this way (down), I have found something that gives me hope!" As well, he puts his faith in alcohol. It is as if he proclaims, "When I feel this way (down), I *believe* this alcohol is going to help me to be the way I am meant to be!"

The problem with what is now happening is that he is using *spiritual* or religious terms. Whatever you put your faith, hope, or dependence in becomes your "god" or your idol. Whatever becomes your god is what gives you your identity. Your god becomes your master, and you become the servant, or slave, of that god. As a slave to this god, you will eventually be given extra potatoes to handle.

Biblical Relevance

Any god you put your hope and faith in other than the living God is not a *loving* god. In other words, any god other than the living God gives you more potatoes to deal with than you have to deal with anyway. This is why the commandment states: "You shall have no other Gods." "You shall not worship idols" (From Exodus 20:3-4).

I believe God gives me this commandment for my benefit rather than for His benefit. It is as if God says to me: "I am not going to give you more potatoes to deal with other than those you deal with anyway. I am actually going to help you deal with the potatoes that come your way. Any god you have or worship other than me is going to end up giving you more potatoes to deal with. So don't worship them."

God actually does not need me to worship Him, for He is complete and without need. He can do very well without me or anybody else to worship Him. But it is His pleasure for me or anybody to be in a positive relationship with Him. I have a feeling of thankfulness and awe to be given the opportunity to worship Him in spirit and in truth.

Since the "god" of alcohol gives our friend extra potatoes to deal with, he ends up juggling more potatoes added to those he is handling anyway. And what does he do with all his potatoes? Right! Into his sack they go! His sack becomes heavier yet. And where does he seek relief from the weight of his sack? He seeks the very treatment that results in him dealing with more potatoes than he otherwise would! He seeks the bottle. More and more potatoes go into his sack. His use of alcohol under these conditions gives him more and more potatoes to handle. He ends up within a vicious cycle of dependence on alcohol, which is something that is undependable.

Biblical Relevance

Nothing in this world is dependable. Not me. Not you. Not my job. Not my car. Nothing, or nobody, is dependable, except the One (Jesus), who is Trustworthy and True (John 14:16; Revelation 21:5).

Since there is nothing in this world that is dependable (including me), I need to find something dependable to anchor myself to. I seek a sense of stability in this undependable world. If my life resembles a ship in the open sea, I appear to be doing well as long as the weather is favourable. But when the storms of life come, I seek a way to maintain my stability. I toss my anchor toward a source to achieve the stability I seek.

I become dependent on any source of stability I discover is successful in keeping me stable. When I am stabilized, I am free to exercise my independence; that is, I am able to achieve my goals as my "ship" carries on with its activities. The value of the strength or stability of the independence I acquire is only strong or stable if what I toss my anchor to hold on to is dependable. Therefore, there is no true independence without dependence (and the value of the strength of my independence is measured by the dependability of what I am depending on).

For example, if I toss my anchor onto the deck of my own ship, I place my confidence in my own strength. I will discover that doing so does not give me the stability I seek in the storm I am in. If I notice another ship that is not too far away, and toss my anchor onto the deck of that ship to seek stability, I will discover no increased stability in the storm (especially if that ship tosses its anchor onto my deck as well).

However, if I toss my anchor overboard into the depths of the sea, I live a life of faith. I do not see the bottom of the murky sea, and I do not know if or when my anchor will take hold, but I place my confidence in something that is unseen. I will discover the results of putting my confidence (faith) in something that is dependable, as my anchor takes hold in the unseen rocks below and gives me the stability I seek in the storm. The rock is Christ.

One risk of a person putting his faith in alcohol to get relief from his sack of potatoes is that he eventually needs to consume an increased amount of alcohol to achieve the effect he is looking for. This is called physical tolerance, and it works like this: Before a person starts to consume alcohol, the cells in his body function efficiently without it. When he introduces alcohol, his cells make adjustments to function efficiently within the context of the added alcohol. In order for him to achieve effective relief from the weight of his potatoes, he discovers he needs to consume more alcohol to override his body's adjustment to alcohol being present. He convinces himself that this is a sign of manhood. He proudly states to his friend: "How much can you hold? I bet I can drink you under the table!" Actually, as opposed to being a sign of manhood, it is merely a statement of how far he is along in physically tolerating alcohol.

As the cycle of tolerance progresses, he is at risk of becoming physically dependent on alcohol. The cells in his body become used to functioning within a certain concentration of alcohol mixed into the "juices" of those cells. If this concentration of alcohol drops below a certain amount, his body starts thinking it is missing out on something. The alcohol becomes like food to him. He clenches his throat with his hands and appeals: "Hey! I'm starving! What are you doing? I need another drink!"

If the cycle of increased alcohol intake continues to progress, the toxic side effects of chronic alcohol use become apparent. He may suffer liver damage, heart damage, or damage to other cells in his body. The process amounts to more health-related potatoes for him to deal with, and he likely adds those potatoes to his sack when he encounters them.

Another risk of alcohol consumption relates to impaired judgment. A sober person may do a good job of keeping his potatoes in his sack. He may be considered the nicest person around. Under the influence of alcohol, however, he may change his demeanour. All of a sudden, he throws his potatoes at whoever happens to be around. He can become violent. Although he throws his potatoes, they actually remain in his sack. But throwing potatoes at people is aggressive and so his actions become a potato to others. If others in turn manage their potatoes by throwing them at him, he is left with handling even more potatoes, which he in turn manages for the most part by putting them in his sack. When he feels the increased weight of potatoes in his sack, he resorts to drinking more alcohol to achieve the relief he seeks. It becomes a difficult cycle of dependence/hope/faith on alcohol for him to break out of.

Sometimes a person under the influence of alcohol does not have a recollection of what he did while drunk. The next day, his friend speaks to him with concern: "Did you know what you were like last night? Do you know what you did?" He may not remember what he did and may believe that his friend is only trying to get him to stop drinking (which he is not interested in, because it is his "treatment"). But even if he cannot remember, the fact of his aggressive behaviour under the influence of alcohol is not nullified.

Although alcohol can give a person a sense of relief, it comes with high risk. Alcohol is therefore a poor treatment for relief from potatoes, and is merely symptomatic treatment. Alcohol does nothing to resolve potatoes and ought not to be linked as a way to manage emotions.

Drugs

The next poor treatment on the symptomatic list is drugs. These may include certain prescription drugs, natural substances, recreational drugs, street drugs, and so on. Any substance that results in a "high," a state of euphoria, or a feeling of escape can fall into this category. A high may represent the energized state of positive emotions and is what is common with many addictions—a person lives in slavery to her emotions and chases the positive emotional high to counter or contrast the down of the weight of her negative emotions connected with the potatoes in her sack.

The dynamics of drug use are similar to the use of alcohol as a treatment. A person requires more and more of the substance to get the effect she looks for and therefore puts herself at risk of an overdose (which is a health-related potato). If she injects the drug, she is at risk for infections such as hepatitis or HIV and AIDS (if she shares and reuses the needles).

Other risks are social. Because of the cost of the substances she uses, she may resort to violent means to get the funds to pay for the substance, or she may sell her body for profit to get access to the substance she depends on. These activities in turn result in more potatoes for her to deal with, which she likely manages by putting them into her sack. To get relief from her heavy sack, she appeals to the very substance that in turn gives her even more potatoes to deal with. She is in a cycle of dependence on the drug, which is difficult to break. Therefore, drug use is a poor treatment to manage emotions.

Smoking

Smoking is another poor treatment for the burden of your emotions. The side effects of smoking, including health issues, financial issues, and social backlashes from anti-smoking groups, add to the potatoes you already deal with anyway. You place the extra potatoes in your sack, and then you appeal to the treatment of smoking to get symptomatic relief from the weight of your potatoes. You are at risk of going into the cycle of dependence on smoking in which you may believe your cigarette is your only friend. The cycle of dependence is difficult to break away from.

Gambling

The next poor treatment is gambling. The way gambling works as a poor treatment is via a sense of thrill or "high" when a person makes a win. He may experience a rush of excitement while playing or he is hopeful for the prospects of a win.

He may be loaded down by a heavy sack of potatoes. He decides to try a certain gambling venture. He may win. It may be a significant amount of money. When he wins, he is on a high. While feeling high, he loses awareness of the heavy sack of potatoes on his back, but it is there nonetheless. He may also believe that he has access to more money than he actually has available to him, and makes promises of buying this or that.

After some time, he comes down from the high of his win, and reality sets in. He starts feeling the weight of his sack of potatoes again, which pulls him downward. In the meantime, more potatoes arrive that he must deal with, and he adds them to his sack. Some of his new potatoes have to do with pay-up time for the promises he made to buy items while relishing the high of his win.

When he feels weighed down the next time, he is at risk. He may remember: "The last time I felt low like this, I played a gambling game, and it sure felt good when I made that win. I made a lot of promises after I made that win, which I couldn't keep. But I think I've learned my lesson. I don't believe I will make those mistakes again. I'm smarter now. I think I'll play again, and it will help me to feel better!" His hope and faith are in making another win to achieve relief from the heavy sack of potatoes on his back.

What he discovers, however, is that it is not easy to get that next win. So he tries again and again and again. Because his faith is in making that win, he continues to play. He notices he is investing more and more of his money in his chosen gambling activity and gets behind in his overall financial picture. He justifies his continued playing, all the while reasoning, "When I make that win, it will make up for everything I have spent on playing the game in the meantime." This dynamic is known as the catch-up phase of a downward cycle of dependence or addiction to gambling. He is at risk of living his life as a slave, serving his chosen game to get relief from his troubles.

Eventually, he may become consumed with gambling. Even placing a bet without knowing the outcome can bring a sense of hope to him. His justification may be: "I've gone 99 times and I haven't come through. That must mean I'm due! And if I don't place that next bet, what hope do I have?" Therefore, just placing another bet carries with it an element of hope and keeps him in the cycle of living for, and being mentally consumed with, gambling as a means of his stress relief.

There may also be an element of excitement (awareness of his positive emotions) connected with the thrill of playing that is a draw for him to keep on playing. He may seek to experience his positive emotions as a way to mask out or balance the effect of the negative emotions he experiences. The gambling in effect becomes a way for him to put a lid on his negative emotions and he places the potatoes affiliated with his negative emotions in his sack.

Gambling is marketed as a form of entertainment, and so it is also called "gaming." The question people need to ask themselves is, "How good am I at keeping the activity of gambling as a form of entertainment?" For instance, a person may be willing to spend, or be out, $100 for the entertainment value of watching an Oilers hockey game. If the game goes into overtime, the entertainment value of the investment is enhanced.

Can he have a similar mindset when he is gambling or gaming? Can he be willing to spend or be out $100 for the entertainment value of his chosen gambling activity? If he wins, will his win be considered as an enhancement of the entertainment value of his investment? Problems can arise when he makes a win, especially if his winnings are significant. His perspective can change. Initially, what he considers a form of entertainment becomes a way to earn income. His purpose for playing is changed, and he believes it is fun!

As an investment strategy, however, gambling provides a low rate of return. Gambling (gaming) is designed to be a form of entertainment; therefore, anyone who chooses this form of entertainment must accept that he has to pay for his entertainment. Just as he pays to see an Oilers game, he pays to play a game in the casino. How much are you willing to spend on this form of entertainment? Not everyone becomes addicted to gambling, but there is certainly a risk involved that everyone needs to be aware of.

Food

The next poor symptomatic treatment is food. A person may feel weighed down by her sack of potatoes. She thinks, "If I just have some of my comfort food, it will help me to feel better." Many of the so-called comfort foods are considered junk foods.

Some foods that you consume are known to increase your body's serotonin levels. Serotonin is a natural chemical in the body. Many antidepressants are effective in treating depression because they favourably adjust the defective serotonin pathways that are present in the brain of a depressed person. I am not aware of studies that link certain foods (chocolate?) as being helpful in the treatment of depression, but I consider the effect on serotonin to be an interesting parallel. The rise a person gets from certain foods may in part have similarities to the use of antidepressants.

An adverse side effect of eating to achieve relief from the effect of the weight of her sack of potatoes is weight gain. As she gains weight, she may develop health-related potatoes (problems) such as hypertension, risk of diabetes, heart disease, and so on. When she gets these potatoes to deal with, she adds them to the load in her sack.

Another risk she encounters relates to social interactions. Obesity is generally understood as a negative term. And so our friend looks at herself in the mirror and does not like what she sees (she judges herself as being a problem and thus has a potato with her name on it to deal with). Or, someone else in her life puts pressure on her: "Look at you! Don't you know you should be doing something about your weight? You're a waste! Get off your ----- and do something!" In other words, the aggressive attitudes of others toward her become potatoes to her. As well, since she has no counter-proposal about understanding her obesity, she may agree (to herself) with others that she is a problem because she is obese. The effect on her is to multiply the amount of potatoes she has to juggle, and she likely adds them to her sack.

Yet another risk is financial. As she gains weight, she may need to replace her wardrobe, which incurs financial stress (potatoes) on her. When those potatoes come her way, she puts them in her sack. She is weighed down even more. She seeks relief from the weight of her sack of potatoes by eating, for that is where her hope lies. She develops a cycle of dependence on food which is difficult to break. Eating is therefore a poor treatment to counter the effects of your negative emotions and to find relief from the weight of your sack of potatoes.

The use of food as a symptomatic treatment can be further complicated in the situation of bulimia and anorexia nervosa, but I will not tackle this discussion in this book.

Exercise

Exercise is the next of the poor treatments to discuss. You may be surprised to consider exercise as being on the list of the poor treatments, for exercise is generally recommended and well respected for providing relief from stress. I believe the helpful component of exercise relates to physical fitness. If a person exercises to maintain fitness, he is training his body to tolerate different levels of activity. His body learns to handle increases in heart rate and respiratory rate well. This effect is helpful in stress or anger management because when he is energized to anger or when he is stressed, he experiences increases in his heart rate and respiratory rate. Since his body is well trained to cope with his increased metabolic rate, he is free to maintain a constructive mindset and thus effectively handle the situations he encounters.

If he is not physically fit and finds himself in a stressful situation or is energized to anger, his attention may be diverted to what is happening to his body. For instance, he may become worried or concerned about his heart if it is noticeably beating and he is uncomfortable about that. Being thus distracted, he is not focusing on the problem at hand and therefore has difficulty dealing with it. Therefore, fitness plays a role in helping a person to maintain a constructive mindset when encountering daily issues.

Exercise becomes a poor treatment when it becomes linked to the "feel-good" component of the activity. This dynamic is linked to the release of endorphins and most often occurs with aerobic exercise such as long-distance running. A person may become addicted to exercise. He may get an exercise high from the endorphin release he attains. He may eventually live for his exercise activity, and thus he spends more and more of his time engaging in his exercise activity. By doing so, he spends less time nurturing his significant relationships. He does not have time to work out the potatoes that crop up in his relationships, thereby keeping them in the sack on his back. There may be demands on his time: "How come you're spending so much time at your exercise? What about me?" Such demands become extra potatoes that he in turn places in his sack. As his sack becomes heavier with the addition of the extra potatoes, he seeks his exercise activity to get relief (another difficult cycle of dependence to break).

Another risk relates to overdoing it. If he exercises too much, he is at risk of developing arthritis at an early age, as he overuses his various joints. Another health risk is hormonal, which is more pronounced in women because of the monthly cyclic variation of certain hormone levels. For example, a woman may develop amenorrhea. Therefore, exercise as a treatment for the heavy sack of potatoes is a poor choice. Remember, however, that the benefits of regular exercise that are not linked with you managing your emotions include better sleep and relief from stress, as explained earlier.

Work

The work of your hands brings you pleasure. For example, you may notice that your garden is full of weeds. You dig out the weeds and admire the enhanced beauty of your garden as a result of your work. You derive pleasure from your accomplishment. As a treatment, work can include a paid position, volunteer position, domestic responsibilities, hobbies, and so on.

Biblical Relevance

Work as being pleasurable is mentioned in the Bible in Ecclesiastes 2:10: "I denied myself nothing my eyes desired; I refused my heart no pleasure. My heart took delight in all my work, and this was the reward for all my labor."

The dynamic of becoming a workaholic is similar to that of exercise as a symptomatic treatment to soothe emotions. A person spends more and more time doing his work and deriving a sense of accomplishment and pleasure from it. He easily justifies spending increased time at work, for the work ethic is honoured in society. But as he spends more time at his work, he spends less time nurturing his other significant relationships and dealing with the potatoes that crop up from time to time in these relationships. The result may be demands on his time: "How come you're spending so much time at work!? What about me? What about the family?" These demands become yet more potatoes for him to handle, which he puts in his sack. He ultimately seeks relief from his heavy sack by performing his work.

Work as a treatment that is linked with a career or profession appears to have been more of a male issue in the past. A man easily derives his identity by his career or profession. Two men meet for the first time and say: "Hi, I'm Ludwig and I'm a doctor." "Hi, I'm Wolfgang and I'm a plumber." I believe one effect of the women's movement has been to adjust the thinking somewhat. The women's movement is in part about a woman seeking an identity of her own, rather than deriving her identity through a man. Instead of identifying herself as "Mrs. So-and-So," she identifies herself by saying, "Hi, I'm Renate and I'm a doctor." Therefore, the treatment of work by a person seeking success in a career or profession to achieve an identity or as power to combat the negative emotions is no longer a gender issue.

Shopping

The next poor treatment is shopping. This treatment involves the "god of materialism." A person's faith and hope is in purchasing or owning a certain item to get relief from the troubles or boredom of life: "If I just go shopping or buy such-and-such, it will help me to feel better." She buys the item and derives a sense of relief from carrying her heavy sack of potatoes. But it is a temporary fix. Over time, her feeling of relief wears off, and she starts feeling the weight of her sack again. In the meantime, she adds more potatoes to her sack as the new potatoes come for her to handle. And so, the next time she feels weighed down, she seeks another item to buy to lift her spirits, or she seeks a high from the activity of shopping.

Sometimes the product she purchases puts her at financial risk. When she comes down from the high of owning the item, she kicks herself for having bought such an expensive thing. "It wasn't that great!" she realizes. She therefore ends up blaming herself, which represents more potatoes against herself for her to handle. Someone else in her life hurls potatoes at her: "Why did you buy that!? What's the matter with you? How are we going to pay for this?" She places these extra potatoes in her sack, and they weigh it down even more. She proceeds to seek relief from her heavy sack by seeking something to buy. The result is another difficult cycle to break, another poor treatment.

I believe the marketing industry is based on the dynamic of placing your faith and hope on material items. The tendency for a woman may be for her to place her hope in purchasing items of clothing or home décor products. Therefore, advertisers expose people to new fashions of the season or new colours of the year. The tendency for a man may be for him to place his hope in purchasing the latest gadgets and gizmos in electronics, tools, or automotive products. Therefore, people hear of the latest innovations or upgrades to this and that.

It is possible to consider the dynamic of shoplifting to fit in with the treatment of shopping. For men, there may be a feeling of power connected with certain items possessed or sold. For women, there may be a sense of power connected with "pulling it off because I deserve it."

Relationships and/or Sex

Another poor treatment is sex. Physical intimacy can be pleasurable. If a person uses intimacy as a treatment to get relief from the heavy sack of potatoes he or she bears, there is a lost sense of relationship with his or her significant other. What there is instead is a dictatorship.

Intimacy in relationship is the result of outward love. If two people are physically intimate with each other with a love for the other's sake, they seek to please the other person or to be pleasing to the other person. The benefits derived are rewarding and fulfilling for both of them.

A dictatorship, however, is inward. A person desires physical intimacy with someone else for his own benefit. His aim is to please himself, or to find a way to please the other person to accomplish a way to please himself. If his sexual encounter does not work out the way he hopes, he feels let down. (How can two people in love truly feel let down if their love is outward? Feeling physically let down does not need to spoil the whole relationship. Physical intimacy is only one of many dynamics of intimacy in a caring relationship.) If he feels let down, yet desires sex to be his treatment to get relief from his sack of potatoes, he is at risk of seeking alternative means to get the effective treatment he desires. The alternative means may involve his use of pornography or his involvement in other relationships. The result of these activities is that there are more potatoes for him to deal with. He places his extra potatoes into his sack. Since his sack weighs him down more as it gets heavier, he seeks sex to get relief from the burden of the weight. Thus, there results yet another poor treatment and another difficult cycle to break.

When it comes to relationships, placing hope in relationships puts a person at risk of co-dependency. Her aim is to please the other person to derive for herself a sense of fulfillment. She exposes herself to the risk of being at the other person's whims to know if she is acceptable or not. There will be more on this dynamic in a later chapter.

Obsessive Compulsive Disorder

Obsessive compulsive disorder (OCD) may be considered a form of symptomatic treatment for the potatoes in your sack. The compulsive act is the treatment to relieve your stress. From another perspective, the compulsive act is your anger management strategy to relieve your anxiety, but you are left with a complicated mess of potatoes as both your anxiety and your compulsive act become potatoes to you that are almost impossible to deal with. The OCD eventually becomes your master or god as you put your faith in the compulsive activities to maintain a sense of well-being. The master of OCD is not a loving master, and you become enslaved to perform the compulsive acts. Not doing so adds to the potatoes you have to deal with, which you add to your sack and put more pressure on yourself to relieve. The result is another difficult cycle of dependence to break.

Final Note about Symptomatic Treatments

You may notice that many of the poor treatments discussed in this section are among the most natural activities in the world. There is nothing inherently wrong with physical intimacy, work, food, shopping, and so on. Such treatments become risky if they have control or mastery over you, rather than you yourself having control of your life as you are meant to have. Your relationships, your work, your food, and so on, form a part of who you are and are indicators of your identity as you express your creativity in these areas. When you have control, your fulfillment accompanies your freedom to be creative.

Biblical Relevance (Repeated)

Any "god" you serve other than the living God is not a loving god. In other words, any god you serve other than the living God gives you more potatoes to deal with besides the potatoes you already have. That is why the commandment states "… have no other Gods before me" (Exodus 20:3). This command is for your benefit rather than for God's benefit. In my opinion, God does not need me to worship or serve Him. He is complete in Himself and does not need me. I, on the other hand, need Him. It is as if God is saying to me: "If you serve any 'god' other than me, you will end up with more potatoes to burden you. I love you. I am with you to help you with the potatoes that come your way. I will not give you extra potatoes to handle."

The Link between the Suppress Method and Clinical Depression

When a person is diagnosed with clinical depression, there are two dynamics that are understood to be occurring. One dynamic is a biological or "body" dynamic. This dynamic is currently understood to be a chemical imbalance of certain brain chemicals, such as serotonin and/or noradrenalin, which leads to an inability of the brain chemicals to function as they are designed to. The dynamic is often compared to that of the chemical imbalance of insulin to mobilize sugar into cells, which results in the illness that is called diabetes mellitus. The second dynamic of depression is psychological and is often explained or understood along the lines of anger turned inward.

The way that the two dynamics of depression are explained can come from either one or the other point of view. For example, a pure biological explanation of the two dynamics suggests that a person, for some reason, develops a chemical imbalance within certain of her brain regions. As the imbalance in her brain gets worse, her ability to manage anger is impaired, and so she keeps her anger inside.

A pure psychological explanation of the two dynamics suggests that she learns to manage her anger by keeping it inside (she is suppressing). Eventually, she has so much anger inside of her that it overwhelms her body, and she develops a chemical imbalance.

It is likely most accurate to understand the illness of clinical depression as a combination of the two dynamics. Depression can be viewed as a spectrum illness, with the biological dynamic at one end of the spectrum and the psychological dynamic at the opposite end (Figure 3.5). An individual's illness is manifested at some point between the two extremes of the spectrum. For one person, his depression manifests toward the biological explanation end of the spectrum; for another, her depression manifests toward the psychological end of the spectrum. Doctors do not at present have a way to accurately discern where on the spectrum a certain person's illness is manifesting. There are therefore various biological and psychological treatments offered to treat the challenging illness of clinical depression.

Biological <--------------> Psychological
Figure 3.5 Spectrum of Depression Dynamics

An alternate way to understand the contribution of the two dynamics of depression is to view the relationship of the biological and psychological dynamics of depression as an interaction between two scales. For that matter, any of the specific illnesses recorded throughout the course of human history find people who are individually at risk to manifest any of the illnesses within his or her gender. But fortunately for us, we do not get all of those illnesses. So, whether you manifest a certain illness in your lifetime or not depends on the interaction between two scales. One of the scales I call a *resistance/susceptibility* scale, while the other is a *risk-factor* scale (Figure 3.6).

For a given illness, you are either highly resistant to it or you are relatively more susceptible. Where you lie on the resistance/susceptibility scale depends on factors such as genetic background. If you belong to a family in which many of your relatives have a certain illness, you are likely to be genetically more susceptible to that illness. Other factors that can affect your position on the scale include exposure to certain viruses, bacteria, or other substances in the early development phases within your mother's womb or the first years of your life (some of which is not necessarily preventable).

The second scale to consider is a risk-factor scale. For a given illness, if you have an identifiable risk factor for it, you are at increased risk of manifesting the illness. If you are able to remove the risk factor, you are at decreased risk of manifesting the illness.

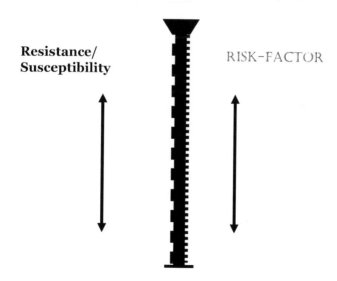

Figure 3.6 Resistance/Susceptibility Scale and Risk-factor Scale

For example, smoking is known to be a risk factor for lung cancer, but not everybody who smokes gets lung cancer. Also, there are non-smokers who get lung cancer. So how are we to understand these truths? Let's look at some different scenarios. One person on one hand has high resistance to lung cancer, and on the other hand is a heavy smoker. Perhaps he has smoked two packs a day for 50 years. This means that he is at high risk for lung cancer. But since he has high resistance to lung cancer, there remains a margin between the two scales, and so he does not get the illness of lung cancer (Figure 3.7).

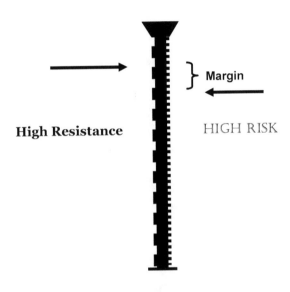

Figure 3.7 Margin Exists Between Resistance/Susceptibility and Risk

If he is more susceptible to lung cancer, and is a smoker, his risk-factor scale may tip beyond his resistance/susceptibility scale. He therefore manifests the illness (Figure 3.8).

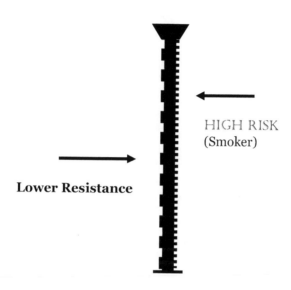

Figure 3.8 Situation of Disease Susceptibility When Risk Supersedes Level of Resistance

With lower resistance and as a non-smoker, he keeps a margin between the two scales, so that he is less likely to manifest the illness (Figure 3.9).

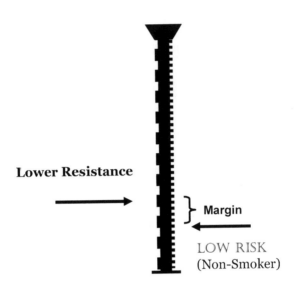

Figure 3.9 Margin Exists Between Resistance/Susceptibility and Risk

In our final scenario, he may be highly susceptible to lung cancer (low resistance). Even though he is a non-smoker, and is therefore at decreased risk to manifest the illness, he acquires the illness nonetheless, and finds himself in a battle against lung cancer (Figure 3.10). He perhaps has other risk factors that tip the scales against him, such as exposure to environmental toxins.

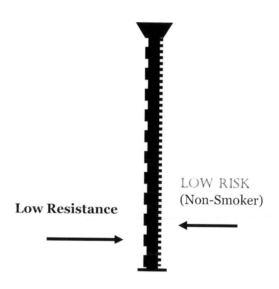

Low Resistance

LOW RISK
(Non-Smoker)

Figure 3.10 Situation of Disease Susceptibility When Risk Supersedes Level of Resistance

From the preceding discussion about the interaction of risk factors and disease resistance or susceptibility, I have come to understand the suppression of anger to be a risk factor for the illness of depression. A person may be highly resistant to depression, yet is a heavy suppressor. She carries a heavy sack of potatoes around, but she is not depressed. She has a margin between her two scales (Figure 3.7).

If she is more susceptible to clinical depression (lower resistance), the interaction between the biological and the psychological dynamics of depression, as discussed earlier (Figure 3.5), come into play. She learns to manage her anger by keeping it inside (the suppress method of anger management = risk factor) within the me-versus-you destructive mindset. She is at increasingly higher risk to manifest clinical depression as her sack gets heavier and heavier with the potatoes she hides inside. Eventually her sack gets so heavy that it puts her two scales of susceptibility and risk for depression in a precarious balance with each other. She becomes unstable. She doesn't know how much more she can handle. When yet another significant life event happens to her, she puts the potato connected with it into her sack. Now her sack is so heavy, the weight of it increases her risk so that the risk scale becomes higher than her resistance scale, and the two scales become tipped with respect to each other. She develops the chemical imbalance of clinical depression, and goes on to manifest the signs and symptoms of the illness (as in the situation in Figure 3.8, but replace "Smoker" with "Suppressor").

Treatment Approaches for Depression

The treatment of clinical depression can be derived from either end of the biological-psychological spectrum of depression. Both treatment approaches have usefulness either on their own or in combination. If a person uses only the biological approach to treatment (such as the use of antidepressants) and does not include psychological treatment, there is no effect of the treatment on the weight of her sack of potatoes. Instead, the biological treatment has the effect of boosting her resistance to depression so that she regains a margin between the two scales of susceptibility and risk. She therefore achieves relief from the symptoms of her depression.

The biological approach to treatment can be effective for many people. The hope of biological treatment is linked to her ability to deal with the potatoes that are in her sack on her own once she experiences relief from the symptoms of her depression. A limitation is that some people are not able to deal with their potatoes anyway. Her potatoes simply stay in her sack. Meanwhile, more potatoes keep coming as is normally expected. If she continues to put her new potatoes into her sack the way she has learned to do, her sack continues to be heavy. Eventually, she decides that she has taken the antidepressant for long enough (it may have been a year). She has responded well to the treatment of her illness, and she wishes to discontinue taking the antidepressant. As she does so, her level of resistance to depression drops back to where it was before. If her resistance level drops below her risk-factor level (set by the weight of the sack of her potatoes), she is at risk of suffering a relapse of clinical depression.

Conversely, she may choose to treat her depression only with psychological treatment and not take medications. This approach does not affect the level of the resistance-susceptibility scale for her depression. Psychological treatments are effective in that they lighten the load of the sack of her potatoes. She acquires relief from the symptoms of her depression as she develops a margin between the susceptibility and risk scales as her sack gets lighter. Psychological treatment can be effective for many people. A risk of such treatment, however, is that potatoes do not stop coming her way. When the new potatoes come and she restarts filling up her sack with them, her sack eventually gets heavy enough to tip the balance of her susceptibility and risk scales once again. She is at risk for a relapse of her clinical depression.

Combination therapies involve a person taking medication and receiving psychological treatment. She may have tried to take only medication and received limited benefit (limited effect to boost her resistance scale). Adding psychological treatment reduces the risk-factor side of the two scales, and she experiences relief of symptoms. Or, she has attempted only psychological treatment and received limited benefit (limited effect on reducing the risk-factor scale, as not many potatoes are removed from her sack). Adding medication increases the resistance side of the two scales, and she experiences relief of the symptoms of her depression. Some people unfortunately have a precarious balance between the susceptibility and risk-factor scales so that treatment is challenging despite using a combination of the therapeutic approaches.

The anger model factors into the treatment of depression in a twofold way. Learning the constructive anger management method is a psychological treatment approach. In other words, the resistance-susceptibility scale will not be affected. On one hand, the constructive emotion intelligence mindset can be *therapeutic* for depression. On the basis of the constructive mindset, we will discuss in a later chapter the favourable treatments that can lead a person to achieve relief from their sack of potatoes. The therapeutic (in contrast to the symptomatic) treatments can lead to a lessening of the symptoms of depression as the sack gets lighter.

On the other hand, learning the constructive mindset to manage anger can be *preventive* for further episodes of depression. The constructive method to manage anger teaches you to deal with your potatoes in such a way that you do not put them in your sack. You therefore keep your sack as light as possible and thus your risk of clinical depression is reduced. This is the rationale for learning constructive anger management techniques for the treatment and prevention of clinical depression.

It is very difficult for someone battling with depression to understand the illness without taking it personally. What I am saying is that the person often blames herself for being depressed and thus tries to snap out of it. If she is unsuccessful in doing so, she tends to blame herself even more for not being able to snap out of it. Add to her dilemma the burden of others who try to understand her illness. They may also blame her for her low mood and other symptoms and believe she can do it if she would just try harder. But even though she tries with all her might to snap out of it, she nonetheless is unsuccessful in accomplishing this task.

The homework assignment applied to the illness of depression can be helpful for you and others to understand what clinical depression is. Let's look at it this way: Clinical depression is an illness. An illness is a potato. People are not potatoes. The illness is the potato! The problem is the depression, not the person with the depression. If you suffer with depression, you are a person struggling with the potato of depression. Any illness is a potato. An illness is a sense of wrongness because you are not meant to be sick. The problem is not you; the problem is the depression. As you understand what the illness of depression is all about, you are able to find ways to manage your potato by the various treatments you attempt. Actually, medical treatment of any sort, for any condition, is an anger management strategy. Your illness is a potato, and the doctor and you are working together to understand your potato and to find effective ways to treat it (the strategy).

The Explosion

The next risk inherent to the destructive method of suppressing anger is the dynamic of the explosion. To understand this risk, let's imagine that a person deals with his hot potatoes in an alternative suppressing fashion. When he understands his potatoes within the destructive me-versus-you mindset, imagine he places his potatoes in a closet instead of putting them in a sack on his back. In this way, he keeps his potatoes out of sight and out of mind to keep the peace. As humans, we all have closets, and we all have sacks on our backs. When a potato comes your way, and you wish to keep your thoughts and feelings inside to keep the peace within a me-versus-you mindset, it is not as if you know where you are placing the potato to keep it out of sight. The sack and closet illustrations are merely two ways to illustrate how you put yourself at risk if you handle your potatoes within the destructive suppress mindset. Perhaps the sack represents memory and the closet represents the capacity to handle stress added to the weight of memory.

The difference between the sack and closet illustrations has to do with capacity. The sack has unlimited capacity and just keeps on getting heavier and heavier as potatoes are added to it. The closet, on the other hand, has limited capacity. A closet holds only a limited amount of potatoes. As long as you have room in your closet to pack in your potatoes, you seem to be doing very well with your stress load. A suppressing person is a nice person.

When someone attends my clinic for counselling, he or she comes for advice. People tell me their stories and their questions about life, and I explain to them my approach to counselling as being to learn how to understand anger and the emotions. Some people listen to my explanation and tell me that this is not the approach they seek, for they claim they are not angry people. "I don't have a problem with anger," they say, and politely leave my office. I cannot help but feel frustrated that I am not able to assist such people with their various dilemmas. Although it is evident in the interview that they are nice people, some of them are nonetheless people who are strong suppressors. Some are burdened by much anger, yet blind to this fact.

Even though your closet has limited capacity, the capacity can vary depending on factors affecting you. For example, I have come to understand that my closet has less capacity when I am hungry and tired. In other words, I tend to be more irritable when I am hungry and tired. My ability to manage a potato if it comes my way when I am hungry and tired is challenged. I am at risk of dealing with the potato in a more aggressive manner: "I don't need this right now! Out of my sight!" However, just because I am hungry and tired does not excuse me to use a destructive method of anger management. Potatoes come whenever they will come. Potatoes have no idea, nor do they care, how well fed or rested I am; they just come when they come. So the onus is on me to maintain a constructive mindset as best I can regardless of how well fed or rested I am.

If I believe I am doing a good job of maintaining a constructive mindset while managing my anger during the times when I am well fed and rested, I may be fooling myself, for the time of testing comes when I am hungry and tired. How will I manage my anger then? Therefore, I have to enter a training program so that I learn to keep a constructive mindset regardless of how well fed or rested I am.

Imagine an Olympic athlete training for the marathon race. The athlete trains only on the plains of southern Alberta. He attains what is considered a world-class time and is considered a contender for the race. But if the race is from Marathon to Athens, he struggles to finish the race because of the hills. He did not prepare for running under such conditions. In the same way, I need to train myself to pay particular attention to my homework assignment when I am hungry and tired. If a potato happens to come my way when I am hungry and tired, I need to be prepared to understand my potato in the constructive mindset. (Sometimes I may even dare a potato to come my way when I am hungry and tired, just so that I get practice dealing with it in a constructive way under challenging conditions. But on the other hand, I really don't need to ask for potatoes, as enough come my way anyway!)

Other factors can affect the size of your closet. For example, hormones may have an impact. The effect is likely more pronounced in women because of the monthly fluctuation in hormone levels. Premenstrual syndrome (PMS) may be considered an event in the monthly cycle of a woman when her hormone levels are such that her closet has relatively less capacity compared with other times in her cycle during which her closet has relatively greater capacity.

Regardless of what causes the fluctuations in the size of your closet, it eventually fills up when you put your potatoes inside. A person eventually gets to a point where he is not sure how much more he can keep inside. Then another potato comes his way. He desperately tries to put it in his closet, but his closet cannot handle the stress load anymore. The doors of his closet burst open from the weight of all his potatoes inside, and he explodes. Blahhhhh! Out his potatoes come! The **power** that he has when his potatoes burst out can be overwhelming not only to others, but also to him. And he ends up doing things he later regrets. For most of the time, he is a peacemaker and seems to be the nicest person around. But when his explosion comes, it tends to come out in an aggressive manner, and he does things he regrets. He and others around him are affected by his explosion.

Explosions can manifest in different forms. In many instances, the explosion is a type of temper tantrum. It can come out as a yelling or screaming fit: "I've had enough!" In other cases, the person pounds his fist on the table or through a wall. He may beat someone up and may get into legal difficulties. On the other hand, an explosion can be inward and instead becomes an implosion. Such a person clams up thinking: "I've had enough!" and goes into his shell. Some people experience clinical depression as a sharp drop in mood within a short period of time when in the presence of a stressful situation. For some people, crying uncontrollably may be the explosion. Binge eating, going on a bender to binge drink excessive alcohol, or having a session of uncontrolled gambling can be viewed as types of explosions.

A person can get himself into further difficulties following an explosion. For the most part, he is a suppressor, a peacemaker. He is likely the nicest person around. But when his explosion happens, especially if it comes out aggressively, he switches his anger management method into the express mode, which is a provocative way to manage anger. When he performs the exploding action that he later regrets, his aggressive action becomes another potato for him to deal with. He is then vulnerable to make himself be the problem in the setting of this new potato. He blames himself or gets down on himself. He may take responsibility for what he has done. If, however, his responsibility is in the context of him believing that he is the problem, he actually may add more potatoes to his closet. These extra potatoes are potatoes of self-blame, and he starts to fill up his closet again.

A person managing his potatoes by filling his closet can eventually be at risk of managing his closet of potatoes in a cyclical fashion. If his exploding event is an abusive event, the dynamic becomes what is called a "cycle of abuse."

An extreme example of a cycle of abuse is illustrated in the following scenario. In the example, the suppressor and subsequent exploder is the husband within a marriage relationship. The husband and wife both love each other very much. He manages his potatoes by putting them in his closet. He is a nice man. But he is not perfect. Neither is his wife, nor anybody he relates to. Potatoes come his way every day. He handles them by suppressing, and his closet fills more and more as time progresses. He may eventually notice that there are a lot of potatoes in his closet, but he continues to fit the new potatoes that come his way into his closet.

Finally, it is the last straw that breaks the camel's back. Another potato comes his way. He tries to get it into his closet, but his closet can't handle all those potatoes anymore. The doors of his closet burst open, and the pressure inside forces most of his potatoes out! He does something rash and with a lot of power. He is out of control. He beats his wife! The **power** he has in doing so is overwhelming to him, not to mention to her. After his explosive release of energy, he settles down and realizes he did more to her than what he intended to do. He realizes he was out of control and is remorseful. He did not mean to harm her in this way.

He is apologetic. He loves his wife. He says to her: "I didn't mean it to happen like this. I'm sorry! Will you forgive me? I promise it will never happen again!" He may indeed be very sincere in his pronouncements.

For her part, she loves her husband. She cannot understand why this abuse should have happened to her, but she desires things to work out between the two of them. She therefore believes his promise, and the two of them enter what is called the "honeymoon phase."

A honeymoon implies that the direction of love is toward the other person. She is everything to him, and he wants to make it up to her. His attention is therefore fully on her, and he seeks to cater to her needs. He gives her a peace offering to make it better or to make up. He may give her flowers, or chocolates, and so on, as a sign that she is important to him.

In the meantime, however, potatoes do not stop coming his way. He is not perfect and she is not perfect, nor is anyone else. So he reverts back to his regular way of dealing with the potatoes that come his way. When the new potatoes come, he starts filling up his closet again.

There is another dynamic in this scenario to keep in mind: During his explosion, many of the potatoes from within his closet have come out. He may have a sense of relief that his potatoes are out. He may believe it is a good thing to vent, to get it out, because there is a sense of relief from the weight of the potatoes when they come out from within the closet. But in many cases, the potatoes that come out are not dealt with. They do not stay out. There is no resolution of those potatoes, and they remain within the destructive me-versus-you mindset of the person who is dealing with them. The unresolved potatoes return into his closet, just as the ocean sends a wave of water onto the shore, only to reclaim the water back into itself.

When his old and supposedly purged potatoes return to his closet, it is not as if his closet becomes full to capacity again. Somehow, the honeymoon phase has the effect of adjusting the capacity of his closet outward, so that there is more room within. The reset capacity of his closet is such that when the old potatoes return inside, it is now a third or half full, rather than completely full. He is once again a peacemaker, and handles his new potatoes in a seemingly healthy fashion, as they come. But he is actually filling up his closet again. His closet gets fuller and fuller. Finally, he reaches the next time when it is the last straw that breaks the camel's back. One more potato comes for him to handle.

He tries to get that potato into his closet, but it cannot hold them anymore. Blahhhhhh! Another explosion! He does the very thing he promised he would not do. He beats her again!

The dynamic of the cycle is developed. A person's closet fills up with potatoes as emotions are suppressed within the destructive mindset. The explosive event happens. After the explosion, the honeymoon phase follows. The cycle repeats itself as new potatoes come and the emotions are suppressed within the destructive mindset—the potatoes are placed into the closet. The next explosion happens, then another honeymoon phase, followed by the next build-up and explosion, *ad infinitum* and *ad absurdum*. Round and round the cycle goes; where it stops, nobody knows.

Over time, the reset point of the closet to accept new potatoes after the explosion is at a fuller and fuller setting. The old potatoes, which wash back into the closet during the honeymoon phase, may refill the closet at a fuller and fuller point. Explosions may therefore happen more and more frequently.

Possible Outcomes of a Cycle of Abuse

Let us explore the dynamics of three possible outcomes of a cycle of abuse. Imagine the spousal couple in the preceding example as the outcome dynamics are discussed.

One possible dynamic occurs when the cycle of abuse continues and the relationship remains together. The wife in our example justifies remaining in the relationship, despite reoccurring abuse at the hands of her husband. She may think, "I do not like what is happening to me, but I made a marriage vow to him, and I intend to honour and fulfill my vow." From a faith perspective, she may include in the justification of her situation the fact that she also made a vow to God to be with her husband "until death do us part." If this is where she ends her internal discussion, however, she places herself in the position of accepting a prison sentence, with no hope of escape. When a person develops a sense of hopelessness, feelings of despair and apathy are not far behind.

It has been observed that prisoners of war incarcerated in concentration camps, who have no hope of escape, can become apathetic. Even if an opposing army appears and attempts are made to help the prisoners to escape, the apathetic prisoners cannot lift an arm to help fulfill their cause of freedom, for to them the situation is beyond belief and is hopeless.

Such is the risk applied to the woman in our example. But, as she becomes more apathetic in her manner, extra potatoes become connected to her, which her husband deals with. Her apathy causes her not to follow through with certain responsibilities, and her husband responds to her lack of action with frustration. He then adds his extra potatoes, which are connected with her behaviour, to his closet. He becomes at further risk of exploding. She therefore does not help her cause by becoming hopeless and apathetic. Her apathy is in fact making things worse for her.

Relationship dynamics in a marriage may not be as bleak as what is observed in concentration camps. The woman may learn to read the signs of the cycle that occurs in her husband. She may learn to anticipate when he is about to explode. She prepares herself and braces for his explosion. She gets through it somehow. Then what? Yes, the honeymoon phase follows. The honeymoon phase represents a break or holiday for her from his emotions. She learns to live for the honeymoon phase, and her holiday may become a justification for her to remain in the relationship. She may think: "I know he has his moments when he has to blow off steam, but doesn't anyone? And after he's blown off steam, I know he really loves me, because he is so kind to me afterward and wants to make things better."

In some circumstances, the woman who receives explosive abuse from her husband learns a different tactic as she anticipates he is about to explode. When she senses the time is right, she provokes him! Her provocation triggers his explosion. Afterwards, she has accomplished her holiday from his emotions. If her husband is called to account for his abusive treatment toward his wife, his defence may be: "She provoked me! What would you do?" Of course he is correct in stating that she provoked him, but she is doing so to get a break from his emotions as his closet fills up. Therefore, discerning the dynamics of anger management interplay between two individuals can be a challenge!

A second possibility of what can happen in the case of this spousal couple is that the cycle of abuse stops because the relationship breaks up. For example, the woman may think: "I don't know how many more of these explosions of his I can handle. I'm afraid for myself and afraid for the children. I made a marriage vow to him, and I intend to honour and fulfill my vow, but he is neither honouring nor fulfilling his vow to me! When he abuses me in the way he does, what has that got to do with loving and caring for me? His behaviour is neither right nor acceptable."

She decides to break the cycle by separating from him. Or, she decides to file for a divorce. There are many degrees of difficulty in going through such scenarios. The final outcome includes breaking the cycle of abuse, which for her is freedom. This freedom is good, because a marriage relationship is not meant to be a master-slave relationship. In terms of the marriage relationship, however, it is an outcome resulting in a break-up. It is therefore a lose-lose outcome that is difficult to recover from, however noble and just her freedom is. But such an outcome is common.

A third possibility of where a cycle of abuse may proceed is one in which the cycle is broken and the relationship is maintained. Such a scenario, although possible, is very difficult to achieve. The reason for the difficulty is that the man, who in our example is the exploder, has to attain the insight that he has an anger problem. Since he is primarily a suppressor in the way he handles his anger, he is likely not aware that his anger management method is a problem. He is a nice guy. Very few people, if any, see him as angry. He may not view himself as an angry person.

The scenario may proceed along the following lines: As the woman receives the brunt of his explosions, she may experience feelings of hopelessness and despair. She may eventually develop symptoms and signs of clinical depression. As she receives treatment for her depression, someone, as part of her therapy, may talk with her about what life is like for her at home. She mentions something about the explosions that she endures from her husband. The feedback she receives may be: "Those explosions from your husband are unacceptable. You are not the problem, and you do not deserve to be treated in this way. Your husband's explosions are evidence that he has an anger problem, but it does not have to continue like that. He needs to talk with someone about his anger problem because the cycle of abuse cannot continue in the interests of your health and the health of your spousal relationship."

Such advice is supportive of her as well as supportive of her marriage. Sometimes the advice she hears may be: "Those explosions from your husband are unacceptable. You are not the problem, and you do not deserve to be treated in this way. Get out of the relationship. You will get better if you do. Your relationship is toxic, and your move is to get out." Such advice is supportive of her, but not supportive of her marriage.

She considers the advice supportive of her, her marriage, and about her husband's anger and thinks: "How am I going to tell him this? Maybe I'll wait until the next honeymoon period because he'll be more approachable then." So she waits for the next honeymoon phase to occur in the cycle (enduring another explosion). When it arrives, she says to him: "I've been told that when you explode and do the nasty things you do, it is unacceptable. Your behaviour shows that you have an anger problem. There is help available for you. Our relationship does not have to be this way. But you need to talk with a counsellor about your anger because our relationship is at risk if your abusive behaviour continues."

He listens to her, considers what she has said, and replies, "Let me think about it." As he thinks about it, he may talk about the situation with some of his friends. He says to them: "My wife is being treated for such-and-such condition, and somebody along the way has suggested to her that I have an anger problem. What do you think?"

What are his friends likely to say in reply? Most of his friends have not seen him angry. He is, for the most part, the nicest person around. His friends reply: "Who is this person that is suggesting you have an anger problem? Does he (or she) know you? Has he (or she) met you? You're the nicest guy around! You handle your stress and anger very well!"

His friends may also question: "What stories is she telling this person? What is her agenda?"

"I know, I know," he replies, somewhat apologetically. But then he goes on to admit to weakness, yet to justify it: "Sometimes I lose it! But doesn't everybody? What would you do if your wife did this or that? Would you be upset?" His friends agree that a lot of what he mentions as problems with his wife would also be upsetting to them if their wives did similar things. People become upset as things are said or done that they believe are wrong. Anger is not the problem. The problem is the problem. But how he manages or what he does in his anger can also be a problem.

Linking his anger with an abusive anger management strategy is where the argument breaks down. Sometimes his conversation with his friends proceeds further: "When I lose it, it is all her responsibility! If she does something wrong, she deserves it!" Unfortunately, there are voices that nod in assent to such a proposition. The rebuttal to such a claim is that two wrongs do not make it right. He may believe his wife has done something wrong, and he may be upset about it, but his anger does not justify his use of aggressive (especially explosive) anger management against her. His challenge is to understand his emotions within the constructive mindset. He is then free to understand the situation and communicate his thoughts and feelings with her when appropriate.

The feedback he gives his wife, after having thought about what she said to him, may therefore be: "I've thought about what you said. I've thought a long time. I've talked about it with some of my friends. This is what I've come up with," and he tilts his head toward her in a condescending fashion, "I don't think I've got a problem! If you would just stop doing blah blah blah, then none of this would have to happen to you, so it is all up to you!"

She hears his words and pauses incredulously. She is already at her wits end trying to figure out what she is supposed to do so that he does not get angry. She already has changed this or that to please him. But no matter what she does or changes, she is still not perfect. She still messes up. It is not as if she is doing things to spite him on purpose. And many of the potatoes he places in his closet have nothing to do with her. She is just like a dog that gets blamed and kicked to take the attention away from the party who is truly responsible. So she is stuck. He does not have insight to accept the responsibility of his own anger.

From another point of view, the message he gives his wife is "My anger is your responsibility! If you would just stop doing those wrong things, then you wouldn't be making me angry!" But this is where she is stuck. He is telling her that *his* anger management is *her* responsibility. But it isn't. His anger is his own responsibility. It is impossible for her to manage his anger. And so the two of them may continue to live within the cycle of abuse in how they relate with each other.

On the other hand, if he has a little insight into accepting responsibility for his own anger, there is hope for both the cycle to be broken and the relationship to be maintained. He may think: "Sometimes when I feel this angry, I feel so justified in how I am treating her! But then I realize I am going too far. I really do more to her than I intend, and I think my emotions get the better of me. Maybe I should see what I can learn about anger and anger management because I agree that these explosive episodes are a problem. I could benefit from some help with my anger so that the explosions don't have to happen."

Now there is hope for the two of them. He takes responsibility for his own emotions, as opposed to blaming his emotions on her. As he learns to manage his anger in a more constructive manner, he gets away from putting his potatoes into his closet. The dynamics of his cycle of abuse are altered and it can be hoped that the explosions cease altogether.

Loneliness

Another side effect of the suppress method of anger management is loneliness. When you keep your thoughts and feelings inside to keep the peace within a me-versus-you mindset, particularly within the context of a caring (for example, spousal) relationship, it can lead to feelings of lack of support and further on to feelings of loneliness.

If you feel lonely, particularly in the context of a caring relationship, you will have the tendency to interpret your loneliness as being consistent with a conclusion that the other person is being selfish. You may think:

"Here I am feeling lonely, and what do you care? You're just thinking about yourself!"

The problem with the preceding conclusion of selfishness is that when your feelings of loneliness are linked to be a side effect of suppressing anger, selfishness is not a part of the picture. In my opinion, you could point your finger at anybody living in the world today, and correctly tell that person that he or she is selfish. Everybody has an aspect of selfishness consistent with being human. Selfishness may be understood along the lines of human nature or the sinful nature. No matter how the selfishness is labelled, everybody has it.

It is true, however, that different people manage their selfishness in different ways. Some people do not know that they are selfish, yet everybody else does. Some people know that they are selfish, but don't do anything about it. And some people know that they are selfish, but try to balance their own needs with the needs of others. They therefore appear to be unselfish people.

Linking loneliness with the suppression of anger is not about selfishness. It is actually about the need for feedback. If two people are in a caring relationship, such as what a spousal vow affirms, then they need to give each other feedback about who they are. They each need to communicate to the person that they care about and who in turn cares about them. A spousal vow basically consists of two people who vow to each other "I will love you and care for you." Just because they make such a vow to each other does not mean that they know how to love and care for each other.

If the marriage ceremony and vows are understood to be the pinnacle of a spousal relationship, where is the relationship likely to go from there? Likely in a downward spiral. The marriage ceremony is therefore not the pinnacle of a spousal relationship; it is rather a *step* in the relationship.

When two people are considering a serious relationship with each other, the time of dating (or courting) is the time when each of them assesses (to themselves) if they have the will to be on the same team with the other person in the game of life, and if the other person has the will to be on the same team as them. If they both conclude that they have the will to be on the same team together in the game of life, they prepare a marriage vow. Such a vow is a statement in which two people proclaim to each other "We will be on the same team in the game of life." But does the vow imply that both of them know how to be on the same team? No, their relationship proceeds and grows stronger as they teach each other how to love and care for each other.

In order for the couple to proceed in their relationship, they each need to teach their loved one who they are. They each need to give feedback to the other, so that the other learns how to love and care for them. Their team thus becomes stronger. This all takes time. The feedback they give to each other also needs to be balanced; that is, they are interested in a balanced communication of their likes and dislikes, their positives and negatives. If the feedback they give is not balanced, they do not teach each other who they are. Each will therefore form a false impression of who the other is and relate with each other according to the false impression they have attained. And when one of them becomes aware of the other's false perspective of who they are, the one may believe that the other is being selfish.

Balanced View

One way to assess balance is when you are shown a glass that is filled to the halfway mark. You are asked, "Is the glass half full or is it half empty?" What would you answer? Is there a "right" or a "desirable" answer?

A popular assumption is that if you view the glass as being half empty, you hold a negative or pessimistic view about life. If, however, you view the glass as being half full, you hold a positive or optimistic view about life. The resulting conclusion is that you ought to teach yourself to view the glass as being half full, for a positive and optimistic viewpoint is considered to be more desirable than its counterpart perspective.

I find that I do not agree with this popular conclusion. My opinion is that the question is a trick question: "Is it half full or is it half empty?" My answer is that the glass is both half full and half empty. I find that if I understand the answer to be both, I am free to **hope** for the good. I believe the true positive attitude I desire is linked with my faith (belief) that the glass is half full in the context that it is also half empty and with my hope for good (half full perspective) to be done.

It is true, however, that if I view the glass as being only half empty, while not realizing it is also half full, I am restricted to an unbalanced view toward the negative side. This is a hard way to live, not only for me, but also for others who are exposed to the results of my unbalanced pessimistic view of life. On the other hand, if I view the glass as being half full and restrict my understanding to the exclusion of realizing that the glass is also half empty, the comeback to my unbalanced optimistic perspective may be "Get real!" The reality is that life has limits. If I do not recognize the limits in life, I put myself at the mercy of unnecessary risky and rash living. Bravery is linked to attaining feats in the context of recognizing risks. I am free to be brave by recognizing the value of fear and understanding fear constructively. As Aristotle[2] points out, bravery is the balance between cowardice (too much fear) and rashness (too little fear).

Therefore, when I recognize that the glass is both half full and half empty, it allows me to hope for the good (the half-full side) in the context of my awareness of the limits (the half-empty side).

Consider the following example as an illustration of the need for people to give each other feedback to develop healthy relationships. In our example, the man is the suppressor. Imagine his wife desires to do something nice for him to show her love for him. She decides to give him a gift, not linked with any special occasion, and therefore purchases a necktie for him. He receives the nicely wrapped gift and asks: "What's this for? It's not my birthday or anything!" She smiles affectionately and urges him to open the present. He opens it and pulls out a tie.

He is now in a dilemma. As he sees the tie, his inner thoughts declare: "What's this? I don't like this! And these colours! There is no way I am going to wear this! But, what should I do? If I tell her I don't like it, she'll get upset, maybe cry, and then I will have to deal with all that! So, what should I do? Ohhh! It's the thought that counts! It's the thought that counts!" His response to her therefore is, "Thanks, I really appreciate this."

If she is not aware of his inner turmoil and is taken by his appreciative response, it is possible we have witnessed a miscommunication between them. According to his feedback, she may believe: "Yes, he is thankful; yes, he likes it." His perspective, however, is contrary: "Yes, I am thankful, but no, I don't like it."

Over time, she proceeds according to her version of truth. The next time she desires to do something nice for him, she gives him another tie. She repeats this scene again and again, each time believing she is doing something he likes, but in truth he does not like it. He starts to struggle more and more as he receives ties from her. Eventually, he thinks: "Why does she keep on giving me these ties? Doesn't she know I don't like them? Doesn't she care?" And now he is struggling with feelings of loneliness and believes his wife is being selfish by forcing her will on him by continuing to give him more ties.

Finally, an explosion happens. She gives him another tie, and he can't take it any more. He blurts out: "Quit getting me these ties! I've had enough of this!" She is shocked. The bubble of her version of truth is shattered. She answers, "What are you talking about?"

In their ensuing discussion, he points out to her, "Didn't you notice I never wear these things?!" Her reply is, "Well, I did notice you never wear them, but I thought it was because there wasn't the proper occasion, or, you didn't have the right shirts for them, so I was thinking of getting you some good shirts!" In other words, she is aware of the same fact that he has pointed out, but she interprets her observation according to her version of truth. She believes that he likes the ties that she gave him (in contrast to his version of truth that he does not like the ties), and so she is acting according to her belief.

Note: And that is the way it is with science and faith. Science has to do with observable fact. Interpretations of scientific observations are based on the foundation of faith—the underlying belief of truth or bias— that the observing person has. There is no dispute between science and faith. Disputes have to do with interpretations of observable fact based on underlying faith systems. Disputes have to do with matters of faith. Good interpretations of science are consistent with the underlying faith system.

When it comes to receiving gifts, there seem to be two components of feedback to consider. One component of feedback has to do with an acknowledgment of the thought of the gift and is communicated with gratefulness or thankfulness. A second component has to do with teaching the other person who you are. The importance of the second component of feedback appears to increase with the closeness of the relationship. For example, if you receive a gift from a distant relative, you are likely to express thankfulness but not likely to mention that you plan to sell the item at your next garage sale!

However, if you receive an item from a person with whom you are in a close relationship, especially a spousal relationship, you are interested in teaching this person who you are. You also must have confidence that he or she is interested in learning who you are. Expressing thankfulness or gratefulness takes priority. The time you choose, however, to give feedback to him or her about who you are requires diplomacy. When an appropriate time and place is selected to give feedback, the man in our earlier example has the freedom to explain to his wife: "I really appreciate that you gave me this gift, but there is something about me that you need to know. I am not likely to wear this tie, because I am not a 'tie' person. In fact, I do not like ties at all."

On hearing such news, his wife may be upset. She may cry. What she hoped would be a good and kind act turned out wrong. It is therefore reasonable that she is upset. But he does not need to be afraid of her tears and emotions. Actually, it is good that she is upset, for she loves him and what she hoped would turn out well has failed. Her tears are consistent with her love for him.

He is free to comfort her. He may gently say: "I know you meant it for good, and I really appreciate that. But because I love you, I am interested in teaching you who I am. And because I know you love me, I know you are interested in learning who I am. It is good for us to work such things out." And so they work it out.

On the basis of working toward an understanding between the two of them, they have freedom. If some event comes up in which he is required to wear a tie, then he is free. As he prepares for the event, he is free to voice his displeasure at having to wear a tie. She is aware of his displeasure and does not blame him for it. She is free to give an understanding reply: "I know you are doing something you would rather not do, and I understand how you feel because sometimes I have to do things I would rather not do. It's a difficult dilemma. But I think you are brave to go through with it."

If perchance he decides that it is not so bad to wear a tie after all, he is free to let her know. He is free to say to her: "All these years I haven't cared to wear ties, but do you know what? It wasn't so bad. Thanks. I'm glad I have the tie. It was good to wear it tonight." He is free to allow himself to accept something new, without a fear of looking bad. People's likes and dislikes can and do change over time.

On the other hand, if he keeps his feelings about the tie inside, and an occasion comes up in which it is protocol for him to wear a tie, he will be double-minded. He puts on a good show for his wife and others. He shows a happy face as he dresses with his tie on, yet inside he is miserable: "Why do I have to go through with this?"

If it comes about that he decides it is not so bad to wear a tie after all, he is at risk not to own up to his change of heart. He may believe that she wins if he admits to himself it wasn't so bad to wear a tie. He may not wish to lose face by admitting to himself that his wife is right, as opposed to defending his original decision not to wear ties. (He battles with the consequences in his own thoughts.) Therefore, he becomes his own worst enemy by preventing himself from accepting something he otherwise would accept. He takes away his own freedom from experiencing or accepting new things in his life, which he otherwise may accept. Suppressing your thoughts and feelings in a me-versus-you mindset takes away your freedom to enjoy life.

Intimacy

Another dimension that factors into relationships and the concept of loneliness has to do with the intimacy levels of relationships. H. Norman Wright, in one of his video presentations[3], discusses intimacy as the sense of closeness two people have with each other in their relationship.

Figure 3.11 can be used as a tool to help discuss issues to be aware of in understanding the dynamics and limitations of relationships, including master-slave relationship dynamics and boundary issues.

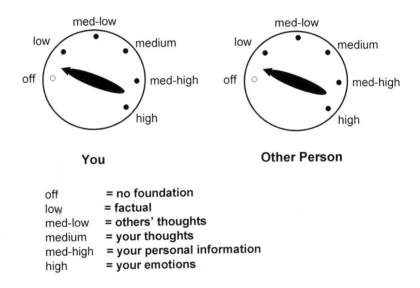

Figure 3.11 Intimacy Settings or Levels

In Figure 3.11, a burner control shows the increasing sense of closeness that you may develop with another person. In proceeding from the "off" setting, in which there is no foundation for a relationship with someone else, there are five intimacy levels, progressing from the low setting to the high setting. Each intimacy level corresponds to an increasingly riskier dimension of how a person thinks and feels about himself and the world in which he lives, as well as his willingness to share information about himself with others.

The low level of intimacy corresponds with the sharing of facts and information, while the high level of intimacy corresponds with the sharing of your feelings and emotions. The low level of intimacy is superficial and safe but is not fulfilling. The high level of intimacy is deep and risky but is very fulfilling if you share a relationship with another person at that level.

An increase in the intimacy level of a relationship has an element of risk associated with it. You may meet someone new and relate with that person at the low level of intimacy. You may wish to get to know him somewhat better and take the risk to do so. For example, you talk to him about some of your own ideas and opinions (a moderate degree of intimacy). If he accepts you at this increased level of intimacy, you feel accepted and good about yourself.

Intimacy is a unity term. The concept of unity is within the spiritual dimension of humanity. The feeling of acceptance that you experience when you achieve an increased sense of unity in a relationship is what I refer to as "spiritual food." It feels good. There is a sense of closeness. Terms such as brotherhood, sisterhood, fellowship, camaraderie, family, belonging, bonding, team, and so on, are used to describe the dynamics of unity. If you try to get to know someone better by relating to her within a higher intimacy level, and she in turn relates with you at that higher intimacy level, you feel good. You experience the sensation of having been fed by the spiritual food of intimacy.

On the other hand, if you try to get to know someone better, and if for some reason she is not interested in a relationship with you at a higher intimacy level, then you will not be fed by the food of acceptance at that higher level. The sense of rejection you feel, however, can be misunderstood. You may understand your rejection as a negative. But in the context of the preceding example, there is no negative whatsoever.

If you try to get to know someone better, and if she is not willing to interact with you at that deeper level of intimacy, then you will only consider the rejection to be negative if your opinion of yourself is linked with being accepted or rejected by the other person. That is, if your sense of self-worth or self-esteem is connected with the acceptance of other people, then you set up the other person to be your judge or to be your god. And since there is no loving god other than the living God, you are at risk, because you have set up another person who lives at his or her own whim to be your judge. You are at risk of living within a dynamic of co-dependence between yourself and the person you link your sense of self-esteem with. It is a hard way for you to live your life and is not in your interests to live within this co-dependent mindset.

Every relationship is a two-way street. Both people have a role to play, a role that is unconditional with respect to the other person, if the relationship is to be healthy. In any relationship you have, it is for you to do your part to enhance it. You must in turn free the other person to do his part. You are interested in allowing yourself the freedom to take risks if you are interested in getting to know the other person better. As well, be free to allow him either to accept you or to reject you. Whatever his response, remember the popular saying "I'm okay—you're okay."

If he accepts you at a higher level of intimacy, it will feel good. But if he is not interested in relating with you at a deeper level of intimacy, then remember: "I'm okay and you're okay. We will not be as close as I hoped we would be, but it is okay. I will continue to relate with you at a lower intimacy level for now. I will possibly try again some other time to get closer, but for now it's okay to be at the level where we are."

Biblical Relevance

To have the assurance of the knowledge of who you are in Christ is a foundation that can help you to stand against the storms of life. If you know who you are in Christ, your acceptance is from God, rather than from something in the world. This faith is your foundation built on rock that gives you the courage to boldly go forward in this world, seeking contacts with others and living out your dreams, despite what the world offers in resistance.

If your foundation is built on something in this world, you seek your acceptance through things that are in the world. Your foundation is built on sand and is at risk of crumbling when the storms of life rage against you. For example, if your self-acceptance comes by being accepted by other people, the whims of those people will affect you. You become at risk of being tossed to and fro by the very whims of those people, who do not love you as God loves you.

Therefore, make sure your foundation is on the rock. Get your identity from the transcendent source, that is, from God, and you will have a foundation that will help you to persevere through the storms that occur in your life. When the whims of the world rage against you (even when you are sincere and logical in doing your good works to benefit others in this world), your foundation built on rock will help you to stand through the storm.

Be free to take risks. For example, be free to try to get to know someone better that you are interested in nourishing a closer relationship with. If she accepts you, it will feel good. But if she rejects you, then remember "I'm okay—you're okay." The saying is valid, not because of you or the other person, but because of God.

The following example illustrates the increasing levels of intimacy that correspond with the depth of sharing who you are when you relate with others. The low intimacy level corresponds to the sharing of facts and information. You may meet somebody new at work, at a club, or at church. You discuss the weather: "Nice day, isn't it? Lots of great sunshine!" She shakes your hand and replies: "Yes indeed! Nice weather!" You may like her. You may think she is nice. But the level of intimacy you have with her is superficial and not fulfilling. You may think as you part: "Well, I'll see you again next week, and we'll talk about the weather again. Bye-bye."

The first step up from low intimacy to medium-low intimacy is when you add to your relationship the sharing of the ideas of other people. This step is the least risky one you can take to increase intimacy with another person because you are not exposing your personal ideas, and therefore yourself, to scrutiny. You may meet your "safe" (low intimacy) friend and say: "Nice weather, eh? My friends think that it's a nice day to go golfing!" If he accepts the thought, you may feel more accepted and closer. You may think: "Whew! I can say what my friends think!" If he does not agree with the thought of golfing as being a valid exercise, yet accepts your statement without judging, you also may feel closer. He may say: "Golfing? I wouldn't want to do that, but it's a great day for it anyway."

On the other hand, if he reacts by saying: "Golfing? Don't talk to me about golfing! What a waste of time! I wouldn't want to be out there on a great day like this, hitting balls in the bushes!" You may in turn think, "Okay, I won't talk to you about golfing." The next time you see him, your conversation may be limited to "Hi, great day we're having!" In other words, you revert back to the low level of intimacy with him, and you set up a wall of protection that limits the two of you from getting into a closer relationship.

The next higher intimacy level setting on the dial is medium intimacy, the level of sharing your own ideas and opinions. You may talk with your medium-low intimacy friend and say, "My friends think it's a nice day to go golfing." Then quickly, as you duck and protect your head with both hands, add "So do I!" Her reply, on the one hand, is: "How can you think of something like that? What's the matter with you?" In response, you may think to yourself: "But I think! If I am not allowed to reveal to you the fact that I think, then I won't!" And so you turn back the knob to relate with her at the medium-low level of intimacy, and you set up your wall of protection between the medium-low and medium levels of intimacy.

The wall of protection you build is a defensive shield to shelter you from an intimacy level that is uncomfortable for you because it does not exist within the constructive mindset. It is your "line in the sand" that separates the intimacy level in which you relate with the other person within the constructive mindset from higher levels in which you relate within the destructive mindset (not necessarily because of you, but in this example because of the other person). Your wall protects you from the me-versus-you destructive dynamics of interacting with the other person in the relationship. The decreased intimacy setting in which you relate constructively with the other person on the protected side of the wall becomes the level that is safe for you to relate together. You have the freedom to share equally within this lower level of intimacy and accept each other, rather than judging each other within the me-versus-you dynamic.

On the other hand, if you believe that she accepts your idea (about golfing) without judging you, even though she does not agree that golfing is a desirable activity, then you feel accepted and thus feel closer to her as a friend.

Master-Slave Dynamics

Now for a word of caution. If you have everything in common with another person, then the two of you may feel closer as friends than you actually are. You will only feel a higher closeness because there has not been an opportunity to find out if he accepts you when you happen to disagree with him. If he reacts to you as if you are not his friend when you disagree with him, then your relationship was never as close as you believed it to have been. You likely experienced a "master-slave" relationship.

In a master-slave relationship, both people believe they have a good friend. The master states: "I have found a good friend. My friend loves to do everything I want to do." The slave states: "I have found a good friend. My friend appreciates everything I do for him."

If you are the servant or slave within a master-slave relationship, you have no rights. The will of the slave must be the will of the master. It is the duty of the slave to be a friend to the master, but the master has no obligation to be a friend to the slave. In such a scenario, if you agree with your master, you are considered a good person (a good slave). If, however, you disagree with your master, you are considered by the master to be disloyal, a poor friend, or a bad person (a bad slave).

In your various friendships, sometimes you encounter the harsh master-slave realities, but you can also learn lessons of life from them. Sometimes you truly believe that the other person is a good friend of yours, but you discover that you are actually living as a slave to him. As long as you participate in the activity that your friend wants to do, everything is all right between you and both of you are having a good time. But as soon as you suggest doing something that your friend is not interested in, he comes up with excuses not to do it or ways to thwart it from coming to pass. You don't really understand why those things don't work out, and so you continue to be his friend and not make a fuss. But your friend maintains control of your relationship and does what he wants to do day after day.

If you think you have a close friendship but discover that you are only friends as long as you agree with him, then your intimacy setting with him is not as high as you believe. You actually are only at the first (low) level of intimacy with him (if even that). Perhaps he expects you to be at the high setting with him, when he is only at the low or off setting with you. A healthy relationship exists only at the intimacy level at which both of you relate to each other at the same setting and puts both of you within the constructive and accepting mindset, as opposed to relating within the me-versus-you destructive mindset. If you are in a master-slave relationship, then the situation is uneven and is not healthy for you.

The fourth intimacy level is at the medium-high setting and corresponds with your freedom to appropriately share personal information with another person. For example, you may say to your friend, "I think it's a nice day to go golfing" (medium intimacy). "But," (as you hold your shoulder and swing it gingerly), "I wonder how it's going to go with my sore shoulder." Her reply may come with ironic concern: "You want to go with your sore shoulder? Well, if you go with your sore shoulder and it gets worse, then you only have yourself to blame! Don't come crying to me!"

Your response to her feedback may be to think, "Don't give me a reason not to go when I really want to go." And so you give in to what you perceive to be her will and out of guilt decide not to go golfing. But the next time you think it is a good day to go golfing, you set in place your wall of protection to shield yourself from being vulnerable at the medium-high level of intimacy. You announce to her: "It's a nice day. I think I'm going to go golfing!" In turn she asks, "How's your shoulder?" You put your hand on your sore shoulder in a protective way, tilt your head to the side, and say, "Just fine, thank you," even though the pain is killing you. Notice the wall of protection that you are operating behind. You do not give yourself the freedom to relate with her at a higher level of intimacy.

Please note: Your lack of freedom is not unreasonable. A healthy relationship exists at any intimacy level, but requires the input of both people to relate with each other within the constructive mindset at that particular intimacy setting. In the preceding case, you are limiting your intimacy in a healthy manner when you realize that when you relate at a higher setting, you are not being allowed by her to be who you are. Your wall of protection, therefore, keeps your relationship at a level in which both of you relate constructively at the same intimacy setting. This lower level will not, however, be as fulfilling a level to relate within, especially in the context of a spousal relationship.

On the other hand, as you speak with her of your concern about your sore shoulder, she may reply with heartfelt concern: "You want to go with that sore shoulder? Well, did you take some medication for it this morning? Good! You might want to make sure you take some more along with you if you golf. If it gets worse as you're out there, you'll be glad to have it available. And another thing! It's okay to stop! Even though you've paid all that money to play a round of golf, it's okay to stop if your shoulder gets worse while you're on the course. And if it's feeling bad when you get back, I'll give you a massage if you like."

From this reply, should you golf or not? Is there a right or wrong answer?

Actually, there is freedom! There is neither a right nor a wrong answer. On the one hand, you may say: "I didn't really think of all those things you mention. Thanks. Maybe I should wait a week to give my shoulder some more rest." Or, you may answer: "Thanks! I'll keep that in mind as I'm out there!" There is therefore neither a right nor a wrong answer. Rather, there is freedom. The freedom you experience is what makes the medium-high level of intimacy so fulfilling, for you do not have to protect yourself from the person you are relating to. There is no protection necessary from the destructive me-versus-you way of relating with the other person.

The highest and most fulfilling level of intimacy is linked with the freedom of both people to appropriately share their feelings and emotions with each other. Feelings and emotions, when communicated at the high intimacy level, are not used as weapons within the me-versus-you way of relating. It is not "Because I feel this way, you have to do what I want you to do!" No. Instead, both people in the relationship allow each other to experience and to communicate their emotions freely as part of who they are as humans.

In the golfing scenario, you may say to her (if she is your spouse): "I wonder how it is going to go with my sore shoulder" (medium-high intimacy). "And if I'm out there and my sore shoulder prevents me from getting the scores I'm used to getting, and if I slow my friends down and have to wave people on to play past us, the whole day may be so frustrating for me," (high intimacy), "that I might be like a monster when I come home!"

To that, she may reply, "If that's what happens, then … before you come home, give me a call … because I don't want to be here!"

If you receive a lack of support for your emotions, as in the preceding reply, you will not easily reveal your emotions to her in the future to prevent uncomfortable me-versus-you interactions. You may think: "If that is how you are, then the next time I go golfing and feel frustrated, I will not come home. Instead, I will go with my friends to the '19th hole' (the lounge)! Why? Because my friends will understand what I went through out there!"

So that is what you are likely to do. If your emotions are not validated within the context of a significant relationship such as with your spouse, then you will be at risk of seeking the validation of your emotions from another relationship. In the golfing illustration, the other relationship is your golfing buddies who are aware of your frustrating round of golf and are free to relate with you in a non-blaming, understanding manner. On the other hand, the person who does not wish to be at home if you return feeling like a monster is judging your emotions to be unsafe (and is therefore judging you). She therefore prevents herself from understanding your feelings and prevents you from being understood. Your relationship with her is left with a limit or a wall that you build to protect yourself from an unhealthy me-versus-you way of relating together when you discuss emotions at the high intimacy level. The two of you are thus limited to relate no further than the medium-high setting.

In contrast, if her reply to your fear of a frustrating round of golf is "Wow! If I thought that I'd be at risk to feel that way, then I think I'd prefer to wait a week instead of trying to golf today. But if you think you'd like to try it out, and it doesn't work well, then I think I can understand how you'd feel. I think I'd feel the same way. But tell you what. If you come home and feel like a monster, I'll see if I can help you by giving you a massage, if you'd like. Maybe later we can do something nice to make up for it."

This second response is consistent with what is considered to be the most intimate and fulfilling relationship. Both people in the relationship allow each other to experience and to share their emotions freely, and they refrain from interpreting their emotions within the me-versus-you mindset.

You will not have many relationships at the high intimacy setting. Ideally, you are interested in relating with your spouse at this most fulfilling level. Perhaps you will have a handful of other relationships at the highest level, such as your best friend or a close family member. If you are relating with somebody at the high level of intimacy, you will not necessarily relate with her at the highest level all the time. You do, however, have the freedom to relate with her at whichever level you believe is appropriate in each circumstance. For example, sometimes you will say, "That is a red car" (low level). And sometimes you will say, "That is a red car, and I really like it!" (high level).

If you are in a relationship in which there is a limit or a block in place at a lower setting of intimacy, for instance at the medium level, then your freedom to communicate with him is limited to within the lower levels. You are, however, able to move your conversation with him among the three lower intimacy settings as appropriate.

A suppressing person is someone who keeps his thoughts and feelings to himself to keep the peace. When this dynamic is applied to the intimacy levels, it can be seen that a side effect of suppressing anger is that the suppressor is limited in his ability to attain higher levels of intimacy in his relationships. If he keeps his feelings inside (to himself), it is difficult for him to attain the highest level of intimacy in a relationship he desires to be a deeply intimate one. If he keeps his thoughts inside (to himself) to keep the peace, he limits his relationships with others to be within the low or medium-low settings of the intimacy levels.

Some people, as strong suppressors, have difficulty relating to anybody beyond the low setting of intimacy levels (limited to facts and information only). In these circumstances, the strong suppressor can struggle with feelings of loneliness. Since intimacy is a unity term, and since unity is a spiritual dynamic, a person who relates to others primarily at the lowest level of intimacy does not feel a sense of belonging (unity) in her world. I consider the sense of unity to be spiritual food. If she feels lonely, her sense of loneliness is a form of starvation. In other words, loneliness is spiritual starvation.

When a person feels lonely, she senses a type of wrongness about the loneliness she feels. She thinks: "This is wrong. This isn't the way life is meant to be. I'm starving!" Along with her sense of wrongness, she will experience negative emotions, as outlined in the anger model. When she is subsequently energized to anger, she may focus her motivational energy for change within the destructive mindset and thus blame somebody. Sometimes she blames herself. She thinks: "Who would want to get to know me better anyway? What have I got to offer?" And so she gets down on herself. On the other hand, if she blames other people for her loneliness, then she may think: "What's the matter with everybody here? They're all so superficial!" And so she believes other people are the problem.

There is, however, a saying, "If you want a friend, you have to be a friend." In other words, take the risk. If there is somebody you meet whom you would like to get to know better, then take the risk to get to know him better by sharing with him something about yourself at a higher intimacy setting. Then give him the freedom to accept you or to reject you at that higher level. If his response is to relate with you in an accepting way at that higher level, then you will feel a sense of satisfaction (your spiritual food—a sense of belonging or acceptance). On the other hand, if he rejects relating to you at that higher level, then remind yourself, "I'm okay—you're okay." You will not be in relationship with him at the higher setting that you hoped to be at, but it is okay. Not everybody will accept relating to you at the intimacy levels in which you would like to relate with them, but not everybody will reject you either.

Be free to allow any relationship to blossom at whatever level it appropriately blossoms to, that is, with both of you growing in the relationship at the same rate. A healthy relationship is not about power and control, but is about acceptance and love. Understanding and applying the homework assignment will help you to keep your relationships as healthy as possible. Keep also in mind the risk of becoming a slave or a master to another person (unhealthy relationship), as discussed earlier, so that you maintain a healthy perspective in your relationships.

Factors in Spousal Relationships

In spousal relationships, potential difficulties arise for the couple to attain the highest level of intimacy because of gender differences in understanding emotions.

For example, there may be a block in the relationship between a husband and wife at the high setting if the man believes "Men don't cry!" He may believe crying is a woman's "thing" and may interpret her crying within the destructive power-based mindset. "She only cries when she wants something," may be how he understands her tears. Therefore, when she is upset and tearful, he is more likely to protect and defend himself from her, as opposed to being free to offer her support. If she cries, he may react in a derogatory way: "There you go crying again! Cry, cry, cry! Well, I'm not buying it!" Does he sound supportive? No way!

Both of them may learn that her tears can be effective in manipulating him to get her way, but her tears do not always imply manipulation. Everybody is free to discern the difference between genuine crying, as an expression of emotion, and crying as a manipulative strategy within the power-based mindset. Your constructive mindset enhances your ability to tell the difference.

If her tears are a genuine sign of her emotions (not connected with any intention of manipulating), and if her husband does not support her by having an attitude that does not allow or acknowledge her emotions, then she may seek her emotional support from a source other than her husband. She may have a close girlfriend with whom she relates within the high intimacy setting. Eventually, her husband recognizes that she is closer with her friend than she is with him. He may take offence at this situation and sternly say to his wife: "What are you doing? Don't you know that the marriage relationship is supposed to be the number one relationship? You're closer with your friend than you are with me! What has your friend got that I haven't?"

Out of fear, he makes it hard for his wife to have the close relationship with her good friend so as to protect himself. But he in turn does not support her at the high intimacy setting. She is therefore emotionally quenched. She is forced to keep her emotions inside because of the will of her husband. Her resulting loneliness is not self-inflicted, but it is due to the demands of an outside force. And if at some time she receives emotional validation from another man, there is a risk of new potatoes presenting themselves as questions of fidelity in the spousal relationship are brought forward.

The husband is therefore interested in allowing his wife to have her feelings and emotions. He must learn to let her cry without the assumption that her natural human function of tears is only to be understood within the me-versus-you destructive mindset. Ideally, if he learns to accept that crying is also part of being a man, he gives himself the opportunity to experience a fuller and enriched life. He opens himself to experiences that include the entire palette of emotions he otherwise cannot imagine is possible to experience.

But if he is uncomfortable within himself to shed tears, he is nonetheless interested in learning to let others cry, especially his wife. Even if she is crying with manipulative intent, he does not have to be fearful or protective, because love conquers fear. He no longer needs to restrict himself to understand tears only within the context of power or manipulation. He can become aware that tears are also a normal function of the reality of emotions. If he does so, he is free to nurture the highest and most fulfilling level of intimacy with her.

A second example of a difference in the understanding of emotions between the sexes can occur in the setting of sports. There is a strong emotional component connected with sports. (In Edmonton, there was a notable contrast of emotional expression within the community not long ago when the local hockey team progressed ever further on its way to the championship, compared to the following season when the team missed the playoffs.) It is possible that the freedom to express emotions in the context of sports is more common in men than in women. (Sports are becoming more heavily marketed to women so the difference is becoming less obvious.) A limit to the intimacy level within a spousal relationship may be interpreted, however, from the woman's point of view in the setting of sports activities. She may be referred to as "the Sunday widow." Her husband plays or watches the game, or gets together with the guys to play or watch the game, and she is left out of the picture. She feels lonely and begrudges her husband's involvement in his sporting endeavours.

To move beyond the emotional block that can occur in a spousal relationship in the setting of sports, I believe the woman must learn to allow her husband to have his likes and his emotions. She may not understand why the sport is so great to him and how it could be so emotional when something happens to the ball or to the puck. Her conclusion, however, cannot be that her husband is not allowed to have his likes and his emotions. She is not interested in the interpretation that his love of the game means that he is against her. Such a negative conclusion will lead her to understand her husband's interest in sports within the destructive mindset. She is, rather, interested to recognize that her husband's likes and emotions linked with a sport are a part of what makes him who he is and whom she loves.

The following suggestion is not to be taken as the correct suggestion; it is merely an option proposed for her to consider. She is free to consider participating with her husband in the sport. If he watches a game on the TV, perhaps she joins him to watch the game together. Her entertainment is not necessarily the game, but could be the emotional outbursts her husband goes through in response to various events that occur during the game.

Over time, she learns aspects of the game. What was once a game she knew little about becomes part of her vocabulary. She may learn to enjoy the game. As her husband becomes aware that both of them are participating in the sporting activity as a team, rather than in a me-versus-you fashion, a freedom ensues. If perchance a different activity arises as something to do together, then he is free to consider: "Maybe watching three games in a day is a bit of overkill. Maybe watching one game today is enough." If this is his conclusion, then the two of them are free to participate in this other activity. If he discovers that he enjoys this other activity, then he is free to let her know. He is free to accept doing other things and free to grow from a bigger bouquet of life experiences. People's likes and dislikes can and do change over time.

On the other hand, he may consent to do something else with her in the context of: "I'm just going to do this with her to get her off my back. She's been nagging me and nagging me. I'll do my duty and please her with this, just this one time." Under these circumstances, he is not likely to let her know that he likes the activity if he discovers he does enjoy it. He becomes at risk to suppress what he otherwise enjoys just because he believes she wins and he does not want to lose face. Therefore, he is neither being a friend to her nor to himself, for he prevents himself from accepting something he otherwise would accept.

Where along the intimacy settings do you assess your relationship with your significant other to be? Are you both at the same setting together or is there an imbalance? Are you in a master-slave relationship? Are you the master? Are you the slave? Try to apply the homework assignment to assess where you are as you consider the difference between healthy and unhealthy relationship dynamics. You are far more interested in relating to others at a setting within the healthy, constructive mindset than within the unhealthy, destructive fashion of slavery or mastery.

Homework

Is there anything new about yourself that you have discovered while thinking about your homework assignment? If you have a tendency to suppress, is the homework assignment helping you to recognize that you are limiting yourself from being free to be who you are meant to be, and free to do what you desire to do, that is, to be creative and have a fulfilling life? My hope for you is that you are starting to recognize when you are becoming a slave to someone else and that you are learning to free yourself to be you and free to take risks in your relationships—my hope for you is that you will discover who your true friends are and that you will learn to accept the limitations in your relationships with those who are not truly your friends.

Chapter 4
Repress

The last destructive method of anger management to discuss is the *repress* method (Figure 4.1). Some presentations of the concepts of anger and anger management may include the repress method as another subset of the suppress method, rather than identifying it as a separate method. This is because the two methods have some common themes. Both methods are based on peace-making intent, but sadly lead to a false peace. Because of these similarities, the suppress and repress methods can be difficult to distinguish from each other and in fact can occur simultaneously. There is a grey area of overlap between the two methods. Presenting them as being distinct from each other is therefore a weakness of the anger model described in this book.

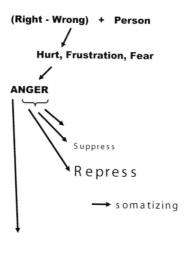

Figure 4.1 The Repress Method of Emotion Management

The reason I list the repress method of anger management as being distinct from the suppress method is as follows. When a person suppresses, she learns to keep the peace by putting a lid on her emotions. In the process, she is aware of feeling her negative emotions. In contrast, when she is angered and uses the repress method, she learns to keep the peace by learning not to feel. Regardless of her intent to curb her emotions, her physical body becomes energized nonetheless because her body is designed to release adrenalin in the face of stress to energize her physiologically.

As she learns to repress her emotions more and more, she becomes less aware of them, even though the energized state of her body continues to occur. If she becomes a very strong repressor, she may cease to be aware of her emotions altogether. Her awareness of her emotions virtually goes into the subconscious realm, yet the energized state of her body is not affected. When her body becomes energized to anger, she does not interpret this energized state as being anger, but may rather interpret it as times when she *feels* stressed (a feeling in her body rather than feeling her emotions).

The cost of the repress method of anger management is what I call *somatizing*. The word *soma* means "body"; therefore, what happens in this method is that your body shows evidence of anger. Any body-related illness or condition that is thought to have a link in some way to stress or anger can fall into the repress category of anger management. For example, certain types of headaches that are thought to be associated with stress can fall into this category. High blood pressure or ulcers (inasmuch as they are thought to have a connection with stress) can be included. Any body ache or pain, thought to have a stress component, can fall into the repress category of anger management.

There are two major ways that a person can learn to repress. If he grows up in a family in which the concept of anger is considered to be bad, wrong, sinful, or inappropriate, he may learn not to feel anger in accordance with such beliefs. He may be a person with the desire to be positive. His noble desire may arise because he does not want to be negative. Experiencing negative emotions is not pleasant. He would rather not have to feel negative emotions. He therefore learns to dull his awareness of his negative emotions because of his desire to be positive.

A third possible way that a person can learn to repress comes from the after-effects of an intense emotional experience. He may have been in a situation in which he almost exploded in anger, but he was able to catch it in time before he did anything drastic. Perhaps he did explode and regrets the consequences. But later he convinces himself: "I never want to feel like that again. I never want to do that again." And so he works toward diminishing his feelings to protect himself and others from his emotions and his wrath. He may develop an "I don't care," or *hakuna matata* ("no worries here"), attitude to life in which he does not have to deal with his own feelings by numbing them out. He may indeed believe he has found the way to peace in his life.

Regardless of how he learns to not feel his negative emotions, he discovers that he cannot be selective. What I mean is if he learns to not feel his negative emotions, he can lose awareness of his positive emotions as well. It is as if there is a range of emotional expression that any person experiences. The normal range (whatever "normal" may be—it is hard to judge what normal is) of emotional expression may be a range that is "this wide," from positive to negative (Figure 4.2). In the middle of the range is what I call "neutral" emotion. This is the horizontal line in the middle of the box in Figure 4.2. On the up side is positive emotion, and on the down side is negative emotion.

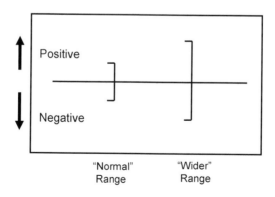

"Normal" Range   "Wider" Range

Figure 4.2 Range of Emotional Expression

If a person is highly emotional, he has a wider range of emotional expression. When he feels up, he swings from the chandeliers in glee.

When he feels down, you could scrape him off the asphalt, he is so low. The crossover from the normal range of emotions a person can have to where the person is at risk for mental instability is a separate topic of discussion that I will not handle in this book.

If the normal spread of emotional expression is "this wide," it will narrow down from the positive and negative ends in a virtually simultaneous fashion, as the person learns to quench (not feel) his emotions. In other words, his emotional range narrows. If he becomes very strong at managing his emotions by learning to quench them, his emotional response in situations becomes so narrow and controlled that it resembles a flat line.

If his range of emotional expression is flat, he is considered a nice person. His ability to manage stress and anger is considered legendary. He "wows" people at how well he takes and handles pressure. But emotionally he is flat. He doesn't react to things with much, if any, emotion. He could attend a party where there are a lot of positive vibes in the air. People are having and showing fun. But the emotional state of our friend is not at the elevated positive level. His emotions are flat.

He may notice that he is not responding to the events at the party with his positive emotions. He may have a sense of wrongness about his lack of feeling. As he seeks to understand this wrongness, he may focus his attention on blaming a person (destructive mindset). If he focuses on blaming himself, he may think: "What's the matter with me? This is a happy place, and I just cannot feel it!" If he focuses on blaming others, he may think: "What's the matter with everyone here? It's not that great a party! Everybody is just overreacting!" Actually, the overreacting that he claims others are doing is within the normal range of emotional expression for them. To him, it seems that others are overreacting because his vantage point for interpreting the situation is from a narrower range of emotional expression. His interpretation is dependent on his own frame of reference (applies to anybody).

One example of how you can learn to repress is as follows: Imagine a four-year-old child growing up in a family whose concept of having anger and negative emotions is considered to be wrong, bad, sinful, or inappropriate. Every time he shows evidence of having negative emotions or anger, the message he receives is along those lines.

Imagine he is playing with a toy and having a great time. One of his parents comes and says lovingly to him, "Put the toy away and come for supper." He looks up, scans the kitchen, and notices Brussels sprouts on the menu. He thinks: "Brussels sprouts! I'm not interested in that!" So he ignores his parent and keeps on playing with his toy.

His parent comes to him the second time and firmly states, "Put the toy away and come for supper." He ignores the command and keeps playing with his toy.

Finally, his parent takes the toy away from him. To our little friend, there is a concept of wrongness before him. His idea of injustice is: "Parent! You do not take a toy away from me that I like playing with!" His response to this indignity is likely to be a combination of frustration and hurt. He is energized to anger. Let us imagine that he manages his anger by throwing a temper tantrum.

Any parent would like to teach his or her child not to throw a temper tantrum when upset. But there is a difference between a parent's message that acknowledges and validates emotion in the child while teaching the child that the tantrum is unacceptable, and a parent's message that assumes the emotion and the tantrum in the child are one and the same.

If the parent separates the emotion in his or her child from the child's anger management method (the tantrum), the feedback to the child is something like: "I know you are upset because I took your toy away, and I can accept that. But we are all going to eat together now, and you can play with your toy again after supper. However, that temper tantrum thing that you did is not necessary and has to go!"

If the parent does not separate the emotion from the management method (the tantrum) of the child, then his or her feedback could be something like a firm command: "I say; you do! If I tell you to put your toy away and come for supper, I say and you do! You do not think! You do not feel! Because I have spoken, you do as you are told!"

Imagine that the parent introduces the consequence of a negative experience to his or her child to send a firm message. A link between the negative experience and the child's inappropriate behaviour is hoped to be a way to curb the inappropriate behaviour of the child. There are many different choices of negative feedback approaches that are available. One example is to send the child to his room (if the message to the child is that his room is a negative place, I think that it is unfortunate, for his room is a private place of ownership and refuge for him). Another example is to make him sit in a corner of the room, facing the wall. Yet a more controversial method is to spank him.

Let us imagine that the child in our example receives a spanking for performing his temper tantrum. The next time he is energized to anger, he may remember: "The last time I felt like this, I threw a temper tantrum, and then I got a spanking. Hmmm. I didn't like that spanking, so I better not throw a temper tantrum." Notice that the use of negative feedback approaches, to curb certain unwanted behaviours, is successful in bringing about change in behaviour. That is why people defend the use of such methods.

But by receiving a spanking, the child does not lose his emotional energy the next time he gets upset. Instead of throwing a temper tantrum the next time he is angry, let us imagine that his attention goes to his body. As you recall in chapter 1 of this book, there are physiological changes in the body due to the release of adrenalin and other stress factors into the bloodstream that produce the energized state when a person is angry. One of the effects mentioned could be the feeling of butterflies in your stomach. Let us imagine that the child's attention goes to those butterflies he is feeling and that he interprets this sensation as a tummy ache. Therefore, the next time he gets energized to anger, he says to his parent, "I've got a tummy ache."

This time around, his parent's response is one of nurture and support. His parent lovingly says to him: "You've got a tummy ache? Awww. That's not so good, is it? How about if we snuggle a bit on the couch, or you lie down and I heat up some of your favourite soup. That will help you to feel better!" He receives positive feedback for becoming sick and is therefore at risk of learning to manage his anger by becoming sick. His first anger management method (the tantrum) is met with negative feedback; his second (the tummy ache) is met with positive feedback. (Note: Another possibility is that the child learns to manage his anger by eating food, but I will not pursue this possible outcome in this chapter.)

He learns to manage his anger by becoming sick. As an adult, he may develop into a person whose ability to manage stress and anger is considered legendary. He is a nice person. He is very strong and stable in his ability to manage his emotions. But emotionally, he is flat. He could be working in a high-stress occupation. The stress he endures may be extreme. His boss may be on his case about this and that. He comes home after a day at work. His spouse greets him, is aware of the stress he is under, and is concerned. His spouse has a wider range of emotional expression than he does. There is fear and trepidation in his spouse's voice, who with pressured speech exclaims, "Ihearthere'salot o fthingsgoingonatworkhow'sitgoing?" (pant, pant)

The response of our emotionally controlled hero is slow, calm, and matter of fact: "Fine," or "Well … it's okay … there are a lot of things I have to do, but … I just have to keep at it."

"ButIhearthebossisinyourfaceandmakingithardonyouhowareyoudeal-ingwiththat?" (pant, pant)

"I just have to keep focusing on what I have to do, and it will be all right," he replies in an almost monotone and soothing way.

The concerned spouse looks upon him incredulously and exclaims: "How do you do it? If I were in your shoes, there is no way I would be able to handle things the way you do! I would be a basket case!"

And so, notice that people who repress are well respected and seem to be very stable and strong in how they manage their challenges. In fact, as you may notice, much of the way repressors handle their affairs appears, on the surface, to be within the constructive mindset.

A little later that evening, however, our repressor may complain: "I think my ulcer is starting to act up again. I'm having a lot of pain. I think it's bleeding! Please take me to the hospital." He is experiencing a real physical phenomenon. His physical damage is not something in his head. In fact, a person can die of a severely bleeding ulcer. Therefore, to repress is a destructive method of anger management with physically destructive consequences.

You may wonder, if the destructive mindset is based on focusing on a person to blame when he is energized to anger, then who does he focus on when he represses his anger? I suggest that the person he primarily focuses on is himself. He either believes it is wrong to have anger or he doesn't want to feel the unpleasant negative feelings of anger. But since having emotions is like having arms and legs, and since having arms and legs is part of what it means to be human, he thus equates himself as being the problem if he experiences negative emotions. His emotions become a potato to him, and that potato has his name on it. It is as if he believes it is wrong to have legs when he becomes aware that he has legs. But he cannot help having arms and legs and he cannot help having emotions, whether they are positive or negative. He therefore gives himself the impossible task to be free of emotions and commits himself to living in slavery to the idea that he should not have negative emotions.

Emotional Leprosy

Another name I give to the repress method of anger management is *emotional leprosy*. Are you familiar with the cause and consequences of the illness referred to as leprosy? Many people think that a person loses a finger or a toe, should he or she be inflicted with leprosy.

Actually, if a person loses a finger or toe when he has leprosy, the loss is not a direct effect of the leprosy. It is an indirect effect. Leprosy is a bacterial infection of the nerves of the skin. If a person contracts leprosy, the damaging effects of the leprosy infection numb his skin, so that he does not feel pain. Different types of leprosy have to do with the type of immune response a person mounts to the infection. If his immune response involves scarring, his leprosy is not as infectious to others. If his immune response involves pus, he is more infectious to others. A scene from the movie *Papillon*, which occurs after the hero escapes from prison and seeks shelter in a leper colony, helps to bear this difference out.

Leprosy is not a common illness in Canada; what is more common is diabetes mellitus. One potential complication of diabetes is peripheral neuropathy, in which the nerves of the skin become damaged related to the disease process. A person with diabetes loses the ability to notice pain.

She could be working in her kitchen preparing a meal. As she goes to and fro, she slips on the floor. In an attempt to brace herself from her fall, she places her hand on the countertop. She succeeds in breaking her fall. She is relieved, and sighs: "Whew! That was close! I could have hurt myself! I should be more careful."

Before long, our friend smells something burning. She does not remember putting that steak on the hotplate. She looks down, and notices it is her hand that is burning. To break her fall, she has placed her hand on the hotplate! But she did not feel the pain! Similarly, this is what happens if a person contracts leprosy—he or she loses the ability to feel pain.

Leprosy continues to exist in regions that are more tropical than Canada. Some of these locations are considered to be underdeveloped compared with Canada. A person living in these regions is more likely to walk to work (which does not make it underdeveloped). But she is not as likely to wear footwear, and the paths she walks on may not be paved or lit. In the tropics, the sun rises and sets at virtually the same time throughout the year: up at 6 a.m.; down at 6 p.m. There is no seasonal variation of daylight hours as experienced within Canada.

Therefore, if she walks home after work, sometimes she walks home past sundown. If there is a full moon, there may be light to guide her on her way. If there is a new moon, her path is dark. Let us imagine our friend has leprosy (and is not yet aware of it). As she walks home, she may step on a thorn. The thorn lodges in one of her toes. She has no idea that this has happened, for she cannot feel any pain connected with the thorn. She just keeps on walking. And with every step she takes, the thorn gets lodged deeper and deeper into her toe.

Eventually, our friend notices that her toe is infected. The cause of her infected toe is the bacteria that the thorn brings with it as it lodges in her toe. She may lose her toe because of the infection introduced from the thorn. The leprosy only made her toe numb, so that she could not feel pain when the thorn pierced her skin.

Leprosy is a very difficult infection to treat. Most antibiotics make it difficult for bacteria to grow and thus antibiotics work together with your immune system to ward off the deleterious effects of any infection you may have. Leprosy bacteria, however, grow very slowly. The arsenal of antibiotics available is not as effective in curbing the invasion of leprosy bacteria, and the bacteria have ways to thrive despite your immune system. Although medical science is finding more effective ways to treat leprosy, a person afflicted with leprosy is also taught not to rely on the sensation of pain to maintain skin integrity. She is taught to pay attention to proper footwear and to visually inspect her feet regularly to assess the integrity of her skin.

Contrast this example of a person walking home who is afflicted with leprosy with that of another person without leprosy who walks home under the same conditions. She steps on a thorn and it lodges in her toe. She feels the pain right away and stops. She lifts up her leg and tries to find the source of the pain in her toe. If she is not successful in finding the thorn, she may seek assistance from a friend to find and take the thorn out. When the thorn is removed, she cleans her foot and bandages her wound.

What does she do the rest of the way home? She likely limps and complains to herself, "I really should get shoes, even though they may cost me a month's wages!" Her limping is a way to protect herself from further injury or damage to her toe.

I suggest that our friend does not enjoy or appreciate feeling pain when she steps on the thorn. But the pain she feels is her friend. Her pain says to her: "Something's up! I need your attention!" And her pain focuses her attention on her toe so that she can take care of herself, and therefore she does not lose her toe.

The same is true of your negative emotions. You do not like to feel them. They are not pleasant. You would rather not have to feel them. But your negative emotions are your friend. They are telling you: "Something's up! We need your attention!" And so your negative emotions, including anger, focus your attention on situations of injustice that you come across. If you believe you should not have negative emotions, or if you try not to feel them, then you place yourself at risk of losing body parts. Such is the risk of a repressor when his feelings go into the subconscious, yet the energized state remains to affect the body. And that is why I call the repress method of anger management emotional leprosy.

Homework

If you strongly use the repress method of anger management, then the homework assignment I have described may be difficult for you to understand. Your challenge is to remember to apply the homework assignment when you feel the energy of your negative emotions (anger). But if you have learned to quench your awareness of this emotional energy, then you may never notice when it is time to think of the homework assignment.

If this is the case, then the cues you are looking for to think of the homework assignment have to be associated with any body response to stress that you experience when you are stressed. For example, if you feel a twinge in your stomach, but do not feel your emotions, and if you know you are under stress, then explore how the homework assignment applies to the situation you are in.

Chapter 5
Confess

This chapter discusses the constructive method of anger management in more detail. The word I use to describe this method, *confess*, is dangerous and risky. It can have a specific connotation, yet it is not my intent to apply the word in this specific way when using it to explain the constructive method of anger management.

The reason that this word is risky and dangerous is that the idea to confess is generally associated with a concept that you have done something wrong. You wish to "come clean" and "fess up" to move on. In this presentation about the negative emotions and anger, however, I consistently mention that your emotions are not the problem. Therefore, you do not confess your anger with the idea that having anger is a problem.

I may have chosen words such as "confirm" or "affirm" to convey a similar train of thought as the way to understand the constructive mindset. Instead, I choose the term "confess" because each of the terms used to describe the other (destructive) anger management methods also end with "e-s-s." And so I try to maintain a continuity of the model by using similarly sounding words to keep the model consistent and easier to remember.

I will divide the constructive method into two phases. The first phase is to confess to yourself that you have anger. This carries the idea of taking ownership for your own emotions. The second phase is to confess to the other person involved, if there is someone else connected with the potato that you are dealing with. To confess to others carries the idea of testifying to them what you believe, or communicating with them who you are. You will communicate what you believe, how you think, and how you feel, depending on the relationship intimacy setting you have with them, as described in chapter 3.

First Phase

Ownership

The first phase of the confess method is to confess to yourself *that* you have anger, or *that* you are angry. It is as if you say to yourself: "I am angry. I have arms and I have legs. I have anger. This is *my* anger." Therefore, by definition, you must convince yourself that **nobody** makes you mad. The saying that a person "makes me mad" is a conclusion that you can easily convince yourself to be true, but it is a nonsensical saying. You may say to someone or you may think "Hey! You're making me mad!" or "So-and-so makes me so mad! Grrrr!"

If you believe other people can make you mad, then you are living in such a way that you give others power over you. You are not interested in living your life this way. It would be as though you approach somebody and say to him: "Hey! You know what? You can make me mad! You can do anything! Did you know that you could do that?"

You are not interested in living with a mindset that gives others power over you. You are rather interested in the freedom to allow others to be who they are and to allow yourself to be who you are. With this freedom, you have the ability to "love others as yourself."

Take ownership of your own emotions. When you get energized to anger, say to yourself "I am mad (or angry)" and realize "This is *my* anger." In truth, it is not "someone making me mad"; it is "*that* I am mad."

Even if you believe that somebody is purposefully doing something to make you mad, you must take ownership of your own emotions and not believe that he or she is making you mad. If it is true that he is intentionally provoking you, you will no doubt experience even more of the energy of your anger, for there are at least two potatoes in play. There is the potato of what he said or did that you believe is wrong, plus there is the potato connected with your belief that he said or did it on purpose. Therefore, more potatoes on your plate means more energy on your part as you experience anger, but you nevertheless must take ownership of your own emotions. Do not give in to the belief that the other person "made" you mad.

When you have the ownership of your emotions, you are able ask yourself the question, "Why am I angry?" Asking yourself this question *before* you take ownership of your emotions easily gets you into the destructive mindset. It is as though you believe the problem is your emotions, your anger, me, or you. You put the accent of asking the question, "Why am I angry?" onto the words "I" or "angry," which makes you think your anger is about me, or you, or your anger, and you thus are drawn into the destructive mindset.

On the other hand, if you have the ownership of your emotions, and thus *accept your emotions* as part of what is a normal life experience, then you are free to ask the question, "*Why* am I angry?" This time around, your question is asked in such a way that the accent is on the word "why." Doing so positions you within the constructive mindset and thus gives you something to work with. Accepting your emotions gives you a sense of self-validation of your emotions. You give yourself the freedom to exist. You are now free to evaluate what your emotions are telling you.

Discernment

The goal of the "why am I angry" question is to discern what represents the injustice that is before you. Sometimes the question is easy to answer, sometimes it is not. There is variable difficulty in arriving at a conclusion, which is reasonable to expect. When it comes to human conflict, the answer is usually along the lines of something said or done, or not said or not done, that you believe is wrong.

One way to seek an answer to the "why am I angry" question is to backtrack up the anger model (Figure 5.1), starting from the word "anger," and explore your emotions. You ask yourself: "Why am I angry? Well, is it because I am *hurt* about something? Is it because I am *frustrated* about something? Is it because I am *afraid* of something?" Try to answer that "something" along the lines of the injustice you currently face. Your answer is usually going to be something that someone said or did, or did not say or did not do, that you believe is wrong. Once you identify the problem, or you at least identify that the situation is about a yet-to-be-discerned problem, and once you are convinced that the person is not the problem, then you are in control of your anger. Your emotions are a tool to help you to discern, as best as you can, how to understand the various challenges that come your way.

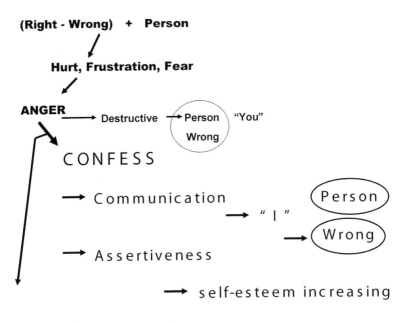

Figure 5.1 The Confess Method of Emotion Management

Hot Potatoes

If you think of the hot potatoes illustration of emotion intelligence, this is the picture: The heat of your potato represents your negative emotions, which alert you to the fact that you are dealing with a potato. The potato represents your belief of injustice that you find yourself in the presence of. You therefore notice that you have a potato in your grasp. As you feel the heat of your potato, perhaps you juggle it back and forth between your two hands, wondering what to do with it (the anger management question). Maybe your attention is focused on blaming the person that is connected with your potato and you are ready to hurl your potato at him. In the nick of time, you remember: "Hey! I've got a potato!" You shift the focus of your attention away from blaming him to the potato that is in your grasp.

Or maybe your attention is focused on the other person, and you are about to place your potato into the sack on your back, thinking, "I better keep this potato out of sight to keep the peace." Then, in the nick of time, before it gets into your sack, you remember: "Hey! I've got a potato!" Your attention shifts to focus your thoughts on the potato.

When you accept that your feelings are there to alert you to the potato, and you in turn focus your attention on your potato, you become ready to assess what your potato represents. In other words, you become ready to discern what kind of injustice you are in the presence of. It is as if you realize: "Hey! This is a red potato! I've never really taken the time to distinguish the difference between red and white potatoes, but this one is red!" You use your emotions to help you to discern what the potato represents. As you focus more and more on your potato, you are able to juggle it less and less as its heat dissipates. You are able to grab hold of it and focus your thoughts completely on it. You gain an understanding of the injustice that your potato represents. Sometimes you attain a complete understanding of the problem, and other times more of a vague idea, but your attention is focussed on the problem rather than on blaming the person.

Now that your attention is on the potato, what will do you do with it? You will not throw the potato at the person responsible for it, nor will you put the potato in the sack on your back. You perform the actions of throwing or dumping your potatoes only in the context of focusing your thoughts on, and thus blaming, the person responsible. So if your thoughts are focussed on the potato, what will do you do with it?

You place your potato on what I call "the desktop of conflict management!" (You can call it a countertop if you like, since it is a potato!) That's right. You let go of your potato and *place it on the desktop*. The action of putting your potato on the desktop gives you something to work with. It is the potato you work with. You are now free to be open- minded, free to find creative ways to manage your potato, and free to persevere in your attempts to change what your anger is motivating you to change.

Creativity and Perseverance

Open-mindedness gives you the freedom to be creative and to persevere. Within your creativity, you are free to assess: "How will I deal with this potato? Should I peel it, cut it up, boil it, and mash it? Should I bake it? Should I slice it up and deep-fry it?" In other words, you discover there are different ways to manage your potato. You are not restricted to thinking there is only one correct way to handle problems; there are rather various options. Indeed, people have unique points of view about what the proper way to fix a problem is, but you don't know how to fix something unless you know what is broken. A doctor needs to know the diagnosis so that he or she can prescribe proper treatment. But once you know what is broken, how you go about fixing the problem is up to the human imagination. This is the realm of creativity.

When you are in an unacceptable situation, you may attempt a certain action plan to change things for the better. After some time, you may hit roadblocks. You shift gears and try an alternate line of action. When your thoughts are within the constructive mindset, you become creatively free to discover an alternate way to bring about change. You become free to *persevere*. Creativity knows no bounds. To summarize: When you hit your roadblock, the open-mindedness of the constructive mindset gives you the ability to persevere with what you are hoping to achieve and to creatively discover alternate paths to attain a solution to the problem.

Open-Mindedness and Identity

Placing your potato on the desktop releases you to be open-minded in how you understand yourself. Your identity relates to how you perceive who you are, and is derived from an idea of truth that you adhere to. You are dependent on your concept of truth to know "who" you are. You are open-minded if you allow your concept of truth to stand on its own merit. Your identity (how you perceive "who you are") and your concept of truth forming the foundation of your identity are not to be considered as one and the same thing.

If you believe that your foundation of truth and your identity are the same thing (like twisting your fingers around each other), then you are closed-minded. This means that your identity is derived from what you believe to be true, and you also believe that your "truth" is dependent on you to defend it as truth in order for it to be true.

To be open-minded, you are interested to let truth be truth and to derive your identity from what you believe is true. You must allow your concept of truth to stand on its own merit. In fact, truth indeed stands on its own merit. Truth is its own standard of reference.

In order for a lie to be recognized as a lie, a standard of truth is required. The reverse dynamic, however, is not the same. In order for you to recognize something as true, you do not require a lie as a contrast to your truth in order for you to recognize your truth as truth. A "standard of a lie" does not exist. Truth stands on its own merit.

For example, imagine I hold a fresh, scrumptious, juicy strawberry in the palm of my hand. As I am about to place the strawberry in my salivating mouth, I proudly proclaim, "How I love these blue strawberries!" What would you think about my proclamation? I imagine that you would react a bit quizzically and think "blue strawberries?" You would recognize my claim that strawberries are blue to be untrue, for my version of truth does not coincide with your version of truth that strawberries are red. Therefore, the standard of truth, that strawberries are red, has helped you to recognize that it is a falsehood to claim that strawberries are blue.

On the other hand, as I am about to place this scrumptious strawberry into my mouth, I proclaim, "How I love these red strawberries!" How would you respond to my proclamation this time? I imagine you would not pick up on anything unusual about my comment. Perhaps you would feel a sense of envy and wish that I would share my meal with you and give you the next one! In other words, you recognize that there is a truth in my proclamation. You agree with me that strawberries are red. But you have not recognized the truth, that strawberries are red, by contrasting this truth with a lie, that strawberries are not blue. You simply agree that strawberries are red on the merit of the truth that strawberries are indeed red.

Therefore, truth does not need the contrast of a lie to be recognized as truth. Truth is recognized on its own merit. In terms of power, there is power in truth. There is nothing more powerful than truth.

Biblical Relevance

John 1:5 states, "The light shines in the darkness, but the darkness has not understood it." If I sit in a room without windows, and it is dark inside, how do I bring light into the room? Right. I flick the light switch to the "on" position. Now that the room has light, how do I make it dark again? Right. I flick the light switch to the "off" position.

What have you noticed? The power is in the light! There is no switch that turns on darkness. Therefore, there is no balance of power between light and dark, between good and bad, between truth and a lie. The standard is light, good, or truth. The standards of truth, light, and good are recognized on their own merit. In comparison, darkness, bad, and falsehood are only recognized as such because they are in contrast with light, good, and truth. Darkness requires light to be recognized as darkness, but light does not need darkness to be recognized as light. During the night I notice that light is missing. In the daytime it never occurs to me that darkness is missing. Light is recognized on its own merit. There is no balance of one needing the other in order to be recognized.

Independence

There is no independence without dependence. The strength of your independence is only as firm as how dependable the foundation of your identity is. In other words, you have a strong independence if the "truth source" you are depending on is indeed true. If the truth source of your identity and therefore of your independence is not dependable, then you are at risk.

If you understand your identity in an open-minded context, then you are free to find creative ways to bring change. Creativity knows no bounds. The open-minded mindset is consistent with the constructive mindset. You are free from taking things personally and have the ability to achieve a strong independence.

Biblical Relevance

Nothing in this world is dependable; the only exception is God. If my identity is derived primarily from God ("First love God with all my heart, soul, and mind"), then I am free to be a creative person in this world.

If my identity is derived from something within the world (money, job, fame, spouse, friend, power), then I am at risk of being tossed to and fro by forces that affect my money, job, fame, spouse, friends, or power. I will live a life full of anxiety because my identity is based on things that are not dependable. My undependable sources of identity and therefore of my independence will let me down, especially noticeable in times of need. My creativity becomes restricted to handle my sources of identity in such a way that they are not affected by their faults. I become a slave to these false gods and lose my independence.

If my identity is on the "rock" that is God (instead of sand), then I have a foundation on which to stand. I can count on a sure footing of stability when I encounter the storms of life. It is God who is dependable, whose name is trustworthy and true. God is not dependent on me to be who He is. When I stand on this rock, I am truly independent.

Closed-Mindedness

If you are closed-minded, then you consider your source of truth and your identity to be one and the same thing. You tend to take things personally. Should your concept of truth be challenged, you understand the "attack" as if you yourself are being attacked. Being closed-minded limits your ability to manage change. You become limited to consider only power-based me-versus-you methods to manage your potatoes. Your creativity is limited, and your thinking is shackled within the destructive mindset.

For example, pretend that I believe blue to be the best colour in the world. I derive my identity from my foundation of truth. My identity is: "I am somebody that believes in blue. Blue needs me to defend it as being the best colour in the world. Blue and I are one and the same."

You may not realize that I identify myself with blue this way. You may come to visit me one day and innocently proclaim: "What's so great about blue? Green is a nicer colour!"

As I think about your statement, I may conclude, "You're shooting down blue and therefore you're shooting down me!" Since my identity is intertwined with my belief in blue, and is understood along the lines that blue and I are one and the same, I interpret your comment as a personal slant and react to you within the destructive me-versus-you mindset. I may think: "I am going to get back at you! Revenge!"

Sometime later, in your presence, I snort out a snide comment about green. I relish the opportunity to get back at you.

You hear my green bashing and feel uncomfortable. You may think: "What is it with this guy? I'm kind of uncomfortable around him now. What was that all about?"

Open-Mindedness and Growth
Compare the preceding interaction with the following: I identify myself as somebody who believes in blue. I derive my identity from the foundation of my belief. I also allow my concept of blue, as the best colour in the world, to stand on its own merit. I am free to be open-minded. I am free from taking things personally. I am free to let me be me and free to let you be you.

You visit me and innocently proclaim: "What's so great about blue? Green is a nicer colour!" Because I let you be you and let me be me, I am free to let you believe in green and free to let me believe in blue. And what is that between you and me? Nothing!

As opposed to reacting defensively against you, I become free to think about your belief in green and how it stacks up to my belief in blue. As I ponder the difference, my conclusion may be: "You know what? Green is okay, too! Maybe I've been limiting myself a little bit. Although blue is a great colour, and I've believed in blue all these years, when it comes down to it, green is a good colour, too! So maybe I should shift my wavelength of truth over a little bit from blue to include green."

With the conclusion to add green as a good colour, I get a sense that I have learned something new. I have a sense of growth. I also feel a sense of thankfulness or gratitude towards you. I may wish to express my gratitude to you at some time. At an appropriate moment, I may say: "I just want to thank you for talking about green the way you did. It has made a big difference to me in how I view the world."

From your point of view, you may not even remember that you had ever talked to me about green! To you, it was merely an innocent comment. In response to my gratitude, you may shrug your shoulders in disbelief and say, "It wasn't me that said anything, was it?"

Notice the contrast of my response to your initial innocent comment. On one hand, if I take your comment personally, I get myself into a vindictive frame of mind. I have restricted myself to a vengeful mindset because I understand my identity within the context of believing that the colour blue and my identity are intertwined as one and the same thing. Instead of defending truth, I defend myself. Life becomes a struggle.

On the other hand, if I understand my identity within the open-minded constructive mindset, then I am free to let me be me and free to let you be you. Because my identity is not intertwined with my belief of truth, I am free from the stress and responsibility to defend truth, as if truth needed me to defend it. I am rather free to firmly uphold what I believe is true, communicating my understanding of truth as opposed to defending myself. I am also free to learn and grow, realizing that there is always something new and exciting to learn. Life shimmers with increasing flair and zest.

There will be times when I will respond to you in a way to uphold my version of truth. I may think: "You can like green if you want! There is no middle ground between blue and green. Blue is definitely the better colour!" My conclusion is to firmly maintain my understanding on what I already believe my wavelength of truth to be. Even though

I come to this conclusion, it does not have to mean that I am against you or that I believe you are against me. There remains an awareness of two differing versions of truth on the desktop to deal with, but the two of us do not need to think that it means we are personally against each other.

The consequences of differing versions of truth between people involve relationship dynamics. There will be a limit to the sense of intimacy in our relationship (as in Figure 3.11), but our differences do not have to mean that we relate within a me-versus-you mindset against each other. Furthermore, even though I do not agree with your version of truth, there may be something about your version of truth that can help me to understand in a more profound way why I believe in my version of truth. I glean a pearl of wisdom from your version of truth because of the challenge to assess your version of truth in contrast to my version of truth. Therefore, I derive a sense of growth in my understanding of life nonetheless, even though I do not agree with your version of truth.

The two most difficult topics to discuss appear to involve religion and politics. When it comes to religion, if I discover that I believe in blue and you believe in green, and if I conclude that there is no middle ground of agreement between our two beliefs, then the unity term to indicate a limit in our relationship is the term *fellowship*. This means that there is a limit to the sense of fellowship (intimacy) in our relationship because of our differing religious beliefs. But it does not have to mean that you and I are against each other (me versus you).

When it comes to political persuasion, if I find that I am somebody who believes in blue and you are somebody who believes in green, and if there is no middle ground of agreement between our two political persuasions, then the unity term that indicates a limit in our relationship is *camaraderie*. According to our differing political viewpoints, we will not share a sense of unity, brotherhood, family, and so on, but we do not have to believe that the two of us are against each other (not necessarily a me-versus-you situation).

I thought a good example of what I am describing came some years ago. I happened to watch Justin Trudeau's eulogy of his father, Canada's former Prime Minister Pierre Trudeau, on television. Justin Trudeau recalled some of his childhood memories while his father was Prime Minister. He mentioned the following scene from when he was about 8 to 10 years old. He was attending a breakfast gathering, which was put on for the parliamentarians and their families. He remembered sitting at a table with his father in a huge ballroom full of people. He mentioned that he was aware that his father was "the leader" of these people and so he felt important to be able to be with his father under such circumstances.

Justin Trudeau went on to recall that he noticed the Leader of the Opposition was sitting at a table across the room. He stated that he pointed him out to his father and made some kind of snide comment about him, thinking that it was "cool" to knock down the opposition and to make fun of him.

He remarked that his father's response to his quip surprised him somewhat. He said his father looked him in the eyes and said something like, "Son, we may not agree with his political viewpoints, but we do not denigrate the individual." After making this comment, his father stood up, took him by the hand, and walked across the room to the table where the opposition leader was sitting. Upon being introduced to him by his father, Justin Trudeau realized and admitted that the opposition leader was in fact "a nice guy."

When I heard this story, I recognized it to be an example of the Prime Minister of Canada giving his son a lesson in constructive anger management (or the constructive mindset). There is no shortage of examples of politicians making personal comments against their foes, especially reported in the press during an election campaign. It is refreshing, however, to notice that there is also a level of respect, despite the differences in policy and the desire to govern, that politicians in opposition to each other are able to have.

Quality Control

The next question for you to assess in the process of understanding your potatoes is what I call the *quality control question*. You may have heard of the terms *quality control* or *quality assurance*. The reason we have concepts of quality control is that the world we live in is subject to decay. The scientific explanation of this is what is known to be the second law of thermodynamics, which states that the order of our universe gradually deteriorates to disorder as time goes by. Things rust out. Things break down and need repair.

Biblical Relevance

Matthew 6:19-20 states: "Do not store up for yourselves treasures on earth, where moth and rust destroy, and where thieves break in and steal. But store up for yourselves treasures in heaven, where moth and rust do not destroy, and where thieves do not break in and steal."

Because of this downward process of decay, there are times when you need to "put work into the system" to maintain a certain level of quality. For example, there are times when you notice that your clothes are dirty. Their state of cleanliness is not up to par. You therefore put work into the system to counteract the decaying level of cleanliness of your clothes. In other words, your work is to do your laundry. But alas, the decaying process takes no holiday. After a while, you notice that it is time once again to put work into the system to improve the quality of the cleanliness of your clothes. You do your laundry again.

In a medical laboratory, quality control looks something like the following. Your doctor wants to know what your blood sugar level is and sends you to the lab. A sample of blood is drawn from your veins and sent to be tested. The lab reports that your result is "5.2." You want to know that if the lab tells you that your blood sugar level is 5.2, that is exactly what it is. And the lab director wants to know that if the lab tells you that your blood sugar level is 5.2, that is what it is. But how do you know that the reported result is trustworthy?

The reason why you can trust the reported result is because of a quality control system that is adhered to in a medical laboratory. The way it works is something like this: When you submit your sample to a medical laboratory and the lab technologists do the testing, your sample is likely not to be the only one they are testing for a blood sugar level. They will do a run of blood sugar tests on perhaps 100 samples from 100 different people. This is an efficient way of running the lab. The blood sugar tests are likely to be run on an automated system.

Your blood sample, before going through the machine, is considered to be an unknown, which means that your blood sugar level is unknown before your sample goes through the machine. In fact, each of the 100 samples that are put through the machine are "unknowns" before they are tested. Extra specimens are also measured in the test run, which are interspersed among the 100 unknown samples, and are known as the quality control samples. The lab tech knows ahead of time what the results of the quality control samples are expected to be. In other words, the quality control samples test the machine to make sure that it works the way it is supposed to.

The reason why the lab tech knows the expected results of the quality control specimens is that they are derived from a pooled source which has already been tested perhaps 50 times as "unknowns." The 50 tests return 50 unique results, which are plotted to make a graph. The name for the graph that is formed is a *bell curve*.

The graph has the shape of a bell because most of the results that are plotted cluster at the average value, which forms the dome of the bell. The number of results per given value that are plotted on the graph continues to diminish the farther you stray from the average, gradually tailing off in both directions, but never completely to zero. The bell-shaped graph depicts a spread of results that stretches from infinity to infinity (Figure 5.2). The horizontal axis is the measured value of the specimen, and the vertical axis is the number of specimens with that measured value.

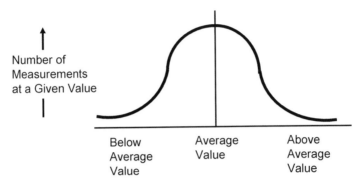

Figure 5.2 Bell Curve

For the graphed results to be of use in the lab, you need to determine a range of values with absolute numbers, which becomes the "normal" range of results for your quality control specimens. This normal range will be a spread from the high side to the low side of the average, and "cuts-off" the tails of the bell at both sides. If a cut-off range is not determined, you will have useless information. For example, if you expect the answer of your quality control specimen to be from infinity to infinity, you will discover that the machine will return any measured result whatsoever when you measure your quality control specimen, and you will have no way to know whether the result represents a quality result or the erroneous result of a defective machine.

Therefore, you require a cut-off range of expected results for your quality control specimen to be of use to run the lab appropriately. The range of expected results selected is usually such that you expect to get a measurement within your selected range 19 times out of 20, or 95% of the time, as long as the machine is working correctly. If you get an answer outside the cut-off range, it is an indication that something is unacceptable. You therefore cannot trust the results of your entire run of unknown samples as being acceptable to report.

For example, imagine that the cut-off range determined for the blood sugar quality control sample is a measurement within an expected range of 6.9 to 7.1. If the lab tech does a run of blood sugar tests, and the control sample is shown to be 7.0, then she will have confidence that the machine is performing accurately. She can confidently report the results of all the unknowns. You in turn receive your result reported as 5.2, and you have confidence that you have received an accurate measurement.

Random versus Systemic Errors

If the lab tech should perform the run of tests and her control sample returns a measurement of 7.2, then the result constitutes an error. The value derived from the quality control specimen is outside the expected range of results that give her the confidence that the machine is working correctly. She therefore will not report the results of this run of tests.

When there is an erroneous result, there are two classes of errors to be aware of. A *random error* occurs when the measurement of 7.2 is understood to be one of the 1 out of 20, or "5% of the time" results that you expect when the machine is working correctly and the measurement for the quality control specimen is outside of the cut-off range of 6.9 and 7.1 (which is your expected measurement 95% of the time). A *systemic error* means that the measured value is outside of the expected range because something is broken and needs to be fixed.

A solitary measured result at 7.2 does not let the lab tech discern the difference between a random versus systemic error. Therefore, she will repeat the run of tests on the machine. If in the repeated run the control specimen returns a result that is within the expected range of 6.9 to 7.1, then the error in the initial run is discerned to represent a random error. The lab tech confidently reports the results of the second run as accurate.

On the other hand, if the result of the quality control specimen in the repeated run falls outside of the expected range a second time (perhaps it is 7.3), then the lab tech is likely to discern that she is dealing with a systemic error. It means that something is wrong with the machine and something needs to be done to figure it out and fix it. The laboratory technologist has a checklist to assist in the diagnosis of the problem. For example, is there a chemical reagent that is at a low level and needs to be topped up? Is there a line that is clogged and needs to be cleaned? Is there an electrode that needs to be replaced?

There are rules that the lab tech follows which help discern the difference between random and systemic errors. Sometimes an error within an initial test run is so far beyond the expected range, it is understood to be a systemic error without the need to repeat the run.

Red Flag

You may be wondering why I have described all of these details and what it all has to do with anger. Imagine it this way: the raised motivational energy of anger is like a "red flag" that alerts you when there is something amiss going on and needs your attention. Your negative emotions tell you: "There is something happening in your presence that is outside the expected range of acceptability."

Anger is a motivational energy to alert you when something needs to change. Since your anger management strategy has to do with how you bring effective change about, you need to discern if the problem is something that is changeable. If the problem is not changeable, then you may do a lot of work and put a lot of effort into bringing change about, yet find that your efforts are fruitless. Such problems constitute the random errors. It means something happened that is unacceptable to you and that you experience negative emotions in response, but there is nothing you can do about it. On the other hand, if you identify the problem to be both unacceptable and changeable, then you are in a position to institute a way to bring about change.

There is no clear distinction between what is changeable or not. It is better to view the distinction as a grey area of uncertainty that can be challenging to understand. For example, sometimes a national commission is set up to ascertain whether an unacceptable event could have been prevented in some way.

Imagine the following domestic challenge: A person has 20 years of experience washing dishes by hand without ever breaking a dish. He is proud of his record! One day, however, as he is washing the dishes, his hand slips to the side and knocks against a bowl sitting on the counter beside the sink. Down the bowl flies and crashes on the floor, breaking beyond repair. And it was a family heirloom to boot!

It is not hard to imagine that he is upset. His emotions and disappointment are very real. He may find consolation in thinking that he had a good record of going so long without breaking a dish. It was too bad that something had to happen, and that it had to be this particular family heirloom, but he must have been due for something to happen. So he decides to carry on with his life. Perhaps he finds a replica of the bowl to replace the broken one, or a different bowl altogether, or perhaps he doesn't replace it at all. It was a random event. No further action is necessary.

As he is washing the dishes a few weeks later, his hand slips again and knocks the new bowl off the counter. This bowl also breaks beyond repair.

He experiences an internal struggle: "What am I? A klutz? I'll never be able to wash dishes again!" (Although this conclusion seems attractive, the realities of life include the use of dishes that are not necessarily self-cleansing!) You may realize that his thoughts show he is focusing his anger against himself, as if he is the problem. He is therefore not likely to identify what his potato is, and is unable to work on an effective solution to bring about change.

On the other hand, he may realize: "Okay! I'm not the problem. But there is a problem. The bowls broke because my hand slipped to the side both times. It means that I need to be aware of a new limitation that I did not have before. My hand is going to slip from time to time; I am just not as young and coordinated as I used to be. But both times my hand slipped to the side. Therefore, I have to make sure not to put anything on the counter beside the sink, so that if I wash the dishes and my hand slips, there will not be any dishes at risk. But I can still wash the dishes!"

Our friend has discovered what his potato represents. A potato for him (his idea of wrongness) is for a bowl to be on the counter right beside the sink when he is washing dishes. When he understands the potato to be the problem, as opposed to making himself out to be the problem, he discovers a problem that has a workable solution. A problem is something that is unacceptable. Within the new limitations of his ability to wash dishes, his problem is changeable. He is therefore free to institute a change and is also free to function within his limitations.

Everybody has limits. If you try to live beyond your limits, you will encounter the evidence of your limitations and will be limited in what you can do. If, however, you live within your limits, you will discover that what you can do is limitless. Our friend realizes his limits and discovers he is capable of functioning within his limitations.

Negotiation

If you discern that the problem you are facing is both unacceptable and changeable, and if there is another person involved in the situation, then you are free to engage the other person in the process of anger management. Up to this point, you have not involved the other person. You have used your negative emotions to discern for yourself, as best as you can, what the problem is, and you have decided whether the problem is changeable or not.

The initial contact is to negotiate a time and a place with him to discuss the situation together. In doing so, you are advised to respect both your own sovereignty as well as his. What I mean by sovereignty is to respect your right to plan your day according to what is right for you and to respect the other person's right to plan his day according to what is right for him.

When you are upset and your emotions control you, you do not necessarily respect the other person's sovereignty. Your attitude, within a power-based destructive mindset, may be: "Because I am upset, you have no rights. Right now, you have to do what I want you to do on my terms, because I am upset!" You therefore tend to "lord it over" the other person.

Biblical Relevance

Jesus said: "You know that the rulers of the Gentiles lord it over them, and their high officials exercise authority over them. Not so with you. Instead, whoever wants to become great among you must be your servant, and whoever wants to be first must be your slave - just as the Son of Man did not come to be served, but to serve, and to give his life as a ransom for many" (Matthew 20:25-28).

Consider the following example: You are at home in the evening, and your significant other is watching a show on the television. You are upset about something connected with him. So you march into the room, stand in front of the TV, and sternly proclaim, "I want to talk to you right now!" (Or, you turn the TV off and declare, "I want to talk to you right now!") How is he likely to respond to you?

He will not like your actions and will therefore be energized to anger. What you are doing is aggressive and provocative. He may not remember to "turn the other cheek" and think "Even though I don't like what you are doing, I know you are upset and are trying to tell me something. What is it?" No. His TV watching is rudely interrupted, and his attention is likely to be on what his issue (potato) is. He is more likely to say: "Get out of my face! I'm trying to watch something!"

In the ensuing discussion, you may declare: "What's more important? Me, or the TV!?" Of course you are more important than the TV, but the person who is attempting to concentrate on the TV could pose a similar question: "What about me? Aren't I important? You are preventing me from doing what I want to do!"

And so there is a risk that the situation will proceed from the provocation to an escalating cycle, or go off on a tangent, as discussed in the "Express" chapter (chapter 2).

On the other hand, if you use your emotions as a tool to identify what the problem is and if you decide that the problem is both changeable and necessary to address, then *you* (the basic essence of who you are), rather than your emotions, have control. If the situation involves your significant other, and if he is watching a television program, then you are free to discern what an appropriate time to engage him in the situation may be.

Triage

A "triage" question helps you discern what the appropriate time to engage the other person involved in the situation is. Triage has to do with discerning the urgency of dealing with a problem. If you decide the situation is urgent and therefore needs to be dealt with right now, and if you notice your significant other is watching TV, then you will go ahead and get his attention. You will tell him that there is an urgent matter to be dealt with. Once you have his attention, you are free to communicate with him what the problem is and free to discover together a way to bring change to an unacceptable situation.

If you decide that the situation is not urgent, but that you would like to deal with it soon (i.e. tonight), then you are free to allow your significant other to continue viewing the television program undisturbed. You are free to seek an appropriate moment to get his attention. You may wait for a commercial break or wait for the program to end. You may decide to sit with him and watch the program together until you find an appropriate moment to engage him in conversation.

When you are at that moment in which you have his attention, the first thing to do is to negotiate a time and a place to discuss the problem. You are interested to respect both your sovereignty as well as his. For example, you may say: "I would like to talk with you about something. It might take 5, 10, or maybe 15 minutes. I would like us to talk tonight. When is a good time for you?"

You have respected your sovereignty by indicating to him what you consider to be the proper time frame to handle the situation. You have respected his sovereignty by asking him when there is an appropriate time for him to handle the situation. You hope the two of you will find a time to meet that fits within your proposed time frame.

Assuming the other person is negotiating with you in good faith, he will respect your sovereignty as well as his own. His reply may be: "I'm just in the middle of this show right now. It might take another 45 minutes or an hour to finish. How about then?" If his proposed time to meet is one that works well for you, you have an agreement. You may say: "That sounds good. Maybe we can have a snack when we talk."

Another possible response of his may be, "This show is a done deal." He turns the TV off and continues, "How about now?" If you are ready to discuss it now, you answer, "Great!" In this scenario, he has turned the TV off of his own choosing, and the two of you are free to proceed forward in your supportive relationship.

When you find an appropriate time and place to discuss a problem, it is recommended that you reduce as many distractions as you can. If you have young children, try to pick a time and a place when they are otherwise occupied or asleep. If your telephone rings often, switch the phone into mute mode, take the receiver off the hook, or use the answering machine function if you have one. If your television is on, turn it off. Two people may have the best intentions to concentrate on each other in a conversation, but if the television is turned on, it is often used as a marketing tool to get your attention and does a good job of achieving this objective. It is like driving down a main street and being bombarded by moving signs that say "Look at me! Look at me!" Therefore, it is better for you to turn your television off during the time you are discussing a problem and seeking a solution.

When you are meeting at the negotiated time and place, you are ready to enter the second phase of the constructive method of anger management. Please refer to Figure 5.1. The second phase has to do with communicating, or testifying to the other person, what you believe is true. You are free to be assertive. And since the person associated with the problem is considered to be separate from the problem in terms of where your thoughts are focussed, you are free to communicate using "I" statements. This freedom is in contrast to being limited to communicate using "you" statements when you are trapped within the destructive, power-based mindset.

Second Phase

Communication

Communication is a skill that is learned. Your ability to learn the skill of communication is enhanced when you are within the constructive mindset. If your thinking is within the destructive mindset, then your ability to learn the skill of communication is limited.

There are stages in a progression of learning when you are studying a subject. The principle involved is called the "see one, do one, teach one" progression of learning. Each stage of the progression enhances the learning of the subject. The first stage is the "see one" stage. This is when you are in the classroom, and you are being taught the theories about how things work. There may be notes on the blackboard to copy or the teacher/professor may be lecturing, and you are trying to take in as much as you can and write appropriate notes.

The second stage of learning is the "do one" stage. This is about practical application, the part that is hands-on. You may be working with materials in a laboratory. You may be an apprentice, an intern, or a resident. When you get experience doing practical work within a defined discipline, the theory you learned within the "see one" stage starts to take on a more practical tone. You understand why you had to go through the "see one" stage, which otherwise may have seemed boring when you found no reason for learning what you believed to be useless material. Now, however, you gain a practical awareness of why you had to learn it! Your learning is enhanced.

The third stage of learning is the "teach one" stage. When you teach others something about any topic, you learn more about the topic yourself. In a classroom, I have heard on more than one occasion, a teacher declare to his students, "I am getting more out of this than you are!" The students are incredulous: "What is he talking about? He is rattling off this information as if he is an authority! What more could he possibly need to learn, since he seems to know all about it!?" But it is true. By teaching others, you learn more about the subject yourself. You discover deeper ways to understand the subject matter when you explain it to other people in ways so they can better understand.

Learning the skill of communication is enhanced when you communicate. The constructive mindset enhances your ability to learn the skill of communication. The destructive mindset hinders your ability to learn the skill of communication.

Communication is a two-way street. There are at least two individuals involved when there is something to discuss. Although each individual has a role to play, the person who wishes to relay a message must be aware of the two directions of communication. The first direction is the *transmission* phase. If you wish to communicate to another person, you need to transmit your "wavelength of truth" to her. The second direction is the *listening* phase. You need to listen to the response of the person you are communicating with. If her response is appropriate in the face of your initial transmission, then you have achieved successful communication. If her response is inappropriate, then you have not communicated successfully.

For example, imagine two people attempting to communicate with each other across a meadow with the use of flashing lights. The first person flashes a signal that says, "Do you read me?" There is no response. Is this communication? No. The first person may hope that the second person received the communication, but there is no assurance that the message is received. Therefore, the first person is likely to try again with the same flashing signal sequence.

Again, the first person flashes, "Do you read me?" This time, the second person flashes the reply, "Did you say something?" Is this communication? Once again, the answer is no. Many people believe that there is communication this second time. What they observe is that the second attempt results in more process compared with the first attempt, and therefore define this process to be communication. In contrast, I wish to define communication in terms of completeness. In the second attempt, the reply is not appropriate to the original transmission. The first person, in response to the incongruent reply of the second person, needs to repeat the original transmission to get her to understand the message appropriately. His attempt to communicate does not return a reply to give him the assurance of success to move on to the next message. Therefore he did not communicate.

For the third time, the first person flashes, "Do you read me?" The reply of the second person is, "Yes, I read you." Is this communication? Yes! The reply is appropriate to the transmission. The first person becomes free to proceed with the next wavelength of truth to transmit.

Communication is a challenge because people speak in different languages. And I am not talking about the difference between English, French, or German. Within the confines of any identified world language, people learn and speak in different languages. I believe that the understanding of the different "languages" people speak is within the realm of education psychology.

One classification system employed to explain the different ways that students learn and think divides people into the following communication styles: oral/auditory (learn and think in oral/auditory terms); visual (learn and think in visual terms); and kinesthetic (learn and think in motion and by doing). This classification system is not intended to compartmentalize people into one style to the exclusion of the others. I believe that any person can exhibit characteristics of all of the identified communication styles, but is likely to be dominant in one of them, which is where the distinction between people comes from.

This classification system can be applied to a classroom setting. It is believed that most traditional classrooms are designed to cater to the oral/auditory and visual learners, but not necessarily to the kinesthetic learners. The kinesthetic learners may be easily dismissed by those in authority as being undisciplined and disruptive in the classroom. These are the students who are in constant motion. They are doodling in their notebooks. They are looking out of the window. Since much of their behaviour is thought to be undisciplined, they are likely to receive numerous disciplinary actions from those in authority, such as their teachers.

As you grow up, your opinion of yourself is in part formed by the way people in authority relate to you. You may see yourself as an undisciplined person if you are a kinesthetic learner and are disciplined often. Many students who are thought to be undisciplined may be diagnosed with attention-deficit hyperactivity disorder (ADHD) and treated for this condition. But another line of thought suggests that many of the students thought to have symptoms of ADHD are actually kinesthetic learners, which is a variation of normal. ADHD is no doubt a real phenomenon. Perhaps medical science needs to fine-tune a way to distinguish between ADHD and kinesthetic traits. It has been observed that a kinesthetic learner, even though he does not appear to be paying attention in the classroom, is actually following the curriculum. When the students do a test, he often performs just as well as the students who are the oral/auditory or visual learners. What the education system does with this information is within their domain of responsibility.

Benefit of Constructive Mindset in Communication

Your first attempt to communicate a message to someone else will tend to be in a way that makes sense to you. There is nothing wrong with this tactic; it is logical. You have gone through the process of figuring out what your potato (the problem/injustice) means to you, according to the way your mind works. Now you proceed to communicate your idea of truth to the other person involved in the situation, according to the style of communication that makes sense to you.

A problem with this tactic is that although your communication language makes sense to you, there is no guarantee that the other person thinks in the same communication style or language as you do. If you sense that she does not understand what you said, then you will likely give her the benefit of the doubt and will try a second time to explain the situation. In your second attempt, however, you will tend to **use the same communication style you used the first time to explain it to her. And you will put a little more oomph and gusto into your explanation the second time. Because if she didn't get it the first time, surely she will get it the second time, especially since you have tried harder!**

Unfortunately, just because your truth makes sense to you within your language, there is no guarantee that it makes sense to her in the way that she thinks, even though you have tried harder. If you get the sense that **she still does not get it,** then you are at risk to be captured by the me-versus-you mindset. You are at risk to spurt out: "You're not listening! You don't care! This makes total sense to me; therefore it should make total sense to you! And the reason it doesn't is because you don't care! Did I mention the fact that you don't care?" And so you are at risk to proceed from there towards the power encounter of an escalating cycle or off on a tangent.

In the preceding example, the destructive mindset prevents you from learning the skill of communication. The challenge of communication is to seek a way to help the other person understand what your potato represents, according to the way that he or she thinks. The first phase of the constructive method helps you to find a way to understand what your potato means to you in the way that you think. The second phase of the constructive method is to find a way to describe your potato so that it makes sense to the other person in the way that he or she thinks. When you keep your thoughts focused on the problem at hand, within the constructive mindset, your ability to learn the skill of communication is enhanced.

When you communicate within the constructive mindset, your first attempt to explain your truth to the other person tends to be in a way that makes sense to you (as in the first example earlier). If, however, you get the sense that she does not understand you, then the constructive mindset frees you to consider, "Why does she not get it?" You are now free to listen to her for the purpose of arriving at an understanding of what her language is. The challenge of communication is to describe your potato to her in a way that makes sense to her. If you understand her communication style or language, then you can help her to understand what your potato is all about.

Consider the following example: A friend of yours, who loves motorcycles, tries to describe a particular brand and model that she is hoping to purchase. She uses auditory language in her description. After she is finished telling you about it, she says, "Do you hear me?" You try to follow her description as best as you can, but there are points that you don't understand. You therefore reply, "I just can't see it." Your friend realizes that you are thinking within a visual communication style and tries again to describe the motorbike, but this time in a way that makes sense to you. She says, "Picture this ..."

If your thinking is within the constructive mindset, you are not limited to any particular classification of communication styles to get your point across. You are free to find creative ways to describe your truth. You are not limited to communicate along oral/auditory, visual, or kinesthetic lines of thought. Other options for you to communicate can incorporate your understanding of what the other person's work, career, or profession is. Perhaps you find a way to describe your potato along the lines of a problem that the other person may encounter at his or her workplace.

Using an example within the world of sport can also be an effective way to communicate. Sport mimics life. The various challenges that athletes face within various sporting endeavours mimic life challenges. It does not matter if you refer to a team sport or an individual sport. There are various sayings that depict this relationship between sport and regular life, such as: "Golf is life." "Hockey is life." "Tennis is life." "Soccer is life."

For example, challenges within a team sport can be effectively used as a way to attempt to communicate family problems. A family is like a team. If a team does not function in unity, various problems are sure to follow. To communicate family problems, you could say: "Imagine a hockey team whose offensive strategy is to dump the puck toward the right corner of the attacking zone. Every player is to enter the attacking zone, gearing their formation so that one or two players head toward the right corner to dig the puck out and feed the puck to another player, who is in position to receive the pass and get a shot on goal. The player with the puck, however, as the team moves toward the attacking zone, dumps the puck to the left corner of the attacking zone. Everyone else on the team is now out of formation, and the team is at risk of being vulnerable to a counter-attack by the other team. And that is what is happening in our family. So-and-so is …"

Observing the emotional reactions athletes exhibit within the various challenges offered in the world of sports can be an effective tool to learn how to understand your emotions constructively and learn effective communication strategies. I have developed a board game that I hope will become a useful resource to help people understand the difference between the destructive and constructive mindset. It is a strategy game that is based on soccer and is called **FC Strategy**®. The premise of the game is to strategize the position and movement of your players, both attacking and defending, to outscore your opponent. The game includes a component that incorporates the concepts of emotion intelligence as outlined in this book. Situations that involve the emotions during a soccer match are incorporated into the game. They are meant to be examples to illustrate the difference between the destructive and constructive mindset an athlete can have when faced with various challenges. For more information, please go to www. fcstrategythegame.com.

To repeat: The challenge of the first phase of the constructive method of anger management is to use your emotions as a tool to help you to understand what your potato represents to you, according to your way of thinking. The challenge and skill of communication is to find the way to describe your potato so that it makes sense to the other person in the way that he thinks. The constructive mindset assists you to be creative when you seek to be understood by others. Please note that communication is a tool, that is, a means to describe your potato to someone else. Communication itself is not a potato. If you are having difficulty being understood by someone else, neither you nor your communication is a potato. The challenge rather is to find the right language to communicate your potato so that it is understood by them.

Assertiveness

Assertiveness is summarized very simply: *You give yourself the right to have your thoughts and feelings.* That's it. Another person may not understand how you could think a certain way, or how you could feel a certain way, but that other person is not you. Being assertive is when you allow yourself to have your thoughts and feelings while not trying to prove them to anyone. You allow yourself the right to think and to feel, and then freely choose to communicate your thoughts and feelings to others according to the intimacy level that you believe is appropriate (Figure 3.11).

"I" Statements

Communicating using "I" statements does not mean that you never use the word "you." Rather, you are free to communicate using "I" statements when your thoughts know how to separate the problem (potato) from the person and your attention is focused on the potato.

You continue, however, to use the word "you." Even though your attention is on the problem (that is, on the thing said, done, or not said or not done that you believe is wrong) rather than on blaming the person, there remains, in the big picture, the person that said it, did it, did not say it, or did not do it. Please refer to the model in Figure 5.1. Although the person and the sense of wrongness are circled separately, there is a "plus sign" between the person and the problem, as is evident in the first line of the model. The person is not out of the picture. The major difference between communicating using "you statements" and "I statements" is based on your attention being about dealing with the problem, rather than on focusing blame on the person who you believe is responsible for the problem.

For example, imagine that I believe something you told me is a lie. I will explore two possible approaches I may take to confront you about the lie. For my first approach, in which I make you and the lie to be one and the same in terms of my understanding, I confront you in a blaming way and say: "You told me such-and-such. I believed you. I acted according to it. I discovered it is a lie. Now, how can you lie to me like that!? What's the matter with you? I'll never be able to trust you again!"

What kind of response are you likely to experience if my approach in confronting you is provocative, as in this example? Most people recognize that their response is most likely to be defensive. You may not remember to "turn the other cheek," as discussed in chapter 2 regarding the express method of anger management. Instead, you are likely to respond within the destructive mindset. Your response may be: "How can you accuse me of something like that? What kind of friend are you to treat me like that?" And the two of us are therefore at risk to get into a battle, such as can lead to an escalating cycle, or off on a tangent, even if it is indeed true that it was a lie.

On the other hand, if I decide to confront you about what I believe is a lie, and if I separate the problem from the person, then I am free to focus on the problem. My approach to speak to you is to focus on the problem and say: "You told me such-and-such. I believed you. I acted according to it. I discovered it is a lie. I am upset that I have been told a lie. I want to know that I can trust you, so the lying has to stop."

How would you respond this time? Most people I discuss this scenario with answer that they are much more likely to respond within the constructive mindset. That is, they are more likely to feel *engaged* with the person confronting them to find a solution to the problem. The confronted person may respond: "I'm sorry! I meant no harm. I guess I didn't realize that it could affect anybody like that. I'm glad you approached me about it. I won't do it again."

The constructive way of communicating, however, does not guarantee that the person you are confronting will take the situation constructively, but it is more likely that he or she will. You may communicate constructively, and yet find that the other person's response is within the destructive mindset. You will need to remain constructive during a challenge such as that. For example, the use of certain words, even though you express yourself within the constructive mindset, is risky. The use of the word "lie" may be responded to in a defensive manner, regardless of your communication within the constructive mindset. Over time, you will discern what the risky words are, and you will find ways to get your point across as constructively as you can.

There is something else to keep in mind: I may believe that you have told me a lie, but it does not mean that you have indeed told me a lie. I do not have the market cornered on discerning truth. In fact, you may have told me a truth. It is only my belief that you have told me a lie that I am communicating to you.

If it is not true that you have told me a lie, and if I have confronted you in an accusatory way (like the first approach earlier, in which I have made you and the lie the same entity), then it is more likely that you will defend yourself against me, rather than educating me that it is not a lie. You may reply: "How can you accuse me of telling a lie? What kind of friend are you?" And on the two of us go, into the me-versus-you way of relating with each other.

On the other hand, if it is true that it is not a lie, and if I communicate my concern to you within the constructive mindset about what I believe is a lie, then you are more likely to respond with the freedom to educate me about the fact that it is not a lie. You will likely feel engaged to help me to understand the situation. You may respond: "I don't think it is a lie. This is the way things are …" In turn, I may respond: "I didn't quite see the things you are talking about. I'm sorry that I thought it must be a lie. I'm glad we had a chance to talk about it." Therefore, you and I have the opportunity to work out the situation together. And the two of us will likely feel good about having done so.

"I" Statements versus "I Feel" Statements

The next point of discussion is that I prefer to let "I" statements simply be referred to as the "I" statements. In contrast, some presentations about communication or anger management may refer to such statements as "I feel" statements, but I believe doing so is risky.

One reason for restricting your communication to an "I" statement has to do with the various levels of intimacy in relationships. As noted in the discussion about intimacy levels in chapter 3, communicating your feelings to another person is considered to be at the highest level of intimacy. It means it is risky to communicate your feelings. You will not be at the highest level of intimacy with a lot of people. Some of the people you wish to speak to are in relationship with you at the low or superficial level of intimacy. Even though it is not wrong to communicate your feelings to others, it is risky. If you get a sense that the person you are talking with allows you to have your emotions, and you thus feel listened to, or heard, then you will be glad that you have communicated with her. Perhaps you will feel closer to her for having taken the risk to let her know how you feel.

Sometimes you are at the superficial level of intimacy with someone, and you wish to tell him that you do not agree with him about something. You do not, however, wish to tell him how you feel. If you think about using "I" statements when you talk to him, then there is no problem to communicate with him. If, however, you believe that you have to use "I feel" statements in order for you to communicate properly, then you may feel intimidated about talking to him. You may not feel comfortable sharing your feelings with him. You may even shy away from talking to him and end up suppressing your thoughts. You may be under the assumption that the communication is either "I feel" or nothing. Even though you could take the risk to tell him how you feel, and you could benefit with increased closeness with him for taking the risk, sometimes you merely choose not to communicate at a higher intimacy level. On the other hand, when you think of speaking to him in terms of "I" statements, it gives you the freedom to communicate at whatever level of intimacy you believe is appropriate.

Boundaries

There are times when it is inappropriate to tell the other person how you feel. These occasions have to do with an understanding of boundary issues. You may be the boss of a company and need to communicate with an employee about a problem affecting your company. The boundary of intimacy between an employer and an employee tends to be at the level of "your own ideas and thoughts," with perhaps snippets of personal information. Therefore, if a boss is concerned about something connected with an employee, the boss is likely to say: "Such-and-such has happened, and I believe it is unacceptable. Something has to change."

The employee may be aware that the boss is upset, but the boss is not seeking validation of his or her emotions. The boss is not saying: "Such-and-such has happened and I believe it is wrong. I'm really upset about it, and you better care about that. Something has to change." No. In the preceding paragraph, the boss maintains the boundary of communicating according to the problem (potato) and his thoughts about it. The communication is effective.

From another frame of reference, the employee may be at risk to take responsibility for the employer's emotions. Even though the boss does not communicate his feelings, the employee focuses her attention on the apparent emotion of the employer and thinks: "My boss is mad. I better get this right or else I am in trouble." In this case, the employee becomes a slave of the employer's emotions, rather than addressing the problem at hand and acting appropriately. It is the employee who crosses the boundary by taking responsibility for the employer's emotions. The problem, however, is not the emotions (employee nor employer), nor is it the person (employee nor employer); the problem has to do with what the potato represents (what the employer is talking about that needs to be fixed).

Feelings versus Truth

Yet another reason why I prefer not to label the statements of communication as "I feel" statements is as follows: If you view effective communication as "I feel" statements, it is easy to convince yourself that the point of communication is about your feelings. The point of communication, however, is not about your feelings. Rather, the purpose of your communication has to do with the wavelength of truth you are trying to transmit, whether or not you include your feelings in the message you give.

For example, you may say: "Such-and-such has happened, and I believe it is wrong. Something has to change." Or, you may say: "Such-and-such has happened, and I believe it is wrong. I'm really upset about it. Something has to change." In both examples, you are focusing primarily on the problem, regardless of whether you include your feelings in what you are communicating.

On the other hand, if you limit what you say to "I'm really upset right now!" have you communicated? How would you respond if someone said that to you? Most people respond with the following question: "Why?"

Exactly! You would ask "Why?" You are seeking a connection between the emotion that is expressed and some sort of problem that is at the root of the emotion. Emotions are conditional on things that happen. If you feel an emotion, or hear of others that are experiencing an emotion, you look for the source that elicits the emotion.

You may, however, be at risk. If someone is interested in getting you to care about and take responsibility for her emotions (whether she is aware of it or not), you are at risk of being captured by her. If she captures you, she can take you anywhere she wants to and you are at risk of being manipulated. You are not interested in living your life in such a manner. You may be a very loving and caring individual. If a friend of yours is upset, you may wish to help her feel better. Although you have a caring attitude, you are at risk of becoming ensnared under the control of your friend. You may become her slave. By taking responsibility of her emotions, which is a realm that is outside of your domain to control, you can become her slave. You cannot feel someone else's emotions. You therefore cannot manage the emotions of your friend. You can certainly empathize and/or be aware of your friend's emotions as she expresses them to you, but you cannot feel your friend's emotions, nor should you take responsibility for them.

You need to understand that the emotions of other people are indicators of potatoes that they are dealing with. Learn to tell the difference between what is a potato to you and therefore is your responsibility to understand and deal with, versus what is a potato to someone else and therefore is his to understand and deal with. When you understand this difference, then you are free to discern where the boundaries in your relationships are and free to uphold your boundaries with your friends to keep your relationships healthy.

Therefore, someone may say to you, "I'm really upset right now!" What that person tells you is that he has a potato. To be a true friend to him is to be aware of his potato and to validate his feelings. Give him the honour of taking responsibility for dealing with his own potato. Too often you may believe you are being a friend by taking the responsibility for dealing with his potato. No! If you do so, you will either become his master or his slave.

When someone indicates to you by his emotions or feelings that he is dealing with a hot potato, you as a true friend may momentarily take hold of his potato, feel with and understand his feelings, and possibly comment or ask him a question about his potato. As his friend, you may reply: "Wow! That is definitely a hot potato! I've had (or I haven't had) potatoes like that before, and I know they are tough (or I imagine they must be tough) to deal with." As you return his potato back to his possession (thereby giving him the responsibility for dealing with it), you add, "How are you dealing with it?" You are now free to give advice if he is seeking your advice. You may be willing to help him in some way to deal with his potato, but you are also free to set limits. You may say: "I could do this or that to help you if you like. But such-and-such is what I am not willing (or able) to do."

If your friend hopes that you take on the responsibility of dealing with his potato on his behalf, he may take offence at your apparent cool shoulder when you return the responsibility for his potato to him. He may accuse you and say: "What kind of a friend are you? I thought you would help me! You're leaving me in the lurch!" What you are finding out is that your "friend" is not being a friend to you. Your friend's idea of a friend is for you to do something for him at his whim and control. And if you do not do what he wants you to do, he blames you for being a poor friend. On the other hand, your true friend lets you be who you are. He lets you set your limits without taking them as a personal affront against him.

Actually, you are being a true friend to him by giving him the responsibility for his potato. It is like you are saying to him, "Because I trust you and respect you, I am letting you have the control and responsibility for your potatoes."

Let us revisit what is at stake in master-slave relationships. You are at risk to become a slave of your friend if you take responsibility for his potato and believe you are being a loving and caring friend. You proceed to do what you can to help him. When you report to him what you have done (believing you have done a good and helpful thing and hoping for his approval), he may reply: "What did you do that for? Didn't you know blah blah blah?" Now you feel bad because you believe you let him down. And you may even vow to do better the next time! But you will never get it right. There will be something that you miss. He will take control of you and you will be his slave, trying in vain to help him feel better. You are in a losing battle. You never win. His feelings are his own responsibility to sort out. The potato is not yours. You may have an idea of what his potato is about, but it is not your potato. There are details about it you will never fully understand, because it belongs to him and not to you. That is why you are interested to keep his potato and his feelings in their proper place, that is, in his possession to deal with.

On the other hand, you are also at risk for becoming your friend's master. You may take control of his potato, believing you are doing something helpful for him. But by doing so, it is as if you tell him, "Because you are so incompetent to deal with your own potatoes, give them to me so that I can deal with them for you." You believe you are being helpful to your friend in need, and your friend believes you are a true friend and is thankful for your help. However, if you take control of your friend's potato, you are actually confirming to him that he is incompetent. Your friend is at risk to experience feelings of inadequacy and to become emotionally dependent on you or others to help him in his affairs.

Both you (the master) and your friend (the slave) may be blind to this dynamic. You may feel fulfilled in your ability to help others that need your help, and your friend feels he has found a good friend. You are, however, in a master-slave relationship. At some point you may be thinking, "Why doesn't so-and-so do what I tell him to?" Or, you eventually desire a break from your friend because he keeps on contacting you for more and more help. You may be thinking, "Get off me!" He is dependent on you. It is becoming more than you can bear and it is hard to get out of because you may appear to be mean if you draw the line with him to get some of your own space.

Therefore, try to set healthy boundaries with your friends as early in your relationships as possible. Learn to tell the difference between a potato that belongs to you and a potato that belongs to someone else. Do not take responsibility for potatoes that belong to someone else. Be free to help others with their potatoes, but do not take responsibility for them. Even if other people try to convince you that it is your duty as a friend to take on their potatoes so that their potatoes become yours to deal with, do not bite.

Biblical Relevance

"Carry each other's **burdens**, and in this way you will fulfill the law of Christ" (Galatians 6:2) (boldface not in original). Is not the law of Christ to "love your neighbour as yourself"? "The entire law is summed up in a single command: 'Love your neighbor as yourself' [Lev. 19:18]" (Galatians 5:14).

"A new command I give you: Love one another. As I have loved you, so you must love one another. By this all men will know that you are my disciples, if you love one another" (John 13:34-35).

A true friend loves his neighbour by bearing his neighbour's burdens, that is, by empathizing and being willing to help. A true friend does not take control of the burdens of his neighbour. If, on the other hand, you are someone who carries a heavy burden, then being a true friend to others means you do not expect others to take the responsibility of your burdens (potatoes). You are, however, willing to ask for help from others within the boundary of maintaining the responsibility for your own burdens.

Self-Esteem Increasing

The first dynamic consistent with increasing your self-esteem has to do with the very act of placing your potato onto the desktop. When you do so, you know there is a difference between the person and the problem. If, however, you place your potato into the sack on your back, then you do this only in the context of making the person you blame the problem, which by now you understand has the impact of lowering your self-esteem. Therefore, when the focus of your thoughts is on the problem (potato), you are free to place your potato onto the desktop. You do not drag your self-worth, or your self-esteem, down. Neither the "who" you are nor the "who" someone else is has anything to do with what the problem is. Your self-esteem is free to stay up.

Another dynamic to increase self-esteem comes when you persevere within the constructive mindset as you deal with your issues. You find that you experience greater success in resolving the issues that come your way. You also find that you are able to resolve your issues within a shorter time frame. You are able to apply the "KISS" principle (Keep It Simple Stupid) in sorting out your problems. When you achieve a resolution, regardless of whether you have an outright resolution or an agreement to disagree, you feel good. You have a sense of accomplishment. Sometimes you may even think, "I don't know how that situation became resolved, but it did, and it sure feels good."

Sometimes, however, your potatoes will stay on your desktop for a long time, maybe years. And as long as they are on your desktop, you will be reminded of them from time to time. They will place a limit in the relationship you have with the person they are connected to (when referring to the intimacy level model in Figure 3.11), but you will not be in the me-versus-you mindset with the other person.

An example of potatoes that stay on the desktop for a long time could be in the realm of political lobby groups. A political lobby is an individual, or group of individuals, who believe that a certain idea of truth is not being maintained in our society. Representatives of the group therefore lobby the electorate and/or legislators to get as many people as possible to agree with the view of truth that they believe society is not adhering to.

For example, there was a referendum some years ago in Saskatchewan about the question of Sunday shopping. The status quo at the time was for Sunday closures. There were voices that appealed for the ability to sell goods on Sunday; to be prevented from doing so was seen as a potato (an injustice). Apparently this was the third time this question was posed to the electorate. On both previous occasions, the will of the majority in Saskatchewan was to maintain closure on Sundays. But to those who believed it is wrong to be closed for shopping on Sundays, the potato remained on the desktop. Further efforts were made to revisit the question on a ballot. The electorate was lobbied to garner support for this version of truth. The third referendum was successful in overturning the law to prohibit the sale of goods on Sunday.

For those who believed shopping on Sunday is correct, their potato came off the desktop. It was no longer an issue, because Sunday shopping became lawful. For those, however, who believed it to be an injustice to allow shopping on Sunday, their potato appeared on the desktop (assuming a constructive mindset in dealing with it). The voices for this opposing view of truth are not heard as strongly at present, but they are there. Various issues arise in which there are differing versions of truth in competition with each other for acceptance in society. The view that holds sway at a particular time in the course of history can swing from one opposing view to the other like the motion of a pendulum.

It is not difficult to come up with numerous other examples to discuss, but it is not the intention of this book to address the issues directly. When you think of the various issues in the world today, how are they being dealt with? What is the ratio of issues being handled within the constructive mindset versus within the destructive mindset?

"Don't Go to Bed Mad"

You may be familiar with the saying "Don't go to bed mad." It is derived from the biblical verse (Ephesians 4:26): "'In your anger do not sin': Do not let the sun go down when you are still angry." Many people within a spousal relationship interpret the saying to mean "If my spouse is angry with me and I am angry with my spouse, then we have to work on a resolution before we go to sleep." Unfortunately, some issues take a lot of time to sort out, and you may be experiencing sleepless nights for a long time if you end up battling it out with your spouse without success.

I believe that interpreting the saying and biblical verse in the preceding manner is a misunderstanding of what is intended. Sometimes the meaning of a saying gets lost in translation. In the English translation of Ephesians 4:26, the words *anger* and *angry* appear similar. In the Greek original, however, there are different words that are translated to *anger* in English. An earlier English translation uses the word *wrath* instead of *angry* in the second part of the verse to indicate that there is a difference.

The way I understand it, the first word *anger* is translated from the Greek word *orgizo*, which is derived from *orge*. This type of anger can be thought of as a state of mind and can be used to apply to righteous anger. This is the kind of anger I believe is consistent with the constructive mindset; that is, you understand your emotions by focusing on a truth or injustice that you are in the presence of. The second word *angry*, or *wrath*, is translated from the Greek word *paraorgismos*, similar to *paraorgizo*, and can be thought of as provocative anger or "beside yourself" in anger.

Another verse in the Bible where the Greek word *paraorgizo* is used is found in Ephesians 6:4. In various translations, the verse states "provoke not your children to wrath" or "Fathers, do not exasperate your children." The idea seems to imply provocative anger, which, according to the anger model, is within the me-versus-you destructive mindset.

A marriage relationship is designed to be a type of team in which the two people are on the same side. If you have provocative anger with your spouse, then you are not thinking the two of you are on the same team. You are not likely to have a restful sleep if you try to sleep but consider your spouse on the other side of the bed to be your enemy. Therefore, when you and your spouse are angry with each other within the me-versus-you destructive mindset, change your thinking into the constructive mindset. You are not the problem and I am not the problem; we are okay. There is, however, a problem that we will figure out a way to understand together and sort out together.

Maybe it will take awhile to sort out what the two of you are upset about; maybe you will figure it out that night. But if your problem is not a breach of your marriage vows so that you can share the mindset of being on the same team, even though your dispute is unresolved, then you can "let the sun go down" and be able to sleep better, knowing that the issue on the table does not threaten your relationship.

Appropriate versus Inappropriate

The last section of the composite anger model, which is a summary of chapters 1 through 5, is illustrated in Figure 5.4 (at the end of this chapter) and is magnified in Figure 5.3. It is introduced by a curved arrow, which tails off the anger management method arrow leading from the word "ANGER" to the constructive method of anger management entitled "CONFESS."

1) Appropriate

2) Inappropriate

a) selfishness

b) perfectionism

c) suspiciousness

Figure 5.3 Appropriate versus Inappropriate Anger

The reason the arrow is curved in this way has to do with another question to ask yourself when you are in the first phase of the constructive method and assessing what your potato represents to you. Although the ideal time to consider this question occurs *before* you describe your potato to another person involved in the situation, sometimes your awareness to assess this question occurs while you are describing your potato to him. When you attain this insight, you backtrack up, around and down the curved arrow to assess this next component towards understanding your potato more completely.

The next question to assess is, "Even though I am upset or angry, is my anger appropriate or is it inappropriate?" Using the terms *appropriate* versus *inappropriate* in this question does not refer to your emotions. I have been attempting to convince you throughout this book that emotions and feelings are not the problem. Therefore, the terms *appropriate* and *inappropriate* are not about whether you should have emotions or not.

What this question is about has to do with the root (or foundation) of your emotional response, that is, what your concept of right versus wrong is (your sense of injustice) that your emotions are alerting you to. Appropriate anger represents a concept of right versus wrong that is defensible. In other words, you can find objective evidence to support your claim that you are dealing with a legitimate concept of right versus wrong.

For example, if you are upset because you were told a lie, you could ask yourself if it is appropriate for you to be upset. Your objective evidence that lying is an issue of right versus wrong could come from the Ten Commandments: "Do not lie." You could look at that commandment and say: "I didn't write that commandment. It was not my idea. Lying is viewed as an issue of right versus wrong. I have been lied to and I am upset. It is therefore appropriate for me to be upset when I am lied to. Now what am I going to do about this problem of the lie?"

If you do not adhere to the Ten Commandments, perhaps you could find a psychological study which shows that 95% of a population of individuals becomes upset when the individuals become aware they have been told a lie with personal consequences. You could then think: "I guess I'm just one of those 95% of the population that gets upset when lied to. I've been lied to and I am upset. It is appropriate for me to be upset when lied to; therefore, how do I proceed from here?"

Inappropriate anger, on the other hand, occurs when you are energized to anger yet have difficulty finding objective evidence to support your claim that you are dealing with an issue of right versus wrong. Sometimes the clue to let you know that you may be in the realm of inappropriate anger occurs when you are dealing with the so-called relative ideas of right versus wrong. Something is right for you, but wrong for the other person (or vice versa).

Relative ideas of right versus wrong, however, do not necessarily always translate into your anger being inappropriate. You and another person may have two differing standards of morality, yet you have objective evidence to support your claim of truth, even though it differs from the other person. In such a case, you are free to stand on your version of truth and do not necessarily have to consider yourself to have inappropriate anger.

There are examples when so-called relative ideas of right versus wrong end up with a common denominator nonetheless and therefore require the "wisdom of Solomon" to sort out. An example is found in the *Tales of the 1001 Nights*. As I viewed a film version of this classic, I noticed a comment made by Sheherazade to her husband the Sultan while she tells him the tale of Ali-Baba and the 40 thieves. As she tells her story, she explains how Ali-Baba notices one day how the 40 thieves enter a cave in which they keep their stolen booty. Seeing his opportunity, Ali-Baba tries it out. He approaches the side of the mountain and calls out, "Open sesame!" And the cave opens! Ali-Baba enters the cave and helps himself to some of the loot. Sheherazade then comments that when the thieves next come to the cave and realize that somebody has stolen from them, they are incensed! Therefore the thieves, who have made a career out of stealing from others, while not believing that they were doing anything wrong, become angry when they realize that someone has stolen from them! In other words, there is a common denominator of right versus wrong when you get to the bottom line.

Inappropriate anger is derived from lenses that you wear. Your mind's eye looks through these lenses to perceive the world in which you live. You derive your interpretations about the world from what you see. Attempts to understand the nature of the lenses lead people to identify them as part of "human nature," or "the sinful nature."

The lenses are not in themselves bad. They each have a purpose and can help you in many ways. However, the lenses are risky and can be dangerous, for they can easily cater to any of your me-versus-you destructive tendencies to interpret your world. The three lenses I identify include the lenses of selfishness, perfectionism, and suspiciousness (or a combination of them).

Selfishness

The helpful component of the lens of selfishness is that it helps you to balance your needs with the needs of others. Without this lens, finding the balance is impossible. Another name for this lens is the lens of *love*.

The Greek philosopher Aristotle explains the difference between a virtue and a vice as a balance, or teeter-totter, in his work *The Nicomachean Ethics*.[2] Placing all the weight on one side of the teeter-totter represents an excess without taking the opposite into consideration. Such a situation represents a vice. The middle zone of the teeter-totter is a point that balances the two extremes, taking both sides into consideration, and is labelled a virtue. Aristotle believes that the virtue is not a clearly distinctive point, but a grey area of balancing two opposites.

When it comes to thinking of your needs versus thinking of the needs of others, Aristotle believes that the virtue is the middle balanced position, taking both into account. You are virtuous if you balance your needs with the needs of others. The vice occurs at either end of the teeter-totter, taking one but not the other into account.

The way I understand it is as follows: If the weight of your thoughts is on the side where you think only of your needs without considering the needs of others, it is considered a vice which is called "selfishness." The opposite scenario is also true. If you think only about the needs of others without considering your needs, it is a vice which I call "slavery." Therefore, the virtue is the balance of the two extremes. It occurs when you balance your needs with the needs of others and is called "love." As one of the cardinal virtues, it could also be considered the lens of justice. It relates truth with the various needs of people. The lens of selfishness (the lens of love or justice) helps you find this middle zone of balancing your needs with the needs of others.

Aristotle's concept of the virtue to balance your needs with the needs of others is refined by Jesus of Nazareth, who states, "Love your neighbour as yourself." This is a paraphrase of Aristotle's teaching. But Jesus also clarifies the point. He states that to "love your neighbour as yourself" is the second commandment. The first commandment is to love God with all your being. It is as though Jesus is saying that you are free to love your neighbour as yourself only in the context of first loving God with all you've got. That is why I also call this lens the lens of love.

Perfectionism

The helpful component of the lens of perfectionism is that you need this lens to set the standards by which you know how to live. If you do not have a standard of truth, life is chaos. For instance, if you drive toward an intersection and the traffic light turns red, your standard of truth is to stop. If you do not have this understanding of truth, you do not know what to do when you approach an intersection. You may not even know what an intersection is. Without an understanding of a standard of truth, your life is one that is chaotic.

Another name for the lens of perfectionism is the lens of *hope*. You have an understanding of a standard of truth (it could be a sense of law and order), and you have the hope that your standard of truth will be attained (by you and others). With regards to the virtue/vice teeter-totter, the virtue in the middle balanced position is hope, which has to do with how you live your life (the choices you make), and can also be called the cardinal virtue of prudence (wisdom). It relates truth with action (deeds). The excesses on either side of the teeter-totter are the vices of perfectionism on one side, and inattentiveness/obliviousness on the other side.

Suspiciousness

The helpful component of the lens of suspiciousness is that you need this lens because you can't trust anybody! You can't even trust yourself! But it does not mean that you cannot trust. Nobody is perfect. To understand the dynamic is to view it as being similar to the teeter-totter example earlier, but I will change the picture slightly. As individual people, everybody is like a glass that is filled halfway. The part that cannot be trusted is the half-empty part. The part that can be trusted is the half-full part. Therefore, on the basis of knowing that you *can't* trust a person (the half-empty part or the limit to your trust), you *can* trust the person (the half-full part).

This lens helps you to be discerning (for example, "Don't put all your eggs in one basket."). Another name for this lens is the lens of *faith*. Faith (such as in people) is not blind to limitations (half-empty), but keeps on believing in the good (half-full). With regards to the virtue/vice teeter-totter, the virtue in the middle balanced position is faith, which has to do with trust, and can also be called the cardinal virtue of temperance. It relates truth with trust. The excesses on either side of the teeter-totter are the vices of suspiciousness on one side, and "foolishness"/naiveté on the other side.

Note: For completeness, the fourth cardinal virtue is fortitude. Another way to understand this virtue can be to call it courage, which is the middle balanced position of the virtue/vice teeter-totter. Courage relates truth with fear and action. As we have seen in this book, fear is an emotional lens that relates with anger, and anger is the motivator that leads to action. The excesses on either side of this teeter-totter are the vices of cowardice (too much fear/too little action) on one side, and rashness (too little fear/too much action) on the other side. The virtue of courage has to do with understanding the mix of fear and action in the context of truth.

Biblical Relevance

Another reason that you can trust is because of Jesus. I believe that as a Christian, I am aware that I am not perfect. I am a sinner. I see evidence in myself that I am not perfect. As a matter of fact, I also see evidence in others that they are not perfect either. But as a Christian, I learn not to put my hope in my own ability to be perfect. I direct my hope and faith in the one (Jesus) who is perfect and without sin. I learn not to trust myself or others. But I do not have to live in fear. I can trust because of Christ, for it is He who is trustworthy and true. He is the glass that overflows. He gives me the freedom to trust myself and others on the basis of knowing that He is the only one who is totally trustworthy. Everyone else is like a glass that is filled halfway. I can trust myself and others (faith—the glass is half full) only in the context of knowing that I cannot trust myself and others (realizing there are limits—the glass is half empty).

Another comment: The three lenses noted earlier are the lenses of faith, hope, and love. Peter and Paul make references to these lenses in their letters, especially 2Peter 1:5-9 and 1Corinthians 13.

Risk

The risky and dangerous components of the lenses of selfishness, perfectionism, and suspiciousness have to do with how easily you interpret your "truth" into me-versus-you thinking, that is, what you see through your lenses. For example, if your version of truth is through the lens of selfishness, you can easily think, "It's my way or the highway!" As a threat, the statement is a me-versus-you challenge. The lens of perfectionism refines the lens of selfishness into greater detail. Perfectionism states, "My way is the only way that holds any water, and your way just does not cut it!" Once again, the statement is a me-versus-you challenge. The lens of suspiciousness is reversed in its dynamics when compared with the other two lenses. When you view the world through the lens of suspiciousness, you find that you may worry about protecting yourself from others, whom you fear may exert power over you. In other words, your view of the world is interpreted in a me-versus-you way.

Imagine that I am teaching you this anger model at my desk and that you are sitting on the left side of the desk facing me. I have a copy of the model on a sheet of paper on the desktop. The words are facing you, but the paper is placed diagonally on the desktop between us, so that a portion of the page is dangling over the edge. Imagine that your version of truth is that it is wrong for a piece of paper to be slanted and dangling over the edge of a desk; a sheet of paper ought to lie on a desktop in such a way that the paper is aligned with the edges of the corner of the desk with a border of about 2 cm between the paper and the desktop edge.

As I am talking with you about the anger model while the page is slanted and dangling over the edge of the desk, you will eventually notice that the paper is not sitting properly on the desktop. Your observation of the misaligned sheet of paper may distract you from listening to me. I carry on with my explanations about the anger model, blah, blah, blah, but you cannot follow my argument because of your distracted state. You are getting energized to anger. You manage your anger by subtly adjusting the way the paper sits on the desktop as we converse, or you may interrupt me: "Excuse me, but I am not following you right now." I may reply, "Do you have a question?" You in turn say, "Well,

I'm having difficulty following you, because the page is bothering me." I may say, "What would you like to do with the page?" You offer, "I'd like it to be centred on the top of the desk." I reply, "Okay, I'll accommodate that," and adjust the page appropriately. You now think to yourself: "*Accommodate* that!? He didn't even apologize! I don't know if I'm going to come back again!" And so you conclude our interaction within the me-versus-you mindset.

On the other hand, when you notice that the page is not placed on the desktop to your liking, and when your emotions kick in to distract you and energize you to change the situation, you can use your emotions as a tool to help you to discern what the problem is. If you are able to discern the problem and you do not blame the person, your conclusion is that it is wrong for the page to be over the edge of the desktop. With your understanding of what your potato is, you are now free to ask yourself the questions: "Even though I am angry, is my anger appropriate, or is it inappropriate? What is my evidence that it is wrong for a page to be over the edge of the table?" In order for you to search out answers to these questions, test the lenses!

Ask yourself, "Is it selfish of me to think it is wrong for a page to be over the edge of the table?" You will notice that you can find creative ways to justify your beliefs. Your answer to the question may be: "I am not being selfish at all! When a page dangles over the edge of a table, the page gets creases in it. The integrity of the page becomes destroyed and has to be discarded. A new tree has to be cut down to produce paper so that I can replace the destroyed information that was on the page in the first place. Therefore, I am not being selfish; I am thinking of the environment!" (In other words, you can find creative ways to justify your beliefs.)

Your next questions become, "Am I being suspicious? Why does the doctor keep putting the page at an angle, so that a portion dangles over the edge? Is he hiding something? Is there a hidden microphone that he is trying to prevent me from noticing?" You lean to the side a bit, take a peek under the dangling edge of the paper, and find nothing there. You notice that your discovery does not relieve your discomfort about the paper dangling over the side of the desk. You conclude that your belief that it is wrong for a page to be dangling over a table is not coloured by the lens of suspiciousness. You therefore realize, "I am not being suspicious."

Testing the next lens leads to the question, "Am I being perfectionistic?" The lens of perfectionism transforms your preferences into absolutes. You may *prefer* the page to lie on the table in line with the edges, with a 2 cm border between the page and the edge of the table. A preference, however, is not an issue of right versus wrong. Everybody has individual preferences. That is part of what makes all people unique in their own way. The lens of perfectionism, however, can transform your preference into an absolute. Your destructive conclusion, through the lens of perfectionism, states, "The paper has to lie on the desktop the way I want it to; your way is unacceptable." Therefore, you interpret your preference into a me-versus-you dynamic through the lens of perfectionism.

As you assess the lens of perfectionism, your conclusion may be: "I think I'm being a bit perfectionistic here. I do prefer the page to be placed on the desktop according to the way I like it (and I could suggest my preference to you). But why are you placing the paper on the table diagonally, so that some of it dangles over the edge? Oh! Maybe it has to do with the angle between us, sitting the way we are. The page is actually straight between us in reference to how the two of us are sitting at the desk. If the page, however, sits at an angle and the words face you, I could not accept that, because I cannot read upside down. I might think that you are trying to convince yourself about how the model works. But the page is facing me! So, I guess that it is okay for the page to sit at an angle on the table, even though I prefer it to be adjusted to the edges of the desk."

If you conclude that it is actually okay for the page to be placed diagonally on the desktop, you have learned something new. Your concept of right versus wrong regarding how a page ought to be positioned on the top of a desk is somewhat adjusted. You will therefore discover that you will be angry less often.

The next time that you are in a situation where a page is lying slanted with respect to the edges of the table, you will likely notice the scene connected with your negative emotions. This is reasonable. You have trained yourself for many years to consider such a situation as wrong, and so your responses will not likely change overnight. But when you notice the situation this next time, you conclude, "Okay. I decided that it is all right." And so you carry on without further action.

Eventually, you encounter at least two possible outcomes. One possibility is that when you sit at a desk where a page lies slanted with respect to the edges of the table, you do not notice it anymore. In other words, the situation becomes a non-emotional event. It means that you are becoming angry less often.

A second possible outcome occurs when you notice the page is slanted with respect to the edges. In contrast to how you noticed the page before, this time when you notice the page, you experience positive emotions. Your response may be: "There he goes! Every time I sit at the side of the table with him, the page is placed at an angle on the desktop so that it appears to be straight between us! When I sit with so-and-so, the page is lined up with the edges of the table. When I sit with so-and-so, the page is projected on the wall. But with him, the page is at that angle!" And as you come to your conclusion, you do so with a slight chuckle to yourself.

What you are accustomed to notice connected with negative emotions has become either a non-emotional event or something that you notice connected with positive emotions. You have opened yourself up to experience positive emotions because you have let me be me.

If you believe that I am your friend only if I do what you want me to do, then you set yourself up to experience negative emotions in the context of our relationship. The result is a dictatorship. Sometimes I will remember that you prefer the page a certain way, and I will cater to your preference because I am thinking about you and desire to be friendly. You are pleased. At other times, however, I will place the page on the table according to the way that is natural to me, but will not be according to your preference. If you notice that the paper is not the way you like it and conclude that I am not your friend because I have positioned the page the way I like it, then you set yourself up to experience negative emotions. You may interpret your emotions within the destructive me-versus-you mindset. I may have no idea that you have become energized to anger. I am oblivious to your response because I have innocently positioned the page in a way that is natural to me and have not had any thought of being against you by doing so. When I notice that you appear irritated, I might think: "What's wrong? What's going on with you?"

On the other hand, if you allow me to be me, then you allow me to place the page on the table without considering the event in the destructive me-versus-you mindset. You are free to experience positive emotions in the context of what is occurring. The reason you experience positive emotions comes from you allowing me to be me. You feel the relationship is closer between you and me (the relationship intimacy levels are enhanced). The line of protection that you maintain between us (referring to the intimacy model in Figure 3.11) is set at a higher level of intimacy, so that we are closer friends (perhaps to the moderate level of intimacy rather than at a lower level of intimacy). We are more accepting of each other in our relationship and exhibit less of the me-versus-you brand of protectiveness.

The more you flush out the me-versus-you effect of your lenses and the more you are able to accordingly adjust your various versions of justice, the less angry you become. You will nurture more fulfilling relationships. No matter how great your awareness of your lenses and their effects become, however, you cannot remove them. They will continue to affect you for your entire life. You will continue to learn about yourself and your limitations your whole life long. This is why life continues to be a learning adventure, and there are always interesting twists and turns along the way.

Therefore, remember that you will continue to have anger. Not only will you become increasingly aware of the tendency of your lenses to get you into "inappropriate" anger, you will also continue to have anger because the issues of justice that are defensible (those issues that have objective sources of evidence to confirm they are issues of right-versus-wrong) will continue to happen. Thousands of years ago, one of the Ten Commandments made it clear: "Do not lie." We as humans do not seem to have figured out what this means yet. People continue to lie, and so you will continue to have issues of right versus wrong to energize you to anger and to deal with.

Fork in the Road

As you travel along the path of discovering the effects of your lenses, and as you work on decreasing any tendencies you may have toward inappropriate anger, you will come upon a fork in the road of your life's journey. One of the branches of the fork will lead you into a life of despair. This dismal path comes with the pressure you put on yourself to be rid of your lenses. You believe that by doing so, you will live a "good life." You believe the fulfilling life is attained by your ability to be rid of your lenses. The more you try to remove your lenses, however, the more you will notice the fact that you have the lenses, and the fact that you cannot remove them. You may try all kinds of techniques to remove the lenses or put your faith in somebody's method of being cleansed of the lenses. You may become a slave to that technique, method, or person. If your idea of the good and perfect life is about not having the lenses nor being affected by them, then you are at risk of living a life of despair and hopelessness when you realize that you are powerless to get rid of them.

Biblical Relevance

We know that the law is spiritual; but I am unspiritual, sold as a slave to sin. I do not understand what I do. For what I want to do I do not do, but what I hate I do. And if I do what I do not want to do, I agree that the law is good. As it is, it is no longer I myself who do it, but it is sin living in me. I know that nothing good lives in me, that is, in my sinful nature. For I have the desire to do what is good, but I cannot carry it out. For what I do is not the good I want to do; no, the evil I do not want to do—this I keep on doing. Now if I do what I do not want to do, it is no longer I who do it, but it is sin living in me that does it.

So I find this law at work: When I want to do good, evil is right there with me. For in my inner being I delight in God's law; but I see another law at work in the members of my body, waging war against the law of my mind and making me a prisoner of the law of sin at work within my members. What a wretched man I am! Who will rescue me from this body of death? Thanks be to God—through Jesus Christ our Lord!

So then, I myself in my mind am a slave to God's law, but in the sinful nature a slave to the law of sin. (Romans 7:14-25)

Taking the path of the other branch in the fork of the road leads you toward a life full of awe, wonder, peace, joy, and love. What takes you down this path is the realization that nobody is perfect. You are not perfect, and I am not perfect. You will be reminded of this truth practically every day. But if you accept this truth, then you will become less judgmental of yourself and less judgmental of others (you will acquire less of the destructive mindset). You will become more accepting that people are not the problem. You will realize that potatoes (concepts of truth or justice) are what the problems are about. You will learn to be less judgmental as you remove the effects of the me-versus-you mindset, which the lenses so very easily lead you into. This is what love is—you love yourself and others when you accept that neither you nor others are problems. Problems there are aplenty, but problems are what people strive to understand and solve; problems are separate from people. You live in a constructive manner when you seek out the truth of the matter to solve, rather than lording it over others to get your way via the power mindset. You will be free to live a fulfilling life the more you live for truth rather than for power.

Biblical Relevance

The Scriptures tell us that the Law is good (see Romans 7 earlier), but the Law is designed to show me that I am unworthy. Therefore, I am not to place my faith in any righteousness that I may convince myself that I have or that I try to put on. In fact, the apostle Paul recognizes this. Paul realizes that if anyone can boast about himself and his accomplishments, he (Paul) could do so about himself. Passages that allude to this and what Paul learned are 2Corinthians 11:16–12:13 and Philippians 3:2–4:1.

In Philippians 3:4-9, Paul states:

> If anyone else thinks he has reasons to put confidence in the flesh, I have more: circumcised on the eighth day, of the people of Israel, of the tribe of Benjamin, a Hebrew of Hebrews; in regard to the law, a Pharisee; as for zeal, persecuting the church; as for legalistic righteousness, faultless.

> But whatever was to my profit I now consider loss for the sake of Christ. What is more, I consider everything a loss compared to the surpassing greatness of knowing Christ Jesus my Lord, for whose sake I have lost all things. I consider them rubbish, that I may gain Christ and be found in him, not having a righteousness of my own that comes from the law, but that which is through faith in Christ—the righteousness that comes from God and is by faith.

Therefore, if I place my faith in Christ and His righteousness, I am free. It is Christ who has fulfilled the Law and is without sin. Not me. I place my faith in His righteousness and in His life and consider myself dead in him. Since He died and has in turn risen from death, the life I now lead is in His risen life! This is the joy, the awe, the wonder of God's love in Christ. I am free to understand what Paul means when he writes, "And I pray that you, being rooted and established in love, may have power, together with all the saints, to grasp how wide and long and high and deep is the love of Christ, and to know this love that surpasses knowledge—that you may be filled to the measure of all the fullness of God" (Ephesians 3:17-19).

Also note: What you experience when you take the more fulfilling fork in the road is written about in Galatians 5:22-23: "But the fruit of the Spirit is love, joy, peace, patience, kindness, goodness, faithfulness, gentleness and self-control. Against such things there is no law."

In the Present

The last point to make about the anger model so far is that it is about "here-and-now" potatoes. The preceding discussion concerns what you can do with the potatoes as they come your way in real time. The constructive mindset shows how you can use your emotions as a tool to identify the potatoes you encounter; to be separate entities in contrast to the person who is responsible for them. You learn to deal with the various problems that arise in a constructive and fulfilling way.

"That is just great! Wonderful!" you may say. But there is something missing. What about the potatoes that you have in your sack, which you have accumulated over the years? What are you going to do about them? Don't they affect you in the here and now? You bet they do!

If you have a heavy sack of potatoes on your back, the weight of the sack affects your ability to deal with any new potatoes that you encounter in the present. You are especially affected if any of the new potatoes remind you of potatoes that you have in your sack—and the potatoes in your sack are there within the me-versus-you mindset. It is as if you try to focus your thoughts, together with your emotions, onto the new potato within the constructive mindset, but your ability to focus on the potato is hampered by the memory of potatoes that are in your sack. The potatoes in your sack are running interference because they have the blaming me-versus-you mindset linked to them. They may remind you of incidents that you blame yourself for or that you blame others for. It can at these times be difficult to tell the difference between the potato and the person. It is challenging to practise the constructive mindset in the here and now, with the new potatoes you encounter. The potatoes from the past inside your sack are "at war" with your intention to handle the new potatoes within the constructive mindset.

So ... what are you going to do about those potatoes in your sack? How can you get relief from their weight?

In chapter 3, the effect of suppressing anger is illustrated to show it is like putting your potatoes in a sack that you carry around with you. Various treatments to help you get relief from the weight of your sack are explored. The symptomatic treatments, which give you a sense of relief from the weight of your sack of potatoes but do not do anything about the potatoes in your sack, are discussed in greater detail. The list of the symptomatic treatments consists of the risky (poor) treatments. In contrast, the more favourable treatments are based on understanding the constructive method of anger management. They are the therapeutic treatments.

Therefore, this is the picture. When you have a memory of a potato, regardless of the reason for the memory, it is as if a potato comes out of your sack and falls into your hands before your eyes. You re-experience this potato in real time. As you relive your memory, you will tend to experience varying degrees of emotions that go along with the potato at hand. You may experience emotional memory, and/or new emotions in the context of the event you remember. Since you are learning that your emotions are not the problem, you will not be afraid to feel them, even though they may be unpleasant to feel. You will allow yourself to feel your emotions. Sometimes your emotions will be extremely unpleasant and difficult to take, but you will allow yourself to endure through the pain and work toward attaining relief from the effects of the potato that are linked with your memory.

Since you allow yourself to feel your emotions, you become free to use them as a tool to help you to discern what your potato represents. You are no longer limited to focus your thoughts in the destructive way, that is, to blame yourself or someone else (whosever name is on the potato that you are dealing with in your memory at the time).

Now that your thoughts are focused on your potato and you have identified it as best you can, you become free to transfer your potato onto the desktop. This is how you get relief from the weight of the potatoes on your back—when you transfer them onto the desktop. There are various rates of transfer that you will experience. Sometimes you find that you can transfer a lot of potatoes onto the desktop within a short period of time; sometimes you transfer one potato at a time over a long time. There is no right or wrong answer for how long it ought to take you to transfer the potatoes from your sack onto the desktop.

The name of the process that transfers the potatoes from the sack on your back onto the desktop is *forgiveness*. Actually, when you manage your anger within the constructive mindset with the new potatoes that you encounter, you are using a forgiving way to manage your anger in the here and now. Forgiveness is a process that changes your mindset from the destructive one to the constructive one—nothing more, nothing less. Therefore, the next item to discuss is a model of forgiveness, a model that includes a list of treatments and strategies that are consistent with the therapeutic process of transferring your potatoes from your sack onto the desktop.

Homework

How are you coming along with understanding and implementing the homework assignment? What are the challenges? What are the limitations? Are you getting good at being as constructive as you can?

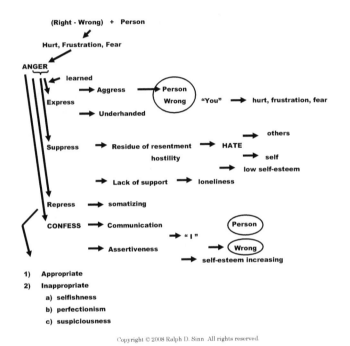

Figure 5.4: The Emotion Intelligence Model, also known as The Anger Management Model

Chapter 6
Love

Before embarking on a discussion about forgiveness, it is relevant to explore concepts that have to do with love. What does it mean "to love"?

To understand the word *love* in the English language poses some difficulties, for there are various meanings of the word, depending on the context. A helpful approach to explore the meaning of love is to examine words from other languages that are translated into the word *love* in the English language. There are at least three Greek words, which indicate three dimensions of love, and are translated into English as the word *love*. The three words are *eros, philia*, and *agape*.

To understand what the three Greek concepts of love are about, I will start the investigation by dividing them into the three dimensions of what it means to be human. Since it is believed that a human consists of the dimensions of a body, a soul, and a spirit, it follows that eros coincides primarily with the body dimension; philia may correspond with the soul dimension; and agape corresponds with the spirit dimension.

Upon closer inspection of the appropriateness of assigning the Greek words to the three dimensions of humanity, I prefer, however, to apply philia as a second dynamic that applies to the spirit dimension. Language has its limitations as a way to describe a concept. For instance, there may be more meaning intended in the term *eros* than being limited purely to body love. C.S. Lewis, in his book *The Four Loves*,[4] attempts to explain the various concepts of love and the limitation of language to express a certain dynamic that you are aware of as a human. Therefore, perhaps it is better to place philia primarily into the spiritual dimension, together with agape, as I will explain later. For my lack of awareness of a soulish Greek word that can apply to what I understand to be the soul dimension, I will use the word *enjoy* to apply to it. I will attempt to explain what I believe are the unique features of body, soul, and spirit. I will attempt to acknowledge the interactions between the dimensions without attempting to explain how they interact.

Humans are complicated creatures. Any attempt to understand your humanness by dividing humanity into the three identified dimensions is inadequate, but you have to start somewhere. Part of the difficulty lies in the fact that there are interactions between all of the dimensions. Therefore, if I explain something about the body dimension of being human, the body does not necessarily function without affecting the other dimensions of your humanity or as exclusive to involvements of the other dimensions. Somehow, the Venn diagram of being human consists of the three circles of body, soul, and spirit (Figure 6.1). But how are the circles to be arranged with respect to each other? Do they all overlap entirely one over the other? Or are there parts that are unique, so that there is not a total overlap? How does one envision a way to search out an answer to these questions?

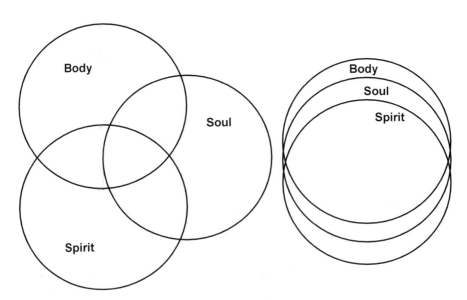

Figure 6.1: What is the best way to understand the interaction of body, soul, and spirit?

Eros: Body

The body component of being human is the easiest to figure out. This is the science dimension, the dimension of the five senses of sight, sound, smell, taste, and touch. Eros love involves body love. It is the sensual or sexual love. This dimension of love is referred to when you talk about "making love." This is the dimension that is marketable in terms of fashion, jewellery, perfumes, romantic getaways, and so on.

Enjoy: Soul

If body is the science dimension of being human, then soul is within a totally different realm. I find it helpful to understand the soul realm by calling it the *arts* dimension of being human. This is the component of humanity that cannot be measured scientifically, yet is nonetheless a part of being human. It is in this realm that I place the emotions, thought, memories, and so on. It is akin to the "cyberspace" of being human, or the "software." It is the stuff of being human that you interact with but cannot grab a hold of, just like cyberspace.

Emotional love is within this realm. In the previous chapters about anger, I indicated that emotions are conditional on events that happen and your sense of justice that is connected with those events. If something happens that you believe is wrong, you experience a negative emotion; if something happens that you believe is right, you experience a positive emotion. Your positive emotion may be labelled as "happy" or as "enjoy." "Feeling in love" or "falling in love" may be expressions of positive emotions that fall primarily within this soul realm. These are the "warm fuzzies" you feel and interpret as love.

To explore the difference between body and soul, we can discuss the difference between sound and music. Science can explain how you twang a stringed instrument, how the sound waves are produced, and how fast they travel through the air. Science can explain how resonant frequencies are formed. Science can explore how your ears are designed so as to collect the sound waves from the air and direct them to your eardrums. You can also understand how your middle and inner ears are designed to change the energy of a sound wave into a nerve impulse, which travels along your auditory nerve to the sound centres of your brain. Science can help you learn how your brain discerns the differing sounds and how the sounds are transmitted to the emotion centres of your brain. But can science explain how or why you respond to certain sound waves with joy and to others with sadness? Is science able to explain how the way a musical instrument is played can be an emotionally moving experience? How do you understand the difference between a technically played musical score and an artfully played musical score? Are these two different dimensions not recognized as components to be assessed in certain competitions? For example, separate marks are given in competitive figure skating for technical merit (the body or science part) and artistic merit (the soul or arts part).

Therefore, soul love is the arts love of positive emotions, which is why I prefer to apply the word *enjoy* to describe this dimension. In contrast, philia love is described as having a dimension of the feeling of pleasure (soul) connected with a common bond (spirit) and is therefore a word that includes both the soul and spirit dimensions of love. Language, as a way to describe the components of love, does not necessarily limit the application of any component of love to any specific human dimension in an exclusive way without including an effect on the other dimensions as well. Perhaps philia is a type of love that describes the overlap of soul and spirit in the Venn diagram of body, soul, and spirit.

Agape and Philia: Spirit

The spirit component of your humanity is within yet a different dimension. I find a helpful way to separate soul from spirit has to do with the concept of "conditional" versus "unconditional" love. Soul, or emotional love, as described earlier, is conditional. Agape, or spirit love, is most often described as being unconditional love. Unconditional love can be understood to be connected to what you have allegiance to. Where you place your allegiance is a matter of choice, and choice is a component of the "will" dimension of your humanness. When you talk about where your heart is, it is yet another way of referring to your will, for your allegiance is associated with where your heart is.

You will have unconditional love for the person who you are in allegiance with. For example, there is a saying that goes "So-and-so is a person that only a mother could love." The implication is that so-and-so must have such repulsive or hideous qualities that people abhor and turn away from him or her, but a mother loves this person. Why? A mother's love is unconditional regarding the so-called repulsive qualities.

A marriage vow is designed to remove conditions; therefore, the love between the spousal pair is declared to be unconditional. The vow states: "It doesn't matter if things are good or bad; it doesn't matter if we are healthy or sick; it doesn't matter if we are richer or poorer. Despite all conditions, I will love you (as you have stated that you will love me)." This love is a matter of the will (choice), and therefore the allegiance is in place. This is not a love that involves feelings or emotions, but is rather an allegiance (spirit) love.

The difference between agape and philia love is the next issue to consider. Philia love is the love of commonality. When two people on an equal power/authority standing in this world share a common interest about something, or when a person of lower standing is in agreement with the view of a person of higher standing, they exhibit philia love. The sense of belonging or togetherness in the context of the common interest (spirit) leads to an allegiance-type of positive feeling (soul). For example, consider people who cheer for the same hockey team.

Agape love, on the other hand, is the love of a person with higher power or authority toward someone with lower power or authority. Agape love defends the powerless (the right to be heard) and upholds the cause of the weak. It is stated in the Bible that true religion is to defend the cause of the widow and the orphan. In other words, to defend and protect the interests of someone who does not have anyone else to defend their interests (as a husband loves [protects] his wife, or a parent loves [protects] his or her child) is to love with agape love the people who as widows and orphans in this world are powerless in a world dominated by the dynamics of power.

If you are in a position of authority over someone else, for example, if you are the boss of a company, then you exhibit agape love toward your workers when you take into consideration, respect, and address benevolently the workers' needs in the decisions that you make. You do not make your decisions in the context of a blaming attitude. Thus, both philia love and agape love have to do with allegiance, but are exhibited within differing contexts of the power status between the individuals involved.

Sometimes the word *philia* is translated to "brotherly love." And this is where I believe the difference between philia and agape love lies. Philia love is used to connote the love when there is a common interest. From a power point of view, the two individuals who share this type of love do so from the vantage point of an equal power standing. Agape love occurs from the vantage point of someone in an advanced power position with respect to someone in a lesser power position. The higher authority person does not necessarily share the common interest or agree with the lower authority person about a certain issue, yet defends or loves her by showing that he is not against her, but is for her.

Biblical Relevance

After His resurrection, Jesus asks Peter three times, "Do you love me?" The first two times that Jesus asks Peter this question, He asks it in the agape form of love. Peter answers, "Yes, I love you." But Peter's answer is in the philia form of love. When Jesus asks Peter the third time, He asks him in the philia form. Peter is upset this time because Jesus asks in the philia form. Peter answers "yes" within the philia form. It is possible that Peter realizes he cannot answer the Lord in the agape form because Jesus has the advanced power position, which Peter is respecting. Yet Peter is upset when Jesus questions even his philia love for him, the kind of love that Peter has already answered in the affirmative.

A Story of Allegiance

You are not always aware that your allegiance is where you believe it to be. Sometimes "love at first sight" is like this. For example, a man meets a woman and falls totally in love with her, at first sight. I interpret this dynamic to indicate that the woman has physical, personality, or other qualities that the man responds to with his positive emotions (soul response—there is something about her that is right), as well as sexual attraction (body response). The man then believes that this woman is right for him, and she becomes the object (source) of his positive emotions. He believes he is in love with her. He may have a sincere sense of allegiance with her (she is "the girl of his dreams"). She in turn may be "swept off her feet," and falls in love with him. They may eventually marry each other, both sincere in their wedding vows.

Over the course of time, however, potatoes accumulate, for nobody is perfect. As our happy couple goes through life together, the man deals with potatoes that are connected with her, as well as potatoes that are connected with himself and anyone else he interacts with. Eventually, if he suppresses his anger and places his potatoes in the sack on his back (within the me-versus-you mindset), then the weight of his negative potatoes may overwhelm the amount of his positive potatoes, that is, his ideas of truth or justice or rightness about her that are connected with her as the object of his positive emotions. He is at risk to lose his feeling of love for his wife.

If our friend realizes that the honeymoon is over, he is at risk. If he happens at this time to meet a woman that he finds attractive and responds to her with his positive emotions, as well as physical attraction, he may think about the relationship with his wife that has cooled down and may in turn be drawn toward this other woman to nurture a new relationship that feels good. Eventually, he may believe that the new woman is the one who is truly right for him (or his "soul mate") and may terminate the relationship with his wife. His wife in turn may notice that her husband has left her, in a spiritual or allegiance sense, long before they actually separate and divorce. The man then marries his new love interest. He may believe that his allegiance is with his new wife, for she is the object of his positive emotions.

Over time, he accumulates the new potatoes that are connected with his second wife. If he continues to suppress his anger, the weight of these new potatoes eventually overwhelms the positive potatoes he has that are connected with her. He is at risk for the process to repeat itself. He may meet a third woman that he finds attractive and respond yet again to this new acquaintance with his positive emotions. He may believe she is right for him and pursue a relationship with her.

In this story, where is the man's true allegiance? In his own mind, he believes his allegiance is with the woman that he "loves." His true allegiance, however, is with himself. What he truly loves (is in allegiance with) is his own positive emotions!

On the other hand, if his allegiance is truly with his wife, then when the honeymoon is over, and his accumulated negative potatoes overwhelm his positive potatoes, he is at risk. If he meets a woman that he responds to with his positive emotions and finds physically attractive, he does not, however, interpret his positive feelings in such a way that makes this second woman right. Rather, he remembers his vow (his pledge of allegiance) to his wife (and his wedding ring is a good reminder) and stays true to his wife. He is not controlled by his positive emotions to believe that the second woman must be the one for him, but rather allows himself to feel his positive emotions within the constructive mindset, understanding the context of his situation. He is free to display true love (allegiance) to his wife by not going astray under the control of his emotions. He may decide to deal with his negative potatoes in a more constructive way so that fewer potatoes accumulate into his sack, and decide to transfer the potatoes in his sack onto the desktop and be free to rekindle his positive emotions for his wife.

A Second Story of Allegiance

Imagine a battle with brutal hand-to-hand combat. Two soldiers come to their general for orders. They view the field of battle together and are aware of the danger. The general looks at the two of them and tells them that they are both needed to fight in the battle in order for the army to be successful. They both look at the combat zone and are aware that they may lose their lives. One soldier looks back at the general and states: "Aye aye Sir! I will do as you command!" And off he goes. This soldier's allegiance is with the general and his army.

The second soldier looks back at the general and declares: "Who are you to tell me to fight down there, where the odds against my survival are so slim that I will surely die? No way! You go there and fight, if it is so important! Not me!" And off he goes on his own away from danger. His allegiance is with himself.

Biblical Relevance

In terms of your faith, the most basic question you need to address is where your allegiance is. Is your allegiance with yourself in this world, or is it with God? What you do and how you act in this world is according to where your allegiance is. In the letter from James, especially James 2:14-26, James writes about the connection of deeds (or works) and faith. James 2:26 states, "As the body without the spirit is dead, so faith without deeds is dead." The way I have come to understand this dynamic is that my deeds (works, what I do) are according to what my faith is in. The two are inseparable. If my faith is in the world (for instance, in my job or in wealth), then what I do is according to my faith in the world. If my faith is in God, then what I do is according to my faith in God. Faith in God does not have to mean living life as a missionary or going to church every day. How I live my life at work, that is, the decisions I make and the way I interact with co-workers (regardless of the type of job I have), is impacted by what my faith is in, whether it is in God or in the world.

Biblical Relevance

A second issue of allegiance I wonder about has to do with the Garden of Eden and the so-called punishment of Adam and Eve to experience death. As argued by St. Augustine,[5] the will is not created. It is an eternal element. The argument shows that eternal beings show their will by their allegiance - they are either for God or not for God.

Adam and Eve, then, by making a choice that is consistent with an allegiance with the serpent, are at risk of making this their eternal choice. But God has already stated to them that by eating of the Tree of the Knowledge of Good and Evil, they will die. Death can occur only within a temporal realm. Therefore, God designs the consequence of the eating of the Tree of the Knowledge of Good and Evil to make this choice of allegiance of Adam and Eve to be that of a temporal being rather than an eternal being. God, in his love, gives us, as men and women, the opportunity to assess our allegiance within a temporal frame rather than an eternal frame. God, by His Son, gives us the ability to choose where our allegiance is. This is an opportunity for us as men and women to examine our allegiance and understand the consequence of our decision. Therefore, the consequence of death to Adam and Eve is actually part of God's loving plan to remedy man's otherwise eternal plight of choosing allegiance against God. The death brought by Adam and Eve is not a punishment; it is, rather, evidence of God's love for mankind.

It is a worthwhile exercise to examine where your allegiance truly is. I believe the adventure is part of a person's life journey of discovery. You discover who you are, and what is important to you, by the varied ventures and relationships you develop over the course of your life. My hope, in terms of a spousal relationship, is that if you discover your allegiance is with yourself, rather than with both your spouse and yourself as a team, then you will shift your allegiance toward the more fulfilling way of viewing your spousal relationship as a team.

Chapter 7
Forgiveness

Please refer to the forgiveness model in Figure 7.1. A copy of the model is at the end of the chapter in Figure 7.2. The model of forgiveness is relevant at the situation of low self-esteem within the anger management model, that is, when you suppress your anger (chapter 3). If you are weighed down by a heavy sack of potatoes, then you are looking for treatments to achieve relief from the effects of the weight. The symptomatic treatments, that is, the high-risk and poor treatments, are discussed in chapter 3. They do not do anything about the potatoes in your sack; rather, they tend to increase your burden.

Conversely, the therapeutic treatments, that is, the better and low-risk treatments, are based on understanding the constructive mindset of anger management. You get relief from the weight of the sack of potatoes because the sack is a lot lighter. You transfer your potatoes onto the desktop. So, buckle up your seats, and here we go to discuss the therapeutic treatments!

Forgiveness

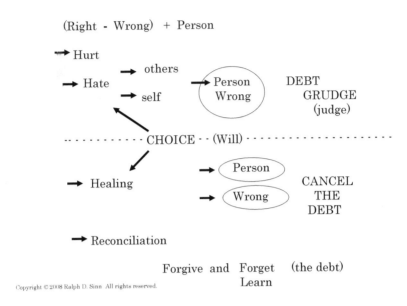

Figure 7.1 The Forgiveness Model

The model of forgiveness begins by setting up the situation when you suppress your anger and accumulate your potatoes in the sack on your back. You have a concept of right versus wrong that is not upheld, plus a person who is responsible for committing the injustice (you or someone else). The injustice is usually about something said or done, or not said or not done, that you believe is wrong. When you are in the presence of an injustice, you are sensitized to your concept of wrongness by your negative emotions. For example, something happens and you feel hurt. If you interpret your emotion within the destructive mindset, then you may eventually understand your emotion within a certain degree of hate. You may hate yourself or hate someone else, depending on whom the person it is that you blame. The person and the problem become encased together to represent your belief that the person and the problem are one and the same thing. The focus of your thoughts is directed at the person and so you blame the person. The situation becomes about the person you are blaming. You find yourself in the forgiveness model at a place that is similar to the anger model when you suppress, eventually hate, experience low self-esteem, and subsequently find yourself at risk.

When the focus of your anger or hate is to blame somebody, whether you blame yourself or someone else, you are holding a grudge against him or her. The word "judge" appears in parentheses under the word "grudge" in the forgiveness model (Figure 7.1). If you hold a grudge against somebody, whether your grudge is against yourself or someone else, it is as if you set yourself up to be a judge against that person. Your concept of right versus wrong is akin to a law that is written and has been broken. Holding a grudge against a person makes you a judge against that person for breaking the particular law that your emotions tell you is broken.

The grudge mindset has to do with debt. If you believe that you have been wronged by someone, then you may believe that the person who wronged you owes you an apology. Notice that the term *owe* implies a debt. Alternately, you may intend to pay that person back, get even, or wish that he or she *pays* in some way for what they have done. All of these conclusions have to do with debt, and in many ways are similar to lending or borrowing money.

For example, imagine that you have a friend who is falling on hard financial times. Your friend approaches you with a request: "Could you please lend me $100?" You reply: "Sure! I can do that." You give your friend $100. As long as your friend has the $100 that you loaned to him, your friend is indebted to you. And that is what it is like to carry around a sack of potatoes. Each potato is like an IOU with a person's name on it who owes a debt to you. You are the one who is carrying around your sack of potatoes. No one else sees it. But you are aware of your sack to some degree or another. Sometimes you feel its weight; sometimes you don't.

You can stay within the debt position and its corresponding judgmental mindset for a long time, carrying your sack of potatoes around with you wherever you go, holding grudges against yourself or against others. The time may accumulate to years and years of holding grudges against people.

Law versus Choice

In order to achieve forgiveness, there is a line to cross over. The way to cross this line is within the realm of choice, that is, within the will component of your humanity ("will" is in parentheses beside "choice" in the model). Therefore, forgiveness is the result of a choice. Forgiveness is not a law. I am not aware of secular, spiritual, or biblical writings in which forgiveness is considered to be a law. It means that nobody "has to" forgive. It is true that forgiveness is a beneficial choice to make, but nobody is required to make this choice.

Sometimes people think of forgiveness as law. You may think "I know I *have to* forgive" or "You *have to* forgive, you know!" Actually, I don't have to and you don't have to forgive. And if I think it is a good idea for you to forgive, I can't make you do it! All I can do is to ask you to make the choice to forgive. I may do a masterful job describing what forgiveness is and what it isn't. I may convincingly explain how you benefit if you make the choice to forgive and how you suffer if you choose not to forgive. I may explain what the limitations of forgiveness are, and so on, but I cannot make you choose to forgive. To repeat, all I can do is to ask you to choose to forgive.

To forgive is a choice. Choice is within the realm of the will part of being human. All people have what is understood to be free will, that is, the freedom to make choices. Since forgiveness is a choice, it is an act of the will. The statement "I can't forgive" is therefore nonsensical. Why? Because you can! (That is, you *can* make the choice to forgive.) If a person claims that he or she can't forgive, it really means that he or she *will not* forgive.

A law is something that is likely not your will. For example, the law states there is a speed limit of 50 km/hr when you drive on residential roads in the city. If it is not your will to drive 50 km/hr, then you likely will not conform to this limit. On the other hand, you may decide to conform to the law, and drive within the posted speed limit although you do not necessarily agree with it. As you continue to do so, the speed restriction eventually does not become a burden. You have made it your will to conform to the law and therefore the law has become a non-issue to you.

At times you notice that another person conforms to your will, but she does not make it her will. You may tell your child, "Say you're sorry!" or, "Tell so-and-so you forgive him!" Your child may do your will but may not make it hers. You will notice this in the spirit in which she conforms to your advice. If she conforms begrudgingly, then she is likely adhering to the "law" (your law) to forgive, but it is not her will to do so. On the other hand, she may agree with you that it is the right thing to do and forgive so-and-so freely. You notice she has made it her will to forgive and follows through with doing so.

Choice Implies Options

A choice implies at least two different options. If there is only one option to choose from, then there is no choice. Therefore, there must be at least a second option for you to choose from if you are not making the choice to forgive (since forgiveness is a choice). If you do not choose to forgive, then what are you choosing to do?

Many people attempt to answer this question by suggesting that the alternate choice, rather than to forgive, is "to not forgive." Actually, to answer in this way sanitizes the situation, so that you are not fully aware of the consequences of choosing not to forgive. If the choice is between black and white, then the choice does not become "white" and "not white." "Not white" is actually "black" in this case. The choice, therefore, of choosing not to forgive is something else. The actual choice you make, if you do not choose to forgive, is to choose to hold a grudge. But the reality is that it is actually a choice to hate. *Hate* is a strong word! Do you like to think that you are making the choice to hate when you are choosing not to forgive? I believe that if more people realized they are choosing to hate when they are making a choice not to forgive, they would instead be more open to choose forgiveness.

Healing

If you choose to forgive, then you enter into a healing process. The term *healing* is meant to be a generic term because forgiveness is not a recipe. It is unreasonable for me to suggest to you that forgiveness is to do this and that, or such-and-such, and then ... bing! Out comes the forgiveness! Congratulations! You've done it! No, I cannot suggest this. Forgiveness is not a recipe. It comes in different ways for different people and not always in the same way for any individual. For some people, it can take a long time, over many years, as the potatoes are transferred from the sack on their back onto the desktop, one at a time. For others, the process may be brief as they unload numerous potatoes from their sack onto the desktop.

Although forgiveness is not a recipe, it is a process nonetheless. The healing process of forgiveness transforms your destructive mindset (with the potato in your sack within the me-versus-you mindset) to the constructive mindset (with the potato transferred onto the desktop). Forgiveness is a process that transfers the focus of your mindset from blaming the person to a focus that separates the person from the problem. Your thoughts become free to focus on the problem (or potato) rather than on the person. This is an important point.

Person Focused

When you forgive somebody, you are doing exactly that. You are forgiving a *person*. You are not forgiving a problem. Forgiveness is a *person-focused* work. In the same way that throwing your potato into your sack is the work of a person-focused mindset when you suppress, the process of transferring the potato from your sack onto the desktop involves a person-focused activity.

When you forgive somebody whom you blame for doing something wrong, you are not in any way suggesting that what the person said or did, or did not say or did not do, is acceptable or all right. No. For example, if you decide to forgive somebody for lying to you, you are not suggesting that lying is okay. Forgiving, rather, frees you to focus on the lie as the problem and frees you to sort out a strategy to respond to the lie, rather than remaining in the blaming mindset against the person. Forgiveness allows you to hold the person accountable or responsible for what it was he or she did wrong.

Emotions

The process of forgiveness involves your emotions to some degree or another. When you remember something, it is as if a potato in your sack returns onto your lap. Your thoughts and emotions connected with the potato are revisited in real time. The various dynamics of memories of the senses and memories of the emotions were discussed in chapter 3. When you remember something, you experience emotions. You may experience a memory of your emotions, and/or new emotions (in the present) linked to what you remember. Since your memory of potatoes from past injustices includes an experience of emotions, the process of forgiveness, in which you transfer your potatoes onto the desktop, involves the world of the *arts* in its various dimensions.

The arts in its various expressed forms represent the languages of emotion. Therefore, as there is a list of symptomatic (poor) treatments to get relief from the weight of your sack of potatoes, so there is a list of therapeutic (favourable) treatments. The list of therapeutic treatments involves the various dimensions of the arts. The therapeutic treatments, although not perfect, are nevertheless more favourable in comparison with the symptomatic treatments.

Therapeutic Treatments

Spoken Word

The first art form to discuss that can lead to healing is the spoken word. This is where the benefits of counselling or psychotherapy come from. However, it does not matter if you are talking with a professional counsellor or with a psychotherapist. You could also be talking with a trusted friend or family member or with a spiritual leader. It really does not matter who you are talking with.

Effective counselling is, in my opinion, connected with the type of feedback the listening person gives you when you talk about your past. When you mention the various things that have happened to you, your emotions become part of your description or are evident when you recall your past. The effective counsellor allows you to have your thoughts and emotions. He or she may not understand your thoughts and emotions, but will nevertheless allow you to experience them without giving you an indication that there is something wrong with you for having thoughts and emotions.

Since you receive a sense of validation of your thoughts and emotions, you become free to transfer the focus of your thoughts away from blaming the person (whether you blame yourself or someone else) onto the potato. You are thus free to transfer your potato onto the desktop. This is the role of effective counselling.

Ineffective counselling occurs when your thoughts and feelings are not validated when you describe your memory to a listening person. You share your thoughts and emotions with someone. His response may be: "Well, buck up! You shouldn't feel that way! It's not godly! Just get over it and move on!" If this is the type of feedback you receive, you are much more likely to maintain an understanding of your potato within the me-versus-you mindset.

Your response to this lack of emotional validation may be, "Don't tell me not to feel my emotions, when there is no doubt that I feel them!" You thus maintain the focus of your thoughts onto blaming the person, and you return your potato back into the sack on your back. Perhaps you add yet another potato to your sack, for you may be offended that the "listening" person did not let you be who you are. Since your emotions are part of the package of who you are, they can represent your right to exist. A lack of validation by someone else therefore results in you hanging on to your emotion and the potato that corresponds to it. You maintain your destructive me-versus-you mindset in a defensive way, protecting your right to exist.

Another form of the spoken word involves *group therapies*. Groups can also occur in different settings. A group could be a formally arranged hospital-based group within the Department of Psychiatry. A group could be a less formally arranged 12-step group, such as the various "anonymous" groups (for example, Alcoholics Anonymous, Gamblers Anonymous, Overeaters Anonymous, Narcotics Anonymous, Cocaine Anonymous). A group could be a family, a community, or a church-based support group, such as a Group Bible Study or prayer group. In addition, any team, such as bowling, volleyball, hockey, or soccer, is a type of group.

Groups that appear to have a measure of success in helping people are the various "anonymous" groups. I believe the reason for this success is based on the dynamic that most people wear "masks" when involved in various interrelationships from day to day. If you are struggling with an issue, you are not likely to let the world know about it. And so, as you get ready to face the world each day, you put on a mask. Your mask declares to the world: "I'm OK! I've got it together!"

The people you come into contact with over the course of the day also wear a mask. And their mask says: "I'm OK! I've got it together!"

The only problem is that you are not necessarily aware that what you see in the other people you interact with is their mask. And so, as you return home to your place of protection at the end of the day and take off your mask, you are likely to struggle. You remove your mask and wonder: "What's the matter with me? Everyone I come across is OK and has got it together. And look at me! I'm struggling with blah blah blah! What am I? An alien? There must be something wrong with me! Maybe I don't really belong here."

And so you wrestle with your thoughts, thinking and believing that you are the problem. Then, you happen to attend a group of some sort. Somebody in that group talks about her potato. But there is something about her potato that reminds you of your potato. You may recognize unique differences, but there are also similarities. And so you respond in your thoughts with astonishment: "Hey! Wait a minute! So-and-so is talking about my potato! But ... but ... it isn't my potato. It is her potato! So ... let me think ... all along I've believed that I am the potato ... but ... so-and-so has a potato that is a lot like mine, but it isn't me. And ... I know that so-and-so is not the problem ... yet there is a problem. Hey! I'm not the problem either (triumphantly)! The problem is the potato!" Therefore, the focus of your thoughts gets shifted from blaming yourself or someone else to understanding the potato as the problem. You are now free to transfer your potato onto the desktop.

Your emotions become validated. You realize that you are not alone when you discover that other people experience similar emotions as you do in the context of similar problems. Sometimes a person claims, "You won't understand, because you've never experienced what I've been through!" The statement represents a declaration that her emotions are unique and need to be validated for what they are. For this reason, people seek and form support groups that are connected with specifically identified losses or problems.

Groups in which the problems of people are different can also be of help to encourage healing. It is more challenging, however, to achieve the sense of an understanding or a validation of the emotions in these groups. The reason for the difficulty is that different people have different potatoes. Something that is a potato to one person may not be a potato to another person.

You may attend a certain group that appears to have sympathetic participants. And so you get your courage up one day to talk about your potato. It definitely is a potato to you, but it may not be a potato to anybody else in the group. You go ahead and describe your potato. The feedback you receive is: "What are you doing here? That's not a potato! This is a place for real potatoes!" And so, with such a lack of validation, you maintain a clutch on your potato within the person-oriented mindset. You reply, "Don't tell me this isn't a potato when it's a potato to me!" You return your potato back into your sack and believe or feel that you have not been understood or validated. The lack of validation you endure becomes another potato to you, as you feel "let down." You place your new potato into your sack. You are therefore worse off than when you started.

You may wish to get a measure of revenge. And so when the other person describes his potato, which is definitely a potato to him but is not a potato to you, you challenge him back: "What are you doing here? You call that a potato? That's not a potato!" And so he clutches his potato within the me-versus-you mindset and returns it back into his sack, thinking, "Don't tell me it isn't a potato, when it is to me!"

Such are the difficulties and challenges of groups in which the participants are dealing with different and unique potatoes. Attention must therefore be given to the fact that different people struggle with different potatoes. Some of the potatoes that people struggle with are definitely potatoes to them, yet are not potatoes to others. The support for an individual comes when his or her emotions are validated. You realize that neither the emotions nor the people are the problem.

Instead, you recognize that it is the potatoes that are the problem. The challenge for any individual has to do with how to manage the potatoes of life. You can be free to conclude that the potatoes are the problem and can become free to listen to individuals who hope to explain their potatoes to you and be understood.

Biblical Relevance

Acts 2:42-47 and 1John 4:7-12 discuss what love is and how love can be unifying: "The world will know we are Christians by our love." I believe that included in this type of love is the realization that "all have sinned and fall short of the glory of God" (Romans 3:23).

Part of my understanding of what it means to be a Christian is that I realize I am not perfect. I am a sinful man, and there are consequences for my sinfulness. But not all is lost, for there is a man who is without sin and is perfect. He is Jesus of Nazareth. I therefore place my faith and hope in Christ and His righteousness, rather than in any righteousness I try to conjure up in my own strength. But just because I place my faith in Him, it does not mean that I will not continue to face challenges of various sorts in this world, for I continue to struggle with that sinful nature that I have. I therefore place my hope not in "my arrival" (that is, the time when I "arrive" and "get it right"), but rather in "His arrival" (the second coming). For when He arrives, I will be changed. In 1Corinthians 15:50-57, it is written that we will be changed "at the last trumpet."

Since this last trumpet is yet to happen, I ought not to be surprised when I realize that I continue to struggle with my sinful nature and, as well, see evidence that others continue to struggle with their sinful nature. But I will try to focus on the potatoes that you and I come across, rather than focusing my thoughts on blaming myself or others, when the evidence of our potatoes and our sinful nature is obvious. To me, this is the love that is written about in the Bible. Another way of saying this is often quoted: "Love the person, but hate the sin." The sin is not about the individual, but has to do with the potato on his or her plate.

No treatment is without risks. Even though the therapeutic treatments listed are considered to be more favourable as compared with the symptomatic treatments, they are not without risks. Besides limitations of the effectiveness of group therapies as previously discussed, another risk in group settings occurs when an individual with a heart to care for others attends and listens to the potatoes of other people. With her heart of love, care, and concern, she is tempted to take the responsibility of another person's potato. She hears someone else's story and responds: "Ohhhh, that's a terrible potato you've been dealing with! Let me help you with your potato." She then takes the responsibility of the other person's potato and adds it to her own burden, placing it in her sack. This loving and caring person becomes worse off.

Both of them may believe they have found a friend to help or be helped by. But they have developed a master-slave relationship. The helping person becomes either the master or the slave, depending on who has actual control of the potato. The master-slave relationship develops because the potato is not in the proper hands of the person it belongs to. The helper takes responsibility for the potato of the person who is helped. The potato is not in its proper court. I have discussed this dynamic previously. Therefore, be aware of boundary issues when you show loving concern to others by listening to them and giving support when they struggle with various potatoes.

Written Word

The next art form that can lead to healing is the written word. Writing out your thoughts and feelings can be performed in various approaches. For example, you could keep a diary or a journal. I believe that the effectiveness of writing as a way to promote healing has to do with the validation of your thoughts and feelings when you write them down. Just seeing your thoughts and feelings in black and white can give you the validation you seek. When you achieve a sense of validation, you become free to focus your attention onto the potato, rather than to blame yourself or someone else. You become free to transfer your potato onto the desktop.

Another effective approach to write out your thoughts and feelings is to write a letter. You can write a letter to yourself, to someone else, or perhaps to God (God or some sort of higher power is often blamed for various things that happen in people's lives). Anybody you can think of who has his or her name on a potato that is in your sack is someone you can address a letter to. The reason why a letter can be an effective way to encourage healing is related to its format. When you write a letter to someone, it starts with "Dear So-and-so," and then you proceed to describe to him your thoughts and feelings about what happened. You are therefore separating the person from the problem by singling out the person you are writing to. When you achieve the sense of validation that can be attained by writing out your thoughts and emotions, you can become free to transfer your potatoes from the sack on your back onto the desktop.

The process of writing a letter, however, also presents risks. Letters are intended to be sent to the addressee. Yet, if you choose to write a letter as your treatment approach to get relief from the potatoes in the sack on your back, then your letter ought *not* to be sent. Sending such a letter can result in more harm in your relationships, rather than promoting the healing that you seek. If your letter is in the form of an e-mail, then you are at increased risk to send it, for it is much easier to click "send" than it is to fold a letter; stuff, seal, stamp, address an envelope, and go to the mailbox.

The reason that your letters ought not to be sent is that you are in the situation that is similar to the first stage of the constructive method. You are trying to understand what your potatoes represent to you. When you write down your thoughts and feelings for the first time after your potatoes have been stashed in your sack, your feelings are understood within the destructive mindset. They may be very strong and can come out aggressively. A person reading such an aggressive letter may take offence to the tone of the letter. There is a risk that the whole scenario may lead further into an escalating cycle or a tangent if she responds to you in a defensive or attacking way (as described in chapter 2 when you express anger within the destructive mindset). You have every good intention of bringing healing to the relationship by letting her know how you feel, but it all comes to nothing as she takes offence with the tone of your letter.

Therefore, if you write a letter as a way to transfer your potatoes onto the desktop, you are advised not to send it. If you have the intention to send a letter, your letter is best sent when your mindset is at the second stage of the constructive method of anger management. At this stage, you understand your potato in a way that the situation is unacceptable, as opposed to believing that the person is the problem, and you have placed the potato on the desktop. You are free to work with your potato and free to write to the person about it within the constructive mindset. Instead of writing "Such-and-such has happened, and how could you have done such-and-such to me," you are free to write "Such-and-such has happened, and it has affected me in such-and-such a way. I am writing to let you know about it and so that you know I am willing to forgive." Of course, such a letter does not guarantee the other person's willingness to sort the matter out, but it will more likely lead to an opportunity to come to peace.

Another form of the written word is to write an *anger list*. This method can be effective on its own, and can also be an approach that ties many of the other treatment approaches together.

To create an anger list, get a blank sheet of paper, and write someone's name on the top of the page. Anybody with their name on a potato in your sack is someone whose name you can write on a blank sheet of paper. You will create numerous pages, each with a unique name. One sheet may have your own name on it. For some people, the anger list of items against the self becomes the longest to write. Other lists may have to do with your spouse, parent(s), sibling(s), friend(s), ex-friend(s), ex-spouse(s), and so on, or God. In other words, anybody whom you blame, regarding anything, becomes a person for you to create an anger list about.

For each individual that you have created an anger list page, write in point form any potato linked with him that comes to mind when you think of him. Write about something he said, did, didn't say, or didn't do that you believe is wrong. You will likely experience feelings of anger, hatred, or bitterness, and understand those feelings within the destructive me-versus-you mindset when you remember those potatoes linked with him. Try to make your list as concise as possible. The anger list format is not intended to become a novel.

Forgiveness is a choice. You are interested to describe your potatoes as concisely as possible when you build your anger list. The quality of your forgiveness will be the strongest when you know exactly what it is you are forgiving "so-and-so" for. Make your forgiveness be an informed choice. If you are willing to forgive somebody, and if you decide to forgive him or her in a general, generic, non-specific fashion, then you may discover the limits and weaknesses of your attempt to forgive. Something new and specific may happen which reminds you of a specific past incident that is connected with the person you believe you forgave. You may discover that you continue to have strong negative feelings toward him and you may understand these feelings within the destructive me-versus-you mindset. You may be confused, for you believe that you have forgiven him. The problem may be that you forgave him only in a generic sense. The effectiveness of your forgiveness is limited. Therefore, the work of forgiveness must include a way to help you make as informed a choice as possible when you forgive yourself and others for the wrongs connected with you and them.

The anger list format is one of many different treatment approaches to transfer the potato from your sack onto the desktop. Even though forgiveness is not a recipe, the anger list method is a good format to explore what is involved in the process of forgiveness. What can you do with the list once you are in the process of creating it? The anger list method of forgiveness has subsequent steps that highlight various stages that are involved in the process of transferring potatoes from your sack onto the desktop. I will discuss these steps in more detail later.

Other ways the written word can be used to lead to healing include writing poetry, an autobiographical account, a short story, a novel, or a play. When you write a story, the characters you develop may be different from your own story, but they deal with potatoes that are very much like those you have. Writing in this way can help you to come to terms with your own potatoes.

The group therapy component of the written word approach to healing occurs when you read someone else's poetry, autobiographical account, short story, novel, or play. As you read the story, you notice that the characters are dealing with potatoes that remind you of your own potatoes. You think: "Hey! The characters in this story have potatoes just like mine! I don't believe that the characters in this story are the problem. I must not be the problem either! The potatoes are the problem!" And so the shared experience you have with the characters in the story can validate your right to feel and think. You become free to realize there is a difference between people and potatoes. You become free to focus your feelings and thoughts on your potatoes and free to transfer them onto the desktop.

Therefore, much of the book industry is a form of group therapy, even though it is not recognized as such. When you open a book to read, you are not necessarily declaring, "I'm going to my group now!" And yet the stories you share with others, and the stories that others share with you, are a form of group therapy.

Movies

Another way to tell stories involves movies or television. When you watch a movie, you become immersed in someone's story. The potatoes that the characters deal with are what the story of the movie is about. Some of the potatoes may remind you of potatoes in your past or of current potatoes, and once again you realize that the characters in the movie are not the problem. You can also recognize that you are not the problem. Your potatoes are the problem. You become free to transfer your potatoes onto the desktop.

The motion picture industry is therefore another multi-million or billion dollar form of group therapy. And yet this phenomenon is not necessarily recognized as such. When you get ready to go to a movie, you are not necessarily declaring, "I'm going to my group!"

Although going to a movie is a more passive way to attend a group than attending a 12-step program group is, movies are nonetheless recognized as a source to promote healing. The book *The Motion Picture Prescription*, written by Gary Solomon,[6] is an example of the recognition of the healing quality movies can offer. The stories portrayed via the medium of movies can be a source to help you understand your own story when you see yourself in the stories of others.

Music

The next art form of therapy is music. The individual therapy component of music occurs when the person seeking healing composes the musical score. It can involve the composition of instrumental music, *a cappella* choral music, or a combination of instrumental music with lyrics.

The group therapy component of music occurs when something about a musical composition you are listening to, whether instrumental or with lyrics, resonates with you emotionally. I believe the healing effect of music transcends musical forms and styles, although certain musical forms or styles may appear to lend themselves more to a group therapy theme. Sometimes jokes connected with certain musical styles are made due to an awareness of the "healing from stories" effect of music.

For example, it is joked that if you play country and western music in reverse, everything turns out all right. The song played forward depicts a story of loss: "I lost my girl, the dog ran away, and my truck died." When the song is played in reverse, the story is "I'm with my girl, the dog came back, and my truck hums."

Music is a way to tell a story. Sometimes the stories set to music involve characters who deal with potatoes that remind you of your potatoes. You hear the song and realize: "The characters in this song are not the potato. It must mean that I'm not the potato either. The potato is the potato!" And so, once again, you are free to transfer your potato onto the desktop. Therefore, the music industry is another multi-million or billion dollar form of media which provides group therapy, even though you may not recognize this fact when you listen to your music or go to concerts. Could it be that McLuhan's phrase "the medium is the message" is about the medium being a form of providing group therapy?

A note of caution needs to be addressed when discussing music as a form of therapy. This caution actually applies to all of the "arts as therapy" methods in this book. Although the therapeutic effect of music applies to all forms and styles, you are interested in being aware of the implied psychology in how the story is presented. Certain musical forms and styles are considered by some to be inherently destructive because of the way the story is told. For example, "hate music" may be considered to be within the destructive mindset.

I believe that music is a way for a person to get a sense of validation, regardless of the form and style used. An individual hopes to have her emotions validated. Sometimes the emotions are very strong and are understood within the destructive mindset when you listen to a musical selection. But as a method for you to achieve healing and forgiveness, music is a way to validate your emotions. The situation is comparable to the first stage of the constructive method of anger management, when you allow yourself to feel and use your emotions as a tool to understand the potato so that you can manage your anger constructively. When you use an art form such as music to achieve the validation of your emotions, you become free to feel and free to use your emotions as a tool to understand the potato that is connected with your emotion. As in the first stage of the constructive method of anger management, you are not at a point when you are involving someone else with your potato; you are working on understanding the meaning of your potato on your own.

The use of music to tell a story, even if the story is presented within the destructive mindset, can help you to achieve the validation of your emotions. However, once your emotions are validated, you need to find a way to transfer your thoughts from the destructive mindset to the constructive mindset. You therefore need to find a way to bring your mindset into this transition.

If your musical form or style of choice, in which you validate your emotions, keeps you within the destructive mindset of understanding your problems and does not lead further to a transition to the constructive mindset, then it may do more harm toward fanning the flames of me-versus-you destructive thinking. You may feel more powerful within the me-versus-you mindset as you believe you have gained support for your particular belief or feeling about something in the world. It becomes more like "us-versus-them" or "us-versus-you," which is the "strength in numbers" that your increased sense of power comes from. You may experience increased hatred toward an individual or a group of people.

The caution therefore is to be aware of the destructive versus constructive psychology in how a story is presented. This caution not only applies to music, but also to stories told in any media form, such as books, movies, etc. In order for you to heal, you need to seek a psychology to help you transform your mind from the destructive mindset to the constructive mindset.

Biblical Perspective

Christian based music in the various forms and styles, such as "psalms, hymns and spiritual songs," (Ephesians 5:19) can be used to contribute to healing. Many of the Christian songs acknowledge trouble and despair and are therefore realistic. The songs also contribute to hope for those who are troubled, which I believe is what contributes to healing. Hope helps a person to understand his problems within the constructive mindset.

If the solutions of problems presented in a song are left within the devices of the way a power based mindset world seeks solutions (such as vengeance – that you attain within your own power, or seek a hero to mete out on your behalf), then hope only goes as far as the power lasts. Most people are not blind to the limits of their power or the power of their heroes, and so the power based solutions leave a person with a fragile hope or without hope altogether.

But if hope is placed in the ultimate hero, God, then this hope does not fail when placed in Him in truth rather than in power. I say "in truth" because your hope is in God to handle the problems according to His way of handling them rather than in your way. There is a trust in God and His love that goes along with this perspective. When it comes to power, there is nothing more powerful than God, because a definition of God is that He is all-powerful. So when I say "rather than in power" it means when you place hope in power, you likely hope God will do your will (such as vengeance) and will feel let down if He does not do your will but instead does His will.

Art

The next art form that can lead to healing is creative art. This approach may involve drawing, painting, sculpting, gardening, architecture, and so on. Anything that has a creative component can lend itself to healing.

The individual therapy component of creative art occurs when you are doing the creative work. The group therapy component occurs when there is something about someone else's creative work that resonates with you in an emotional way. It could be the way the strokes of the brush are made on the canvas to indicate emotion, or the way a scene is depicted to indicate an emotional event. Going to an art gallery, for example, could be considered to be a form of group therapy.

Sport

The last artsy method of therapy I will discuss is sport. I consider sport to be art because there is a significant emotional component that goes along with sport. In the spring of 2006, the community of Edmonton became immersed in the emotions of the fans of the local professional hockey team. The successes of the team continued to mount toward the possibility of winning the championship.

The individual therapy component of sport occurs when you perform the sporting activity. You could be involved in an individual sport or team sport. The group therapy component of sport occurs when someone else is the athlete and you are the spectator. Going to a game at the arena or stadium, or watching a game on television, is therefore a form of group therapy. Once again, this is a multi-million or billion dollar form of group therapy, but you are not necessarily claiming to be "going to your group" when you are going to the game!

As discussed in connection with music as therapy, it is good to be aware of the sport psychology involved when you play or watch a particular sport. There is a destructive sport psychology and there is a constructive sport psychology. But since sport is competitive in nature, is sport not an inherently destructive activity? For example, in an individual sport, such as tennis, there is one player against his opponent. In a team sport, such as hockey or soccer, there is one team against another team. Is such a situation not consistent with what is described as the destructive mindset? Aren't the games inherently about me-versus-you or us-versus-them situations?

Not necessarily so. The destructive versus constructive sport psychology has to do with how the game is played or how the story of the game is told. Every game is a story in the making. What will be the outcome? How will the obstacles be overcome? Who will triumph?

In a team sport, the destructive sport psychology occurs when the athletes have a me-versus-you mindset. To win the championship, the approach of the team is to prevent their opponent from winning. The players may attempt to "take out" the players of the other team. They believe the last team standing wins. In the destructive sport psychology, players are more likely to get injured as they battle each other in their quest to win. There is more emphasis on power rather than on skill. The athletes and spectators tend to make the game be about pushing or bending the rules. They try to get away with close calls regarding the decisions of the referees and make the game be about how the referee is calling the game.

In contrast, the constructive sport psychology is goal oriented. To win the championship, the approach of the team is to outplay their opponent at their best. A sense of honour goes hand-in-hand with the constructive sport psychology. The athletes honour their own abilities as well as the abilities of their opponents. The goal is to outplay the opposition when they are at their best. There is more emphasis on skill rather than on power. The athletes honour the rules and the referees. They may at times disagree with the interpretation of a call, but work at outplaying the opponent within the rules of the game.

I believe it is more fulfilling to win a championship by outplaying the opponent when they are at their best. In this way, you know that you are the best. If your team wins by "taking your opponent out" or "getting away with the calls," then you are actually conceding to the other team that they are better than you are. Your hope of winning is to lower the standard of excellence of your opposition down to your level or play the referee (instead of your opponent) to your benefit. To me, this is not as fulfilling a way to win a championship.

During the telecasting of the Olympic Games, I have noticed on a number of occasions that the program host interviews someone who is interested in promoting sport as a means to enhance self-esteem. The promotion involves helping children in disadvantaged situations to have access to and participation in a sporting activity for the purposes of increasing a sense of self-worth or self-esteem.

Sports can be a beneficial way to enhance self-esteem and lead toward psychological healing because it has to do with an activity that is goal oriented. For example, you may have a goal to complete 50 push-ups a day. You work toward attaining your goal by proceeding in a step-wise fashion. For the first week, you do 3 push-ups a day. The second week, you do 5 push-ups a day; the third week, 8 a day; the fourth week, 10 a day; and so on. As you make strides toward attaining your goal, you develop a sense of accomplishment. You have evidence of success. You can do something. Your accomplishment feels good. You become free to realize: "All along I have believed that I am 'a nobody,' but now I have evidence that I can do something! So ... the problem isn't me! I know now that there are things that I can do and succeed! So ... even though I have a heavy sack of potatoes, I know that I am not the problem. The potatoes are the problem! But if I try to deal with my potatoes all at once, it may be a bit overwhelming. If I deal with my potatoes one at a time, eventually I will deal with all of them, just as though I am working toward doing 50 push-ups a day, a little at a time."

The sense of accomplishment you are able to attain in a given sport can therefore be a helpful way to enhance your self-esteem. You become free to transfer the potatoes from your sack onto the desktop.

A sense of accomplishment is not always connected with winning the event. An athlete in the throes of a challenging game or a person in the struggles of life can derive a sense of "the joy in the journey." The success of playing a game well, although the game is lost, can lead to joy and a sense of fulfillment. This joy may defy the logic of winning for success. Instead, you have a winning mentality, which is a constructive mindset applied to sport and life in general.

Note: A risk of the various group therapies is that they may be used as an escape. For example, people may attend groups, go to movies, or read books to "get away from reality." The therapy becomes a symptomatic treatment for the potatoes rather than therapeutic. There is only temporary relief from the sack of potatoes. If this is the situation in your case, please become aware of the context of your activity so that you can transfer the activity into a therapeutic method and derive greater benefit regarding the burden of your potatoes.

Anger List

I mentioned previously that I would return to discuss in greater detail the anger list method of healing as a way to transfer the potatoes from your sack onto the desktop. The anger list method is broken down into steps. I was first introduced to this approach when I read a book entitled *Finding the God-Dependent Life* by Joanie Yoder.[7] She writes about her experience toward healing following crippling panic attacks and agoraphobia. She describes steps toward healing that involve creating an anger list. I will incorporate her steps in the following discussion, and add relevant input as to how the homework assignment applies in the process. The goal is to understand your emotions in as constructive a way as possible as you proceed through the healing process.

Step 1: Create the List

The first step of the anger list method is about creating the list. Take a blank piece of paper and write someone's name at the top. Any person whose name is on a potato in your sack is someone to create a list for. Include a page that will become a list with your own name on it (this could end up being the longest list you create, for people are easily the severest judges of themselves); other pages can be for lists about your spouse, ex-spouse, family member (for example, parent, sibling, uncle, aunt, grandparent, child, grandchild), friend, ex-friend, co-worker, neighbour, God, and so on.

When you think of the person whose name is on a given page you created and remember something about him that includes feelings of anger, hatred, or bitterness toward him, start compiling your list. You will likely understand your emotions within the destructive mindset when you feel them during a particular memory. Write in point form about the offensive issue connected with that person, as you remember them. Try to keep it concise; you are not using the anger list method to write a novel. Try to describe something about what he/she/you said, did, didn't say, or didn't do that you believe is wrong. Continue compiling your list as appropriate.

The anger list method can be attempted specifically on its own when you sit down with pen and paper and try to remember the issues of the past, or with the idea to compile it as you normally do things from day to day and experience memories that happen to occur when you are involved with the other art forms. For example, you may happen to be watching a movie or listening to music. Something in the movie or song triggers a memory of a potato from your past. Take the memory as an opportunity to write on your anger list what the potato represents to you.

Some days you may have little to write; other days you may have much to write. If you find the task of writing your memories somewhat overwhelming, then try not to overdo it. Sometimes you may feel a flood of emotions, about to breech the dam, and you may feel like you can't take it anymore. If so, try to limit yourself to perhaps 10 minutes a day to work on your list, or call a friend for emotional support. If you are overwhelmed with your emotions and start feeling suicidal or homicidal, arrange for professional help or arrange to have a supportive friend alongside you during this time. A supportive friend reminds you that you (and others) are not the problem. This is helpful when you struggle with the memories of your various potatoes in which your primary focus is to blame yourself or someone else.

When you are reminded of the various potatoes of the past, the feelings you experience alongside the memories may be intense. You may feel a churning of emotion inside. Since you are becoming better at allowing yourself to feel your emotions, you will be better able to persevere through the churning you endure. You will remember that the emotions and the inner struggle of experiencing them are not the problem. You will let your emotions give you insights you may never have thought of before. Let your emotions teach you about yourself and the challenging dynamics of life. Sometimes you will cry out to the Fates: "*Why*, why me; take this feeling away from me!" But by persevering through the pain and letting yourself feel, you will find the freedom to declare: "*That*, that this happened; that this happened to me. This was my role and this was so-and-so's role in what happened. This is what the potato is."

The process of healing to achieve forgiveness is work. It can be a difficult path to venture on, but the benefits make it worthwhile and fulfilling. The first step of the anger list method is a path that leads you toward making an informed choice. To forgive is a choice, and the process of healing helps you identify what your informed choice is about (so that you know what it is you are forgiving "so-and-so" for). You will experience a stronger sense of forgiveness and greater benefit by understanding what it is (the potato) you are dealing with. Forgiveness is the beneficial outcome of the choice to forgive and the work of healing that accompanies your choice.

To proceed to the second step of the anger list method, the first step does not have to be exhaustively completed. The process itself is what is important. The first step identifies the various potatoes. It brings them out of your sack and into real time in terms of the thoughts and feelings that accompany the memory of each potato you have. You feel the potato in the grasp of your hand and understand the thoughts and emotions that accompany it within the destructive mindset. You will tend to blame the person responsible for the potato that is in your hand (which is why you need to exercise caution, as noted earlier, if you feel very strong emotions against the person you are working on to forgive).

As an alternative to writing out an anger list, you may consider to keep the situations within your mind as you remember them. You will follow the remaining steps of the anger list method in your mind without writing the issues down. The validation of your emotions and the understanding of your potatoes within the constructive mindset will be sorted out as you remember them. It may take time to sort the situations out. When you persevere to attain the constructive understanding of your emotions and thoughts, you will become free to proceed onward with the process of transferring the potatoes onto the desktop.

Step 2: Forgive

Now that you are compiling your list, what do you do with it? The second step is to forgive. For each of the incidents of injustice written on your list, consider them separately, one at a time, and say to yourself something like, "I forgive 'so-and-so' for the time he said, did, didn't say, or didn't do such-and-such." You may consider performing this step in a spirit of meditation or prayer. Please note that you are *not* at this time communicating with the person that you are forgiving. Rather, you are working toward understanding your own emotions in as constructive a way as possible.

If you believe in a higher power, or if you have the understanding that God is with you in the process of the forgiveness you are working on, then you will find the sense of His presence to be a powerful and valuable resource to help you to persevere with the second step of the anger list method of healing. A reason for your sense of comfort is that you will feel you are not alone when you work toward understanding your thoughts and emotions. The feeling of unity with the higher power is an identity that is very powerful, helpful, and beyond understanding.

Biblical Relevance

One of the requests prayed within the Lord's Prayer states, "Forgive us our debts, as we also have forgiven our debtors" (Matthew 6:12). When you pray the Lord's Prayer, you are not praying to your debtors. You are praying to God. Therefore, the first relationship dynamic when you forgive someone else (or yourself) is actually between you and God rather than between you and your debtor (the offending person). That is why knowing God is *with* you (as opposed to against you) when you work out your forgiveness, and knowing that He is willing and able to forgive you becomes a powerful, helpful, and freeing dynamic to base your identity on. You become free to do your part to forgive others and to forgive yourself.

The second step of the anger list method shifts the focus of your thoughts onto the potato. Instead of your thoughts being focussed so as to blame the person (whether you blame someone else or yourself), the second step redirects your focus so as to understand there is a potato. You understand your feelings and thoughts in a way to recognize what was said, done, not said, or not done that you believe is wrong, rather than to blame the individual responsible. But the potato is still in your grasp. You haven't transferred it onto the desktop yet. Therefore, there is a third step in the process.

Step 3: Transfer and Release

The third step of the anger list method of healing is the release step. You release the control of your potato by placing it onto the desktop. This step is also a "transfer" step. To perform the third step, go through your anger list a third time. For each issue of injustice you have written on your list, release (or transfer) your role as judge to a *judge in truth*.

What I mean by a "judge in truth" is a judge that presides over civil law, criminal law, or ultimately, moral law. In a system of government, there are two main offices to maintain order. One office is a legislative office. This is a person, or a group of people, that make the laws. In the Canadian federal and democratic system, this office is composed of the House of Commons and the Senate. The second office is a judiciary office, which interprets and upholds the law. In Canada, this is the police and court system, which pyramids up to the Supreme Court of Canada.

In a monarchy, the King or Queen presides in both offices and delegates the responsibility of administration to citizens or servants who execute the functions of the offices. The administrators fill the offices either by appointment or via a democratic process.

In the ultimate sense, a higher power or God presides in both offices. God is seen as both law maker and judge.

In each of these systems of government, neither you nor I function within these roles. If you are a member of a law-making body such as the Canadian House of Commons, or if you are a member within the judiciary system, you ultimately have responsibility to a higher cause than yourself. For example, you are responsible to *the people* in a democratic system. You are aware that a law is written and you are aware that you will be judged if you do not adhere to the law.

If you see yourself in the role of a judge, then you believe a deception. You must transfer your (self-deceptive) role as a judge to a judge in truth. For example, if you have been wronged by someone (if someone told you a lie), then you become aware of the wrongdoing (your emotions alert you). But when it comes down to it, you have neither written the law of telling the truth, nor will you be the presiding judge assessing the person's responsibility regarding upholding this law. You actually have been victimized by the person who at your expense did not uphold the law of telling the truth. You must view yourself as a victim, as opposed to viewing yourself as a judge.

I am not talking about getting yourself into a victim mentality. A victim mentality occurs within the power-based, destructive mindset. When you are in a victim mentality, you see yourself as powerless and unable to prevent others from having their way over you. On the contrary, you understand the situation within the constructive mindset when you have been wronged by someone and see yourself as having been victimized by him committing the wrong against you at your expense. Therefore, your freedom to transfer your role as a judge comes when you see yourself as a victim instead of as a judge. You become free to transfer your role as a judge to the judge in truth.

The third step of the anger list method brings freedom. It is the step that places the potato, along with its weight, into the proper court. The transfer does not make the potato go away, but rather liberates you to understand your potato in its proper context. You are free to place your potato into the proper court and address it appropriately.

Step 4: Freedom, Benevolent Regard, Prayer

As a way to signify the sense of freedom that the transfer step can bring, some people burn their anger list. The smoke as it rises signifies the spiritual dynamic of release, that is, a release from the burden of their potatoes. The sense of a weight loss of potatoes is liberating and renews the life-spirit of the individual.

For people who believe in a God and pray to their God, there is an alternative approach to dealing with the anger list they have created. In the context of a relationship with God, the fourth step is a possible "action" step. In this step, you go through the incidents you recorded on your list a fourth time. Your anger list, however, now becomes a prayer list. You are free to pray *for* the individual whose name appears at the top of your list. You are free to exercise a ministry of intercession, in which you pray for the person.

If you wish to pray regarding a concern of yours that is connected with someone else, you are not likely to pray for her if the potatoes with her name on them are in your sack within the destructive mindset. You are more likely to pray *against* her. Your prayers may sound something like, "Father, make so-and-so *pay* for what she has done!" I believe such prayers are not consistent with praying in truth or with worshipping God in spirit and in truth. Praying in this way sets you up to be "the boss," as you request God to do your will to make the person pay or suffer for the things he or she has done. You thus seek God as the source of power to do what is according to your will to be done.

If your potato is on the desktop and you understand that God is the judge instead of you, then you become free to pray for the person connected with the potato. Your prayer may sound something like: "Father, bless this person. Give her eyes to see and ears to hear. There are potatoes associated with her that I know both you and I are aware of, and I know that her potatoes prevent her from living a fulfilling life. What she has done is not only against me, but is also against you. Therefore, bless her, so that she may receive eyes to see, and ears to hear. May you give her the understanding to turn from doing harm to herself, to you, and to others." Such a prayer is what a ministry of intercession is all about.

Biblical Perspective

As a Christian, Jesus is your High Priest, who currently serves His ministry of intercession within the Heavenly realms. Hebrews 7:23-28 states:

Now there have been many of those priests, since death prevented them from continuing in office; but because Jesus lives forever, he has a permanent priesthood. Therefore he is able to save completely those who come to God through him, because he always lives to intercede for them.

Such a high priest meets our need—one who is holy, blameless, pure, set apart from sinners, exalted above the heavens. Unlike the other high priests, he does not need to offer sacrifices day after day, first for his own sins, and then for the sins of the people, He sacrificed for their sins once for all when he offered himself. For the law appoints as high priests men who are weak; but the oath, which came after the law, appointed the Son, who has been made perfect forever.

An individual who is a Christian is also a priest (1 Peter 2:9 states, "But you are a chosen people, a *royal priesthood*, a holy nation, a people belonging to God, that you may declare the praises of him who called you out of darkness into his wonderful light"[italics not in original]). As a Christian, it means I accept that I am not perfect and accept the perfection of Christ to stand in my place. I am thankful to Him for being perfect and willing to stand in my place. I understand that others are not perfect either and also need the perfection of Christ to stand in their place. I become less judgemental of myself and of others. I am liberated to serve within a ministry of intercession, as I prayerfully intercede on behalf of those who are in need. I understand that I am also in need, and am thankful that Christ is interceding within the heavenly temple on my behalf and on the behalf of others.

If it would be possible for me to be perfect in this world, then there would be no need for Christ as my High Priest to intercede in the heavenly realms on my behalf. But He *is* interceding for me, as the scripture declares. Therefore I also intercede on behalf of others who in this world are not perfect. I pray *for* them, as opposed to against them; I pray in a *loving* manner, as opposed to a judging manner.

Once you are in the process of transferring your potatoes onto the desktop, you will notice greater freedom in dealing with the new potatoes as they come your way. And when the new potatoes do come your way, you will deal with them as best as you can within the constructive mindset. Notice that forgiveness does not prevent new potatoes from coming. As long as this world continues to function as it presently does, you will continue to deal with potatoes throughout your life.

Example

I will attempt to describe a difficult situation. I realize there are many factors I will not be able to address, and there are many differing opinions for handling and interpreting such situations. I understand that I will not get everything right, but I will attempt this discussion anyway. Imagine there is a young woman who has been raped. She is bringing the man accused of being responsible for the crime against her to justice. I will explore two basic and differing mindsets the young woman may have in going through such an ordeal.

If her mindset is destructive, then the man who committed the crime becomes the focus of her emotions and thoughts. To her, the man is the problem. Within her destructive mindset, there is a high probability that the ordeal of going through the court process will be very emotional for her. She may not be able to look at the man, for to her, he represents evil. Attempts may be made for her not to be required to testify on the stand, for doing so may be extremely emotional and difficult for her. After all is said and done, the accused man may be found guilty and a sentence pronounced. On hearing the verdict and sentence, it is likely that she will feel outraged. She does not believe he received the punishment that he deserved. She is of the opinion that nothing is good enough to make him pay for his crime. Her mindset sets herself up as being the judge, and so nothing but what is according to her will is good enough in her eyes.

Contrast the same situation when the young woman's approach is within the constructive mindset. She has forgiven the man (put her potato on the desktop), but is holding him accountable for the crime (dealing with the potato on the desktop). I am not about to suggest that her constructive mindset prevents her from feeling emotions in this scenario. Her emotions continue to be a part of who she is, but she is free to understand them within the constructive mindset. She is free to experience a sense of control. She allows her emotions to assist her attain the goal, purpose, or conclusion of the case at hand. She is free to demonstrate in court that a wrong has been committed and that the man accused is the person responsible for having committed the crime against her. She is free to let the judge decide if the event in question constitutes a crime within the spirit of the law and if the man charged with the crime is the person responsible for having committed the crime. The man may be found guilty and a sentence pronounced. The young woman may believe that the severity of the sentence does not match the severity of the crime, but her concern relates to a problem within the justice system. She is motivated to speak in terms of matching sentences to crimes, rather than to punishing more severely the man who "didn't get what he deserved."

Cancel the Debt

A way to define forgiveness is to "cancel the debt." Remember what it means to hold a grudge against somebody. When you do so, your mindset goes into a debt position. You believe the person who wronged you owes you an apology. The debt position is similar to the example of somebody who owes you an amount of money. A friend of yours asks you to loan him $100 and you comply. Let us follow the scene further, to see what possible outcomes can arise.

Some time passes. Maybe it has been a long time. You haven't heard a word from your friend about when he will pay you back the $100 you loaned to him. So you start thinking about the situation: "Should I mention something about this to my friend? Well … if I do, maybe he will take offence and be upset with me. I might lose him as my friend, so maybe I won't say anything." At this point you are suppressing. You are keeping the peace between the two of you within the me-versus-you destructive mindset.

More time passes. You still haven't heard a word from your friend regarding when he intends to pay you back the money. So you think further: "What should I do now? Is it wrong for me to mention something about the $100 I loaned to him, wondering when he will pay me back? Well … it was an agreement after all. There's nothing wrong with asking!" So you get up your courage and ask him.

You politely ask, "Remember the $100 I loaned you?" "Yes," he replies. "Well, I haven't heard anything from you regarding how or when you are planning to pay me back. What is your plan?"

You have neither said nor done anything wrong. It is not wrong to ask such a question. If your friend takes offence that you have asked him this question, then perhaps you are finding out that he is not such a great friend to you. Unfortunately, everybody learns lessons about the limitations of their friendships from time to time.

One of the options to deal with the situation of unreturned money loaned to a friend is as follows. (This is not to be viewed as the "correct" option when it comes to money. It is only a suggested option for discussion purposes.) You approach your friend and say: "It's been a while since I loaned you $100, and you haven't paid me back yet. I've noticed that things are still fairly tight for you financially, so tell you what. Keep it. It's a gift. You don't owe me anything."

This proposal illustrates forgiveness. Actually, both phases of the constructive mindset are in play in this scenario. First of all, you have made the problem to be the unpaid loan (the potato), rather than your friend. Your focus is on the unpaid loan (the potato), which is what forgiveness is all about. The main point is to make it be about the unpaid money and not about the person. "I am out 100 dollars," rather than "you owe me 100 dollars." But notice that the potato is still there to be dealt with. You are still out $100. The unpaid loan has become an item on your desktop for you to handle.

The second phase of the constructive mindset is in play as well. A hidden transaction has taken place. When you say, "keep it; it's a gift," it is as if you say to your friend: "The problem is that I am out $100. You are the person responsible to pay me $100 to cancel out your debt. But since I know that you are not able to afford to pay me what you owe me, I give you $100 so that you can pay me the $100 that you owe me." This is the hidden transaction. You are actually paying off on his behalf the debt that your friend owes you. Therefore, the potato is off the desktop or into the "out" basket. Your potato has been managed. (To repeat, I am not suggesting that this is the correct way to handle the situations of private loans. It is merely an option to consider.)

But let us carry on with this example yet further. Some time has elapsed since you cleared your friend's debt on his behalf. He is debt free toward you because you have forgiven his loan. Your friend, who continues to be financially at risk, comes to you the second time and asks, "Can you loan me another $100?" What would you do? How would you answer your friend? Take some time to think about your response.

Some people answer quickly and emphatically: "No!" Others are more hesitant and suggest that the answer depends on various factors. Still others say they would comply with loaning more money to their friend, some with conditions, others without.

My suggestion: The next time your friend asks if you can loan him another $100, it is a fair question. Your friend has not done anything wrong by asking you for another loan. If you have truly forgiven the first loan to your friend, then there is no right or wrong answer regarding his second request. Forgiveness liberates you to answer either yes or no. You are free to let your "yes" be "yes" and your "no" be "no." There is actually no right or wrong answer when the freedom of forgiveness liberates you to deal with new situations within the constructive mindset.

If you choose to answer "no," your friend may reply, "Why not?" You may believe that it is a difficult and loaded question to answer. You may wish not to hurt your friend or not to look bad. My suggestion is to freely discuss the situation with him as you focus on the problem within the constructive mindset. By doing so, you are free to answer something like: "I loaned you $100 some time ago, and you were not able to repay me. I know I told you that you don't owe me anything anymore and that is still the case. But this is a new situation, and I don't believe that it is a good idea for me to loan you more money this time around. I am uncomfortable with doing it again."

You are at risk. Your friend may take offence. He may state: "Why are you bringing up what happened before? I thought you forgave me! What kind of friend are you anyway? Can't you see I need more money? I'm desperate!" Actually, in such an unfortunate situation, your friend is not being a friend to you. Being a friend to someone does not mean you are his or her banker. A banking relationship is a business relationship and may be friendly, but it is not a friendship relationship. You are therefore free to answer: "I did forgive you last time. You do not owe me anything. But this is a different situation."

Your friend may not be a friend to you. Someone who is truly a friend to you will allow you to be who you are. He may be disappointed by your answer not to loan him more money, but he will understand. He will not hold your decision against you. He will seek other avenues to attain his desired loan, and you may feel free to assist him if you like (but it is not necessary). On the other hand, your friend's perspective may be: "You are not a friend to me because you are not doing what I want you to do. And what I want you to do is to give me the $100 I asked you for." Such a person is not letting you be who you are and is not letting you do what you believe is right; therefore, he is trying to be your master and is expecting you to be his slave and to do his will. He is not your friend. Sometimes you discover the true dynamics of the friendships you have, difficult and gut wrenching at times as those lessons can be.

On the other hand, you are also free to answer "yes" to your friend's second request for money. You can change the dynamics of the loan if you wish: "I have noticed that you continue to be under financial pressure. I loaned you $100 before, and you don't owe me anything on that. I am willing to loan you another $100, but because of what happened with the first loan, I think this time we should have some kind of agreement. Last time, nothing was said as far as an understanding between us on how you would repay, but this time I think it would be better to have an agreement. How about you agree to repay me within 3 months? Or, you agree to repay me $10 a month over the next 10 months starting next month?" You could handle the situation in this manner. There is actually no "correct" way to handle the terms of the loan; there are options to consider. You may consider words of advice or wisdom from the experiences of others as to how to approach the issues of lending money to friends, and you have the freedom to consider what is best for you in your situation.

As another option, your reply to your friend could be: "Sure, I am able to loan you another $100. But based on what happened last time, when you could not pay me back—here! Take it as a gift. You don't owe me anything." Whether or not your friend is willing to agree to such terms is another matter. Your friend may insist on repaying you at some future time.

Yet another possible reply could be, "Yes, I can loan you another $100." You give him $100 without further discussion (just like the first time you loaned him $100). You think to yourself, "I'm not going to see this money again." But this time it is a choice you have made. You have made the choice to help your friend in this manner. You may consider it to be a bonus if your friend repays you, but you are not expecting to be repaid, nor are you relating to your friend within the me-versus-you way to see if your friend can prove himself to you by being responsible.

Forgiveness gives you the freedom to sort out your various challenges and how to relate them to yourself and others. You attain the freedom to consider each new challenge on its own merit, as well as to build on the foundation of your previous experiences. You have freedom from the mindset of guilt or blame to deal courageously with your challenges.

Trust and Reconciliation

Yet another situation may arise. Imagine that a friend of yours has lied to you, and that you have decided to forgive her for the lie. Does your forgiveness mean that the next time she tells you something, you are to believe her? Does your answer depend on anything, and if so, what would it depend on? Please take some time to think of what you would do.

The situation has to do with trust. When it comes to matters of trust, there are two major components to a trusting relationship. The first component is that trust is *given.* The first time you see a doctor, you give the doctor trust that she is who she claims to be. The first time you take your vehicle to a mechanic, you give the mechanic trust that he is who he claims to be, that is, someone who can figure out what to do about the problems of your vehicle.

The second component of trust is that it is *earned*. Over time, as you get to know your doctor or mechanic, she/he earns your trust as she/he continues to take care of your health needs or the health of your vehicle. Therefore, the trust in your relationship grows.

If your friend has lied to you, then the trust in your relationship is broken. The relationship is severed. When you have chosen to forgive your friend for lying to you, then the main factor to consider if you believe her or not the next time she tells you something has to do with whether or not you have reconciliation with her.

Reconciliation is the ultimate healing that can take place when you are wronged or hurt by someone else. But reconciliation requires both people in the relationship to do their part. Every relationship is a two-way street requiring both people to contribute to make it a successful one. When a person is wronged by someone else, both people are involved in the outcome of the relationship. The person responsible for doing what was wrong, at the expense of the person wronged, is the "hurter" (the offender, or in some cases, the "bully"). The person who is wronged by someone else is the "hurtee" (the victim). In order for reconciliation to occur, both people have a role to play.

The role of the hurtee is to forgive. Most of the discussion in this chapter involves the process of forgiveness as a choice.

The role of the hurter is … this is where the concept of sorrow or apology comes in … the role of the hurter is to choose to say "I'm sorry" or "I apologize." There needs to be an awareness of remorse for having done the wrong. The strongest term for what the hurter can choose is "to repent," which has to do with allegiance, and means: "What I did is wrong, and I am aware that it is wrong. I have been acting according to allegiance with myself, as opposed to allegiance with you or anyone else. I am sorry for what I did, and I apologize. I choose to follow a new path of allegiance, a path that takes your needs into consideration for the way I live my life and that does not include me doing the wrongs I have done, such as the wrong I did against you."

If the hurtee has chosen to forgive and the hurter has chosen to apologize or repent, then the relationship has achieved reconciliation.

But reconciliation is not guaranteed. The relationship is a two-way street. Both people have a role to play to make the relationship successful, independently of each other. As the hurtee, you may be willing to forgive, but the hurter (the offending person) may not be willing or able to apologize. Perhaps she is deceased, or is unwilling to admit responsibility for the wrong committed. In these situations you will not achieve reconciliation, although you as the offended person have forgiven the offending person. Your potato is placed on the desktop and remains on the desktop. The unresolved potato on your desktop places a limitation on the relationship, but you do not understand the relationship with the person you have forgiven within the me-versus-you mindset.

Therefore, if you forgive your friend, but she for her part has not apologized/repented, then the next time she tells you something, you are not interested in taking her at her word. You do not have reconciliation with her. The achievement of reconciliation gives you a new foundation on which to give your friend trust. If you have not attained the achievement of reconciliation with your friend, you do not have the foundation to give her trust. It means that the next time she tells you something, you are interested in checking out the information from another source before accepting it as reliable.

On the other hand, if you achieve reconciliation with your friend, then you have a foundation on which to give her trust the next time she tells you something. How you approach the situation this next time, however, can be variable. There is really not a correct answer for how to proceed. A more conservative approach would be to check out the information from another source before accepting it as reliable. If everything checks out fine, then she is earning your trust once again. You hope that you will eventually feel comfortable with taking her at her word without having to check from your other sources regarding the reliability. A less conservative approach would be to take her at her word the next time she tells you something and to find out as you go whether everything works out fine from then on.

Unfortunately, sometimes you believe that you have a sense of reconciliation with your friend after she has lied to you, but the next time she tells you something, it turns out to be another lie. You have forgiven her, and she has apologized to you. You believe you have achieved reconciliation. What you have discovered, however, is that her word to you is neither reliable nor trustworthy. She is not being a friend to you. On the intimacy scale of the relationship with your friend (Figure 3.11), you may not even be at the lowest level of intimacy with her, for she is not a friend to you. There is actually no foundation on which to have intimacy or trust with her. Even the factual information she gives you is not reliable. Her apology may be her way to get you to think what she wants you to think. Her intention is to achieve her own purposes. She is protecting herself and is therefore blind to achieve the benefit of a healthy trusting relationship for the both of you as friends. If you have ever encountered such a scenario, you will learn the challenges and limits to relationships in this world.

Because there is no perfect person, someone whom you have achieved true reconciliation with and have re-established a trusting relationship with will let you down again. Eventually, your friend may lie to you again. But it does not necessarily have to mean that you never trust her again. Your trust level does not have to go back to the bottom, that is, to no foundation. What keeps your trust from bottoming out is the knowledge that you can confront her and that she will come clean with you. You will come to understand this experience you have with her as your relationship grows over time.

Unconditional

The decision to forgive on one hand, or to apologize/repent on the other hand, needs to be unconditional with respect to what the other person in the relationship decides to do. If your choice to forgive or apologize is conditional on what the other person chooses, then you relinquish your freedom of choice to the will of the other person who therefore has the control of the relationship. It is not in your best interests to give away your freedom to someone else in this way.

For example, if your perspective is "I'll forgive you *if* you say you're sorry," then are you likely to forgive him if his reply is a harshly spoken "OK! I'm sorry! All right!?" You are less likely to choose to forgive him if his reply is harsh. Therefore, in this situation your choice to forgive is conditional with respect to the way the other person replies and you prevent yourself from having the freedom to choose for yourself what is right for you to do. You are rather interested to be free to forgive regardless of what the offending party's attitude is. It is for you to transfer your potato from your sack onto the desktop.

On the other hand, your choice to apologize or repent cannot be conditional on whether the other person chooses to forgive or not. If you think "I'll apologize *if* you forgive me," then the sincerity of your apology is in question, being conditional on the other person's choice. This situation does not make sense in terms of nurturing healthy relationships. Although it is true that one person's forgiveness may lead to the other person's apology, reconciliation is doubtful if the apology is conditional on the forgiveness.

As previously discussed, there are times when you make the unconditional choice to forgive, but you do not achieve reconciliation. The offending party may be deceased or is unwilling to own up to having done anything wrong. Your potato is on the desktop, yet remains an item to keep in mind from time to time until you have attained reconciliation with the person who is connected to it.

Conversely, there are times when you do not achieve reconciliation when you have chosen to apologize but the offended party is not willing to make the choice to forgive. In this situation, the offended party keeps his potato in his sack although you are willing to take responsibility for your role in the offence. But if he is not willing to forgive you, it does not mean that you become his slave. How many times are you required to say that you are sorry (and sincerely mean it) to prove to the offended person that you are truly sorry (and thus make his forgiveness conditional on his own terms, as your judge)? No, if the offended party is not willing to forgive, then you do not achieve reconciliation, but you do not become his slave.

Forgive and Forget

There is a saying that is often quoted and is supposed to represent wisdom. The sage advice is to "forgive and forget." But is this a good saying? Is it possible to do this? What do you think or believe about this advice?

I believe it is a good saying and is possible to fulfill. But I also believe that it is a misunderstood saying. The problem with the concept of "forgive and forget" is related to the word *forget*. Perhaps the word *forget* can have multiple meanings, depending on the context. Examples of other English words with similar challenges include the word *love*. The New Testament of the Bible is originally written in Greek. There are at least two Greek words in the Bible that are translated into the word *love* in an English translation. The Greek words *philia* and *agape* are forms of the English word *love*. An example of where the two Greek words for love are used in the Bible is a scene that occurs after the resurrection of Jesus, when Jesus and Peter are engaged in conversation. Jesus asks Peter three times, "Do you love me?" Three times Peter answers, "Yes, you know that I love you." In an English translation of this event, the transcribed language uses the word *love* each time. In the original Greek text, however, some of the occurrences of the word *love* in this scene are written in the philia form, while others are written in the agape form. I will leave it for your own research to understand the significance of this variation in the original text.

Another example of multiple meanings for a word is the word *anger*. In chapter 1 I have discussed that there are at least two categories of definitions for how the word *anger* can be understood. I believe that the word *forget* is another word with multiple definitions, depending on the context. The primary understanding of the word *forget*, however, has to do with memory. And so the tendency is to interpret the word *forget* in terms of memory, in the saying "forgive and forget." And this is the error that leads to confusion when attempting to understand what the saying "forgive and forget" is meant to say.

If your understanding of the word *forget* is in terms of memory, then the word *forget* in the saying "forgive and forget" captures the prime importance of the saying. The tendency becomes to change the saying around, to make forgetting, in terms of memory, to be what the important work of forgiveness is about. It is as if the saying is changed to "forget in order to forgive." If this is how you understand the saying "forgive and forget," then you are at risk to believe that you must forget things that have happened to show that you have forgiven.

The problem with understanding forgiveness in this way is that if you believe you must forget to forgive, then you are in a dilemma. When you "forget in order to forgive," what are you actually doing? **You are suppressing!** Forgetting, in order to forgive, is what you hope to accomplish when you suppress. But suppressing is done in the context of the destructive mindset. You may be sincere in your intention to forgive, but if you hope to achieve your forgiveness by forgetting, then you are at risk. When you experience a memory about some past hurtful event, and when you feel some emotion connected with your memory, then you may be confused, especially if you understand the emotion component of your memory within the destructive mindset. You may think: "I thought I forgave! So why do I feel this way? Isn't forgiveness possible? Maybe it is just an impossible thing to accomplish, and it isn't real! Forgiveness must be a con!" And so you are confused. If your religious faith includes the concept of forgiveness, then you may have a crisis of faith, believing forgiveness is not possible at all and doubting any faith that has anything to do with forgiveness. But the bottom line is that you have sincerely attempted to forgive, while all the time you have actually attempted to forget in terms of memory.

Another problem that can occur is related to how you handle the memories you experience. You may believe that the truth or effectiveness of your forgiveness depends on whether or not you have memory of the hurtful event at some future time. Sometimes you are challenged by someone else: "Hey! I thought you forgave me! Why are you bringing up what happened?" And so you may become confused about having memories.

I do not believe that the word *forget* in the saying "forgive and forget," is about memory. I believe it is reasonable to remember events in your past. In the same way that having emotions is like having arms and legs, well guess what?! Having memory is like having arms and legs as well! Our bodies are designed to have memory!

The main subject of the saying "forgive and forget," is to **forgive**. Therefore, what is added to the primary subject needs to be consistent with what forgiveness is. Remember that a strong forgiveness is one that is connected with an informed choice. In other words, you need to know what it is that you are forgiving "so-and-so" for. To have memory is reasonable and is a necessary component of true forgiveness. Therefore, the word *forget* that is added to the subject "forgive and …" cannot be about memory.

In fact, if the definition of forgiveness is about the cancelling of a debt, then what is it you are to forget? **The debt!** Therefore, the way to think of the saying "forgive and forget" is to view it as "forgive and forget *the debt.*"

Memory

If the concept of memory is to be brought into the discussion, then what is the purpose of memory? (Hint: It is a principle of education.) Right! You have memory because memory helps you to *learn*. Therefore, to be consistent with what the purpose of memory is, the way to include the concept of memory into the saying "forgive and forget," is to reword it to say "forgive and *learn*." Now the two words are compatible with each other in the context of their unique definitions.

Since you have the ability to forgive and learn, you become free to learn from any situation. If something turns out well, then you learn from it to keep it that way. If something turns out poorly, then you learn from it to change it into something good.

It is suggested that there are two main education systems in this world.[8] The education system of most organized schools involves the student being rewarded for doing well (good marks, good behaviour) and being punished for doing badly. Making mistakes is viewed as negative, and students are at risk of becoming stressed about making mistakes. This is the "see one, do one, teach one" education system. You sit in the classroom so that you can "see." If you are considered competent in a particular subject, then you move on to enhance your learning by "doing." You engage in the practical application of working within the subject matter. As examples, you could be doing practical work in a school laboratory, or working as an apprentice or practical residency program. The theory of the "see one" stage takes on practical relevance in the "do one" stage. In the "teach one" stage, you learn more about a particular subject by teaching it to others.

The second education system could be coined "learning on the street." In this alternative system, the student learns from his mistakes. Making mistakes is seen as an accepted component of the education process (as long as the mistakes are understood constructively, that is, the person is not the problem and is not blamed). A saying goes along with this system: "You learn from your mistakes." This second education system could be called the "do one, see one, teach one" system. You learn by doing; doing is the foundation for you to "see" or understand.

Consider the following example. Imagine that you wish to start a home-based business. As you keep track of your revenue growth over time, you may notice that your revenues are increasing at a slow pace. It is time for a decision. You make what you believe is the best decision. Following your decision, the revenue growth climbs at a greater rate. When it comes time for your next decision, you are interested in looking back at your first decision to understand what you got right. You hope to apply what you learned from the outcome of your first decision, so that you can use it to assist you to make the best decision the second time around and thereby keep things going as well as you can.

On the other hand, if your revenue growth starts to go downhill after your first decision, then when it comes time to make your second decision, you are interested in looking back at your first decision to understand what you got wrong or missed. You hope to take what you learned into account to help your second decision to be as good a decision as possible so that you can turn things around. Your revenue growth may then readjust in a positive direction.

Whatever the outcome of your first decision, whether it turns out well or not, you learn from it. The wisdom you gain helps you either to keep things going well (or even better) or to reverse the downward direction that came as a result of your mistake back toward a positive direction. Therefore, you learn from your successes and from your mistakes. There is no difference between the two outcomes in your ability to gain wisdom.

However, if you do not learn from your experiences as discussed in the preceding example, then you will nonetheless learn something as your life proceeds. Your body is designed to have memory. Therefore, you are guaranteed to learn various things as your life proceeds. What you are likely to learn, however, is that when you make decisions, sometimes the outcome is good and sometimes the outcome is bad. But you will not have a clue as to why or how the decisions turn out well or poorly; you only know *that* things can go well or poorly. You are likely to become anxious when it comes time to make decisions. You may wring your hands and struggle with thoughts such as: "I don't know what to do! If I do such-and-such, it might go well. But it might go poorly. It would be great if it went well. But it would suck if it turned out wrong. What am I going to do? I don't know!" You are at risk to be indecisive and anxious when you are faced with decisions.

But if you learn as you go, regardless of the outcome of your decisions, then you become free to increase your confidence about the decisions you make. You also make better decisions as your wisdom increases over time. And you are not afraid to make mistakes. You are confident that if a mistake is made, you will be able to sort it out and turn things back into a positive direction, for that is your experience. In addition, you discover that a mistake is an opportunity to learn. When you make a mistake, you are free to think, "I am going to learn something that I didn't know before." Everybody has to pay to get an education. It is as if the cost of the mistake is the payment you make to get your education.

Biblical Relevance

Romans 8:28 states, "And we know that in all things God works for the good of those who love him, who have been called according to his purpose." All things work together for good to those called according to His purpose! That means that everything, whether good or bad, works together for good, according to those whose purpose is in Christ. If your purpose is according to the world, then how can all things work together for good? If you are behind the "Joneses," then you are behind! How can you catch up again? But if you are called according to the purpose of God, then everything that happens, whether good or bad, can be viewed as something that can be turned into good (the silver lining in the cloud).

Concluding Remarks

And that is forgiveness in a nutshell. I hope that you have enjoyed, and benefited from, the discussion in this book about anger and forgiveness. I wish you every success as you *put your potatoes on the desktop!*

Biblical Relevance

A final question can be asked. If you are looking for a reason to make the choice to forgive, what is the ultimate reason that will help you consider the choice to forgive as a valid option? I find that if my search for a reason to forgive is limited to something within this world, I am likely to find a reason *not* to make the choice to forgive. Since the world is not perfect and is subject to decay, I am likely to think, "Why should I forgive 'so-and-so' when 'so-and-so' always gets away with everything anyway?" And so I struggle with considering the choice to forgive as a valid option.

I believe that the ultimate reason to help me to choose to forgive is contained within the gospel message. Please refer to the forgiveness model in Figure 7.1 or 7.2 and follow the argument: God shows us the difference between right and wrong, and we are the people. Since there is no perfect person, nobody fulfills God's law. Romans 3:23 states, "for all have sinned and fall short of the glory of God." Therefore, God is hurt by the wrongdoing of the people, and He is energized to anger. As people, we are in the situation in which the person and the problem (the wrong or the sin) are considered to be one and the same entity. There is a debt to pay. Romans 6:23 states, "the wages of sin is death." All people have a death sentence hanging over them. It is said that there are two certain things in life: death and taxes. We are indebted to God and we are indebted to the governments of the world. As soon as a person is born, we know that this person is going to face death at some point.

Fortunately for us people, God has made the choice to forgive. He has brought about His forgiveness by sending His Son, who is a new creation. Jesus is like a second Adam. 1Corinthians 15:45 states, "'The first man Adam became a living being'; the last Adam, a life-giving spirit." Jesus is therefore a new creation. He is not created from the dust of the ground as the first Adam was. Rather, Jesus is created within the womb of a virgin. The "stuff" of His flesh, that is, the building blocks that go together to form his body, comes from the bread (another name for "food") that Mary, His mother, eats. Therefore, when Jesus states "this bread is my body," He is correct! Bread has life in it, and Jesus says that "bread" is His body. If I should eat of the stuff of my flesh, that is, if I eat dirt (the dust of the ground), then I discover that dirt does not give me life. But out of the ground comes the food that gives me life, and when I eat this bread, I have life.

Jesus also lives a perfect life. He is without sin. When John baptizes Him, the heavenly voice declares, "This is my Son, whom I love; with him I am well pleased" (Matthew 3:17). Jesus also withstands the temptations in the desert. Since Jesus is without sin, He does not have a death sentence on Him. To repeat, as the second Adam, Jesus continues without wrongdoing or sin. He therefore is life, for He lives without a death sentence.

When Jesus decides to give up His life, as the sacrificial lamb, He does not die to pay the debt of His own sin. Since "the wages of sin is death," however, there must be a death to satisfy law and justice. Jesus' death fulfills all righteousness, in that Jesus dies, not for Himself (He does not have a death sentence), but for those who have a death sentence. God offers forgiveness to us; to the people who are created in the flesh of the first Adam, who are against His law (by falling short of it) and who are under a death sentence. In Christ, God separates the person (us) from the problem (sin) and fulfills the death sentence by dying on the cross. We as people are therefore set free from the burden of our wrongdoing or sin through Christ.

If Jesus did not choose to die, I believe He would still be walking among us today. He would be the oldest person in the history of the world and perhaps not look a day over 29! This is because the stuff of His body (bread) is different from the stuff that we are made of (dust or clay). The celebration of Christmas is in essence the celebration of creation. Jesus is a new creation, made out of nothing, made in the womb of the virgin. Perhaps it could be argued that He is a new species of man, who comes from the womb of a virgin.

But Jesus does choose to die. And He does not die for himself, for He is sinless and without a death sentence. In Matthew 26:52-54, Jesus is arrested, and the servant of the High Priest's ear is cut off: "'Put your sword back in its place,' Jesus said to him, 'for all who draw the sword will die by the sword. Do you think I cannot call on my Father, and he will at once put at my disposal more than twelve legions of angels? But how then would the Scriptures be fulfilled that say it must happen in this way?'" Therefore, Jesus chooses to call off His troops and accept His upcoming fate to die on a cross.

We live in a stage of history when God is offering people His forgiveness. In order for us as individuals to do our part in the relationship with God, it is up to us to repent. It is for us to apologize to God. If both forgiveness and repentance are in place, then we have achieved reconciliation with God. This then is the ultimate reason that I believe helps me to make the choice to forgive, that is, to forgive myself and to forgive others. Since God offers to forgive me and has proved He is serious by accepting death in my place by His Son, then I can be free to choose the option to forgive myself, and I can forgive others. As in the Lord's Prayer, I am free to forgive, as He has forgiven me.

Note: I find it interesting to ponder the concept that the body of the first Adam, as being formed from the dust of the ground, is formed from clay. Jesus' body, on the other hand, is formed in the womb from bread, which is another word for food. Both clay and bread form a type of dough. Both of the doughs of clay and bread are kneaded, formed into a mould, and baked to produce the desired result.

The following verses from Psalm 49 and Psalm 51 show that there is no man or woman created as a descendent of the first Adam who is able to be without sin and to satisfy the payment of his or her own sin or the sin of others. Only Jesus, who is created as the second Adam, is without sin and is able to satisfy the payment of the sin of others. We know this because His body does not see decay, but instead is resurrected. We must live in this faith, that is, believe that He exists, even though we do not presently see Him. If we believe in the Son, we believe in the Father who sent Him.

Psalm 49:

> [7] No man can redeem the life of another
>   or give to God a ransom for him-
> [8] the ransom for a life is costly,
>   no payment is ever enough-
> [9] that he should live on forever
>   and not see decay.
> [10] For all can see that wise men die;
>   the foolish and the senseless alike perish
>   and leave their wealth to others.
> [11] Their tombs will remain their houses forever,
>   their dwellings for endless generations,
>   though they had named lands after themselves.
> [12] But man, despite his riches, does not endure;
>   he is like the beasts that perish.
> [13] This is the fate of those who trust in themselves,
>   and of their followers, who approve their sayings.

Psalm 51:5 states, "Surely I was sinful at birth, sinful from the time my mother conceived me."

Forgiveness

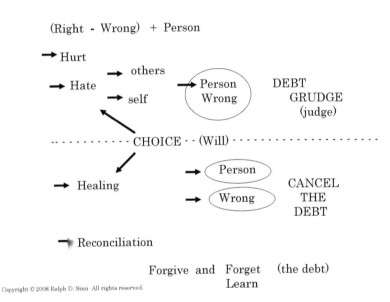

(Right - Wrong) + Person

Hurt

others

Hate   Person   DEBT
      self   Wrong   GRUDGE
                              (judge)

- - - - - - - - - - CHOICE - - (Will) -

Healing   Person

          Wrong   CANCEL
                         THE
                         DEBT

Reconciliation

Forgive and Forget   (the debt)
              Learn

Figure 7.2 The Forgiveness Model

Chapter 8
FAQs and Other Issues to Keep in Mind

This chapter deals with questions and issues that have relevance to the discussion about potatoes and your emotion management of them. Some of the issues may be relevant to a specific chapter of this book, while other issues are general in nature. Some of the concepts in this chapter may be a repetition of the main text of the book.

Concept of the Potato

The potato represents a notion of right versus wrong. Your potato can apply to a sense of law, truth, or justice, which you adhere to for whatever reason. Your primary negative emotions of hurt, frustration, fear, or a combination of them sensitize you to the fact that you are in the presence of an injustice (potato) and in turn energize you to the secondary negative emotion of anger. The energized state of anger is the heat, which makes your potato a "hot potato" and alerts you to the fact that you are dealing with a potato (injustice). The energized state of anger is the motivational energy to inspire you to come up with a way to address the injustice and change the situation to one that you believe is just. Anger management concerns how you handle the potato in your grasp to achieve the change you are motivated to work toward.

Homework Assignment: What Is the Problem?

When you take offence at something, think about the homework assignment. There are three ingredients in the mix:

1. The problem or potato (the thing said or done, or not said or not done, that you believe is wrong).

2. Your negative emotions and anger (and if you believe it is wrong to feel negative emotions, then you believe that you are the problem because you feel them).

3. The person responsible for the problem or potato (you or someone else who said it, did it, did not say it, or did not do it).

Of these three ingredients, only one of them is the problem. Which is it?

The problem is neither your negative emotions, nor your anger, nor you. The problem is not the person responsible for the wrong. The problem is the problem (the potato)! Nothing else. Once you have this truth sorted out in your understanding, you become free to discern and communicate the problem within the constructive mindset and hold accountable the person who is responsible for the problem.

When you are upset, try starting a statement with "that" to help you to understand the problem: for example, "*That* I am upset. *That* such-and-such happened." A "that" statement will help you to focus your thoughts on the problem at hand rather than on blaming the person. I suppose the effect of doing so is that you are self-validating your emotions and you become free to make the issues of life be about truth rather than about emotions.

Warning

As you learn the application of the emotion management model, please refrain from using the model as a weapon against yourself (or against others). The model is designed to assist you to gain insight about how you make sense of your emotions and the thoughts that go with them when you are upset about something. If you discover that you are managing your emotions within the destructive mindset, then you have achieved insight into a dynamic that you may have previously been blind to. Therefore, you are growing in wisdom!

The model is not about right and wrong. If you discover that you are managing your emotions within the destructive mindset, then it does not mean that you are doing it wrong or that you are bad. Think of the model as a way to help you gain insight into the destructive versus constructive mindsets, rather than viewing the mindsets as right versus wrong or the good way versus the bad way.

Disclaimer

The bias of my writing style is from the foundation of a person with faith in Jesus of Nazareth as the Christ. I am like any person who seeks truth, but I believe truth to be embodied in Christ. My attitude toward other faiths is to understand the differences constructively. It is not my intention to demean any faith that believes in an alternate understanding of truth.

"Why" Question

I have found it helpful, in my experience, to turn a "why" question into a "that" statement. Sometimes I am bewildered by the things that happen. I tend to ask myself "why" or "how come"? I discover that these questions are very difficult, if not impossible, to answer. I believe a reason for the difficulty lies in the tendency for these questions to get me into the destructive me-versus-you mindset. The focus of my thoughts is on the person. For example, my question, "Why did I do that?" easily restricts my focus to blaming myself. I then have difficulty answering my question. It is difficult because I am not the problem!

On the other hand, if I change my "why" question into a "that" statement, I discover that I have the ability to focus on the situation within the constructive mindset. I now have something to understand and to work with. My "that" statement self-validates my emotions, so that I own them and use them to discern the problem (potato) to deal with. For example, my statement, "*That* I did that! What now?" somehow gets me to accept my feelings and understand that something unacceptable has happened. I become free to focus on the problem and free to go forward from there to learn about and hopefully understand the situation. Instead of being stuck with the impossibility of answering the "why" question, I become free to ask, "What now?"

A Weakness of the Model

There seems to be a fine line of distinction between the "suppress" and "repress" methods of anger management. Although I list the two methods as being unique, the two can very easily coexist. There is likely a grey area, rather than a clear distinction, between these two methods. Distinguishing between anger "coming out," as with the "express" method of anger management, and anger "staying inside," as occurs with the "suppress" and "repress" methods, is more clearly understood, but the distinction between the two inward methods ("suppress" and "repress"), in which anger is kept inside, is less clear.

Action or No Action

Being assertive within the constructive mindset does not necessarily mean that you are forced to voice your opinions to others regarding all the issues (or potatoes) that you have on your desktop. Sometimes the action is "no action." From a third-person perspective, if you choose not to say anything, or "no action," it can appear the same as if you choose not to say or do anything to keep the peace within the suppressive destructive mindset.

From the perspective of your inner thoughts, however, there is a big difference between your positive choice not to speak versus not saying anything because you are frozen with fear (no action by default). Your decision of no action, within the constructive mindset, is a positive and in-control decision, rather than the weak "being controlled by others" decision of no action to keep the peace, in which your emotions are actually in control of you. Either you feel good about yourself and feel confident to handle your problems as best as you can or you feel anxious and inadequate to handle the problems that come your way. The constructive mindset liberates you from "sweating the small stuff."

Running and Chasing Dynamic

When two people are in the heat of the moment of a discussion, a "running and chasing dynamic" is sometimes encountered. In such circumstances, the chaser is motivated to get his or her point across. The runner, on the other hand, is uncomfortable with the situation and runs away from the chaser for safety. The more the runner runs away, however, the more motivated the chaser becomes to deal with the situation. He continues to chase after the person who is running. The runner in turn increases her effort to run. The chaser increases his effort to chase, which leads to more running, and on and on.

Eventually, the runner needs to turn and face the chaser. Being aware of the homework assignment can be helpful for both the runner and the chaser to work through the situation. The runner can gain the confidence to listen to the chaser and to address the problem at hand, while the chaser can assure the runner that the situation is about a potato and that it is not about blaming anybody. The chaser can be free to have patience with the runner, yet also be free to encourage the runner to deal with the issue.

Deceitfulness of the Destructive Mindset

Since life is based on love, and since love implies relationship, there is a tendency to blame a person when there is a problem. A problem leads to a break in relationship, and so you tend to focus your thoughts in a way that blames the person for putting the relationship at risk. If you do so, you find yourself relating with others and yourself within the destructive mindset, which places the relationship at further risk.

In contrast, when a problem happens, it means that there is a break in the strength of the relationship. You are interested in focusing on what the problem is (the constructive mindset) to work toward restoring the relationship to its former strength. Or, on the other hand, you accept that the relationship is not strong and recognize where the appropriate boundary of the relationship stands.

A Connection between Hope and the Fork in the Road

As you learn about the lenses that affect your interpretation about what is true (end of chapter 5) and flush out the tendencies to experience "inappropriate anger" from looking through the lenses within the destructive mindset, you may become at risk to believe that someday you will "arrive," that is, someday you will "always get it right." I have learned, however, not to put my faith in my arriving. On the contrary, I put my faith in **His arrival**. When Jesus returns to this Earth, only then will I be changed. 1Corinthians 15:51-53 states: "Listen, I tell you a mystery: We will not all sleep, but we will all be changed - in a flash, in the twinkling of an eye, at the last trumpet. For the trumpet will sound, the dead will be raised imperishable, and we will be changed. For the perishable must clothe itself with the imperishable, and the mortal with immortality." Therefore, my hope is in His arrival, for when He arrives, I will be changed. Any change I undergo before Jesus returns does not result in my arrival (that is, in my becoming perfect). On the contrary, something I change about me involves my own progress toward increasing the application of constructive thinking to the various challenges I face. I gain an awareness and acceptance of the limitations that other people and I have.

Forgiving Yourself

If you have been hurt by another person, then the two-way direction of forgiveness and apology/repentance to achieve reconciliation of the relationship is understandable. But what if you blame yourself for something wrong that you have done? For example, you blame yourself for hurting someone else or you take the blame when someone yells (but the person did not specifically yell at you). How do you achieve reconciliation with yourself?

To attain reconciliation with yourself, the two-way street dynamic of forgiveness and apology applies as well. In contrast to the process of reconciliation when you and another person are involved and your role is to either forgive or apologize, you are responsible for both directions of the two-way street when you seek reconciliation with yourself! When you have hurt yourself, or if there is anything that you blame yourself for, then you are both the "hurter" (offender/perpetrator or bully) and the "hurtee" (victim or the bullied). As the hurtee, it is for you to forgive yourself. You are to transfer the potato with your name on it from the sack on your back to the desktop. The action of doing so places the potato into the proper court to be dealt with by the appropriate judge. As the hurter, you become free to apologize or repent to yourself and to the judge (for example, God) who is overseeing your case. The constructive mindset frees you to take responsibility for your actions and to bear the consequences. You are also free to learn from your mistakes and to gather wisdom from your experiences.

In this process, it makes more sense to forgive yourself first. If you desire to apologize to yourself before you have forgiven yourself, then you do not know what to apologize to yourself for since you are in the destructive mindset and therefore blame yourself. It does not make sense to apologize to yourself for existing. Therefore, forgive yourself first. Doing so opens up your ability to understand what the potato (problem) is. You become able to transfer your role as judge against yourself to the judge in truth, which may be a higher power or God. A higher power is something bigger or more powerful than you—it may be your family, society, a supernatural force, or God. You attain the freedom to take responsibility for the problem and to apologize to yourself for the wrong you did against yourself. You therefore achieve reconciliation with yourself.

Measure of Forgiveness

How do you know if you have forgiven somebody? I suggest that when you remember a hurtful event from your past and experience the emotions that accompany your memory within the constructive mindset, then you have forgiven the other person (or yourself). The focus of your thoughts and emotions are on the issues.

On the other hand, if you experience the emotions that accompany your memory within the destructive me-versus-you mindset, then the potato linked to your memory has come from the sack on your back and you have not forgiven the other person (or yourself). If this should happen, then your memory is like a gift which reminds you of a burden that is affecting you. You become free to transfer the potato connected with your memory onto the desktop and achieve the freedom of forgiveness.

Write a Story

If life is about stories, that is, about love and relationship, then a useful approach when working toward forgiveness is to write a story. For example, you could write a letter, address it to God, and tell Him the story about you and "so-and-so" when "such-and-such" happened. Or you could tell your story in a song. Journaling your experiences can be a way to give you a voice when you seek the validation of your emotions as you tell your stories. There are many other formats in which to tell your stories, and the work of forgiveness is enhanced by the stories you write.

Limits and Boundaries

It can be a challenge to be aware of and accept your limits (boundaries). Since people are *finite* beings, you have limits (the definition of finite). If you attempt to live outside the boundary of your limits, then you will encounter the reality of your limits. For example, your boundary/limit may be that you perform a certain skill at the Grade 6 level. If you attempt to perform actions that are at the Grade 10 level, then you will struggle and likely show evidence that you are not at the higher level. You may become anxious, expecting yourself to perform at a level that you are not yet capable of attaining. If your parent expects you to perform at the Grade 10 level when you actually perform at the Grade 6 level, then your anxiety may be intensified. Although you try to please your parent, you fail to perform at the higher level that your parent inappropriately expects you to attain (you may eventually attain the higher level with appropriate challenges over the course of time).

If you live within your limits, then what you can do is limitless. It means that if you live within the boundary of your limitations, you can discover limitless possibilities. For example, a person may be limited by a particular illness. The achievements of people with physical disabilities are inspiring. We have seen the contributions of Christopher Reeve, Joni Erickson-Tada, and Stephen Hawking, who despite severe disability, are not limited by the intellect or the infinite creativity of singing, speaking, mouth-art, writing by mouth, and so on.

Stress

What about stress management? Does the homework assignment have a role? If you are under a lot of stress (there are issues with your work, issues with your family, issues with your pets, bills to pay, repairs to do, and so on), then the homework assignment definitely has a role. Each of the issues represents a kind of potato. You are interested in keeping all of the potatoes on the desktop. The homework will help you to prioritize and appropriately address them.

If you fret about your ability to deal with all of your stresses (potatoes), then your anxiety makes it harder on yourself. You may think: "I'm never going to get all this done! I should be able to do it! Is there something wrong with me? Why can't I get this done? If only I didn't have so much to do!" These statements are consistent with the destructive mindset. You make yourself out to be the problem, but you are not a potato. You are not the problem. If you treat yourself as the problem, then your hands are tied because you cannot change who you are. Your stress magnifies and you are left spinning your wheels, getting nowhere.

Rather, see yourself as having many issues (potatoes) to deal with. You are not the problem; the potatoes are. The constructive mindset frees you to believe in yourself and to believe in your ability to work with your potatoes as best as you can. Be free to prioritize them and to appropriately address them. You are also free to set limits on what you can do and to know when to say *no* when you consider taking something on.

Group Dynamics

For most of this book, the discussion concerns "one-on-one" relationship interactions. But what about group dynamics? How can the understanding of the homework assignment help you to understand power dynamics in a group of people? Although there may be many dynamics to study, there have been two group situations that I have encountered and thought about the application of the homework assignment.

In one situation, I attended a social gathering of about 10 people who were all seated in a circle. I noticed that one person (the "alpha") especially seemed to have the dominant role in leading the discussion of the group, for virtually all of the conversation was directed by this person. There was a second person who "co-dominated" with the first; that is, the second person was particularly animated by the discussion and became the primary source for feeding the alpha person. Nearly everyone else in the group quietly focused their attention on the two dominant players, sometimes contributing a chuckle, sometimes contributing a minor comment. This dynamic carried on for a long time, and eventually I wondered if it would be possible to talk with anyone else or at all.

I took a chance and asked a fellow "spectator" sitting close by a question in a normal tone. We started a separate conversation. I believed it would be acceptable to have a second conversation going in a group of this size and the setting of the gathering. The outcome was that the alpha person cut into the subject of our conversation and regained control of the entire group, relating the subject, and the group, once again to his/her control. On a separate occasion with similar dynamics and a similar attempt to become active in a conversation, the two conversations were maintained for a short time, and then the alpha person became quiet.

In a different setting, I attended a board meeting. I noticed that all of the board members focused their attention on the chairperson, except for one of the attendees. This person was distant and appeared uninterested, but was recognized by all of the board members as an authority. There was much discussion surrounding a certain topic at the meeting. Before a vote was taken, the chairperson asked the apparent disinterested authority figure for a comment. Around the room, all became silent, and all eyes focused on the authority figure. This person made a quiet comment or two, and his/her comments became the "law" of the group. All previous discussion was nullified. The authority figure then resumed doing something else while continuing to attend the meeting.

In group situations, think of applying the homework assignment. Get an awareness of the power dynamics of the group and of your role within the power structure. Neither you nor other people are the problem. Rather, the group is a way to discuss and share information about the various potatoes in the world. If you maintain the constructive mindset, you will be free to be assertive. You will be free to let yourself be who you are, that is, to understand your point of view and to be free to communicate it. You become free to let yourself have your thoughts and emotions and free to let others have theirs. You become free to recognize the peculiar power dynamics within certain groups of people and free to be bold and respectful but not intimidated.

Quotes

Consider the impact of the homework assignment and your awareness of the destructive versus constructive mindsets as you think about what the following quotes are about:

"Nearly all men can stand adversity, but if you want to test a man's character, give him power." – Abraham Lincoln

"Courage is the mastery of fear—not absence of it." – Mark Twain

"Hatred stirs up dissension, but love covers over all wrongs." – Proverbs 10:12

"But godliness with contentment is great gain. For we brought nothing into the world, and we can take nothing out of it." – 1 Timothy 6:6-7

There are so many profound and wise quotes to be inspired by. What is your favourite quote? Does something about the quote fit in terms of the homework assignment?

Notes

1. Christopher Reeve, *Still Me* (New York: Random House, 1998).

2. Aristotle, *The Nichomachean Ethics*, trans. H. Rackham (Cambridge MA: Harvard University Press, 1926).

3. H. Norman Wright, *Marriage Renewal Video Series: Holding on to Romance: Keeping Your Marriage Alive and Passionate after the Honeymoon Years Are Over*, VHS (Ventura, CA: Gospel Light, 1994).

4. C.S. Lewis, *The Four Loves* (Glasgow, Scotland: Geoffrey Bles, 1960; repr., Collins / Fount Paperbacks, 1977).

5. Saint Augustine, *Confessions*, trans. R.S. Pine-Coffin (London, England: Penguin Books, 1961), p. 290.

6. Gary Solomon, *The Motion Picture Prescription: Watch This Movie and Call Me in the Morning* (Santa Rosa, CA: Aslan Publishing, 1995).

7. Joanie Yoder, *Finding the God-Dependant Life: A Personal Story of a Life Transformed by the Secret of 'God-Dependence' over Co-Dependence* (Grand Rapids, MI: Discovery House Publishers, 1992).

8. Robert T. Kiyosaki, *Rich Dad Poor Dad: What the Rich Teach Their Kids about Money—That the Poor and Middle Class Do Not!* (New York: Warner Business Books, 2000).

Other Reading: I wish to acknowledge the following authors and their writings that have influenced my understanding of the human condition.

1. Neil Clark Warren, *Make Anger Your Ally*, 3rd ed. (Colorado Springs, CO: Focus on the Family Publishing, 1990).

2. Sandy Livingstone, *Dealing with Anger*, 2nd ed. (St. Albert, AB: SL Discovery Consulting Services Inc., 1997).

3. Daniel Goleman, *Emotional Intelligence: Why It Can Matter More Than IQ* (New York: Bantam Books, 1995).